# Best Hikes Asheville, North Carolina

SECOND EDITION

**Johnny Molloy**

**FALCON** GUIDES

ESSEX, CONNECTICUT

# FALCONGUIDES®

An imprint of Globe Pequot, the trade division of The Rowman & Littlefield Publishing Group, Inc.
4501 Forbes Blvd., Ste. 200
Lanham, MD 20706
www.rowman.com

Falcon and FalconGuides are registered trademarks and Make Adventure Your Story is a trademark of The Rowman & Littlefield Publishing Group, Inc.

Distributed by NATIONAL BOOK NETWORK

Photos by Johnny Molloy
Maps by The Rowman & Littlefield Publishing Group, Inc.

British Library Cataloguing in Publication Information available

**Library of Congress Cataloging-in-Publication Data**
Names: Molloy, Johnny, 1961– author.
Title: Best hikes Asheville, North Carolina / Johnny Molloy.
Other titles: Best hikes near Asheville, North Carolina
Description: Second edition. | Essex, Connecticut : FalconGuides, [2024] | Previous edition: 2017. | Summary: "This guidebook covers 40 family-friendly hikes within 100 miles of or about 1 hour from the Asheville, North Carolina, area"— Provided by publisher.
Identifiers: LCCN 2023030691 (print) | LCCN 2023030692 (ebook) | ISBN 9781493075775 (paper : acid-free paper) | ISBN 9781493075782 (electronic)
Subjects: LCSH: Hiking—North Carolina—Asheville Region—Guidebooks. | Walking—North Carolina—Asheville Region–Guidebooks. | Trails—North Carolina—Asheville Region— Guidebooks. | Asheville Region (N.C.)—Description and travel. | Asheville Region (N.C.)— Guidebooks. Classification: LCC GV199.42.N662 A756 2023 (print) | LCC GV199.42.N662 (ebook) | DDC 796.5109756/88–dc23/eng/20230828
LC record available at https://lccn.loc.gov/2023030691
LC ebook record available at https://lccn.loc.gov/2023030692

∞™ The paper used in this publication meets the minimum requirements of American National Standard for Information Sciences—Permanence of Paper for Printed Library Materials, ANSI/NISO Z39.48-1992.

# Contents

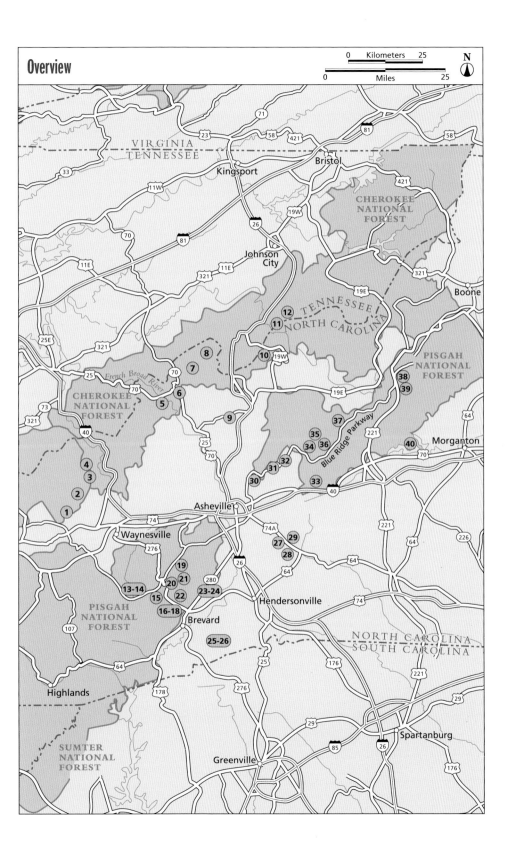

Overview

0 — Kilometers — 25

0 — Miles — 25

N

# Acknowledgments

Thanks to my wife, Keri Anne, for her help. Thanks also to those who build and maintain area trails, and folks at FalconGuides. Also thanks to Kelty for their fine tents, sleeping bags, and other camping gear used while exploring the trails of greater Asheville.

# Introduction

Welcome to the second edition of *Best Hikes Asheville, North Carolina*. The city and surrounding communities from Marshall to Hendersonville, from Canton to Swannanoa, are blessed to sit in the heart of the wild western Carolina mountains, an area blanketed with trail-laced public lands. It all starts with area residents acknowledging and preserving western North Carolina's scenic splendor. The citizenry could see that the special places would remain special if they were held by the public for the public to use and enjoy, and so they created parks and preserves, including Great Smoky Mountains National Park, the Blue Ridge Parkway, and Pisgah National Forest. Other preserves came to be, such as DuPont State Forest and Mount Mitchell State Park.

With their backdrop being the North Carolina highlands, greater Asheville hikers can immerse themselves in the region's forests, mountains, and river valleys along which travel hiking trails. Hiking trails extending all four cardinal directions can be found in this guide. To the west, you can climb to the High Rocks, stealing far-reaching views along the Appalachian Trail (AT). The view from Lovers Leap near Hot Springs is a fine year-round walk. How about the one and only Great Smoky Mountains National Park? Hikes here include the historic and wildlife-rich Cataloochee area. Stay above 5,000 feet the entire gorgeous route to Hemphill Bald and its stunning views. Alternatively, visit the preserved Little Cataloochee Church where early Carolina residents worshiped, or soak in national-park-level scenery on the Big Fork Ridge Loop where you can ramble through groves of rhododendron along untamed waterways and atop hardwood-clad crests.

East of Asheville, you can hike to Crabtree Falls, which creates a 70-foot parade of lather crashing into a rocky pool. The walk to Rattlesnake Lodge visits the fascinating ruins of an early-20th-century mountain getaway where a pioneer Asheville conservationist and his family communed with nature. The hike to Douglas Falls also includes a stop by long and wild Cascade Falls, near Craggy Gardens, after using a portion of North Carolina's long-distance master path—the Mountains-to-Sea Trail. How about the vistas from mountaintop meadows on the Trombatore Trail near Gerton?

To the south, Pisgah National Forest boasts wilderness and backcountry areas, unique geology, and botanically fascinating destinations. The hike to Looking Glass Rock takes you atop a massive stone face rising above the mountain terrain, presenting fantastic views. And how can you forget hikes to the plentiful waterfalls of this area—High Falls on the South Mills River, Twin Falls near Buckhorn Gap, and Cove Creek Falls near John Rock. And then there's Shining Rock Wilderness with its open meadows, white quartz outcrops, and panoramas extending as far as the clarity of the sky allows. Or make the climb to the Mount Pisgah Fire Tower, gaining mile-high views. The trek to Mount Pisgah is one of several hikes that start at or near the Blue

Ridge Parkway, and also includes the multiple waterfalls of the Graveyard Fields. The Pink Beds, a natural wildflower garden, provides a chance to view thousands of blooming wild rhododendron. DuPont State Forest is down this way also, and has more than its share of cascades and overlooks, including Wintergreen Falls, Grassy Creek Falls, and Bridal Veil Falls.

North of Asheville you can walk atop Black Mountain, the lofty ridge where Mount Mitchell—the highest point in the East—stands proudly. This trek also includes bagging other 6,000-foot-plus peaks and extensive views amid spruce-fir forests that cloak only the tallest mantles in the land. Or take the River Loop along the South Toe River, visiting recreation areas, crystalline waterways, and see Setrock Creek Falls along the way. Solitude, waterfalls, and extensive vistas can be had while looping Hickey Fork Creek. The Shelton Laurel Backcountry offers additional waterfalls and vistas near Whiteoak Flats and Big Firescald Ridge.

To the east you can hike along Lake James and experience yet another side of Asheville hiking. Just over the state line in Tennessee you can check out craggy Rock Creek Falls deep in the Unaka Wilderness.

And there is still more. Grab sights and hike along one of the highest elevation streams in the East on the Flat Laurel Creek Loop. Climb from the Davidson River to John Rock, a granite dome rising above the valley, creating a grandstand to look out on the nearby Blue Ridge. The trail along Big Laurel Creek takes you through a rugged, rocky gorge where a large mountain stream fights its way to meet the French Broad River, passing the historic town site and ruins of Runion. Or hike up the lower South Mills River, where wildflowers grow in springtime profusion while trout lurk in translucent pools, or alternatively visit the site of historic Cantrell Creek Lodge. It all adds up to an impressive array of hiking destinations!

After having the privilege of researching potential hikes for this update, hiking the hikes, taking photographs, finding the ones that made the grade—and the ones that didn't—exploring the parks beyond the trails, mapping the hikes, then actually writing and updating this compendium, I am excited to share these best hikes near Asheville with you. The hikes are an ideal mix of views and waterfalls, places where the human history of western Carolina mixes with the natural history, where a wealth of flora and fauna makes hiking in greater Asheville a singular experience.

I think of the treasure trove of trails near Asheville, and how the hikes in this guide reflect the wide array of experiences to be had in this part of the Southern Appalachians. I hope the trails offered in this book will help you explore, understand, and appreciate the natural and human history of greater Asheville. Enjoy!

## Weather

Asheville, Hendersonville, and the mountains enveloping them experience all four seasons in their entirety, and sometimes all at once when you take into account the elevation variations of the region, ranging from a little above 1,300 feet along the French Broad River at Hot Springs to Mount Mitchell at 6,684 feet. Summer can be warm, with a few hot spells, though cool breezes can always be found along mountain streams and in the high country. Morning hikers can avoid the common afternoon thunderstorms that arise in the mountains. Electronic devices equipped with internet access allow hikers to monitor storms as they come up, though coverage can be spotty in remote national forest lands, especially deep in stream valleys. Hikers increase in numbers when the first northerly fronts of autumn sweep cool clear air across the Southern Appalachians. Crisp mornings, great for vigorous treks, give way to warm afternoons, more conducive to family strolls. Fall is drier than summer. Winter will bring frigid subfreezing days and chilling rains, and copious amounts of snow in the high country. We are talking over 60 inches annually at 5,000 feet, though the city of Asheville averages only 14 inches per year. Winter also brings fewer hours of daylight. However, a brisk hiking pace and wise time management will keep you warm and walking. Each cold month has a few days of mild weather. Make the most of them, and seek out lower elevation hikes. Spring will be more variable. A mild day can be followed by a cold one. Extensive spring rains bring regrowth, but also keep hikers indoors. March can bring heavy snows in the high country. However, any avid hiker will find more good hiking days than they will have time to hike in spring and every other season. A good way to plan your hiking is to check monthly averages of high and low temperatures and average rainfall for each month in Asheville. This will give you a good idea of what to expect each month. However, remember temperatures can be significantly cooler and precipitation higher in the adjacent highlands.

| Month | Average High (degrees) | Average Low (degrees) | Precipitation (inches) |
|---|---|---|---|
| January | 47 | 28 | 2.9 |
| February | 50 | 31 | 3.2 |
| March | 58 | 37 | 3.3 |
| April | 67 | 45 | 3.0 |
| May | 75 | 53 | 3.3 |
| June | 82 | 61 | 3.4 |
| July | 85 | 65 | 3.3 |
| August | 84 | 64 | 3.4 |
| September | 77 | 57 | 3.2 |
| October | 68 | 46 | 2.1 |
| November | 58 | 38 | 2.9 |
| December | 49 | 30 | 2.8 |

## Flora and Fauna

The landscape of greater Asheville varies greatly, from the deep valley of the French Broad River and other desiccated waterways to high peaks extending in every direction around Asheville. Widespread public lands create large swaths for wildlife to roam. At the top of the food chain stands the black bear. You can run into one anywhere in the region and on any trail included in this guide. Although attacks by black bears are very rare, they have happened in the Southern Appalachians. Seeing a bear is an exciting yet potentially scary experience. If you meet a bear while hiking, stay calm and don't run. Make loud noises to scare off the bear and back away slowly. Remain aware and alert. In addition to bruins, a wide variety of wildlife calls these landscapes home. Deer will be the land animal you most likely will see hiking area trails. They can be found throughout the western Carolina region. A quiet hiker may also witness turkeys, raccoons, or even a coyote. Do not be surprised if you observe beaver, muskrat, or a playful otter along mountain streams. If you feel uncomfortable when encountering any critter, keep your distance and they will generally keep theirs.

Overhead, many raptors will be plying the skies for food, including hawks, falcons, and owls. Depending upon where you are, other birds you may spot range from kingfishers to woodpeckers. Songbirds are abundant during the warm season no matter the habitat.

The flora offers as much variety as you would expect with such elevational range. Moisture-dependent forests are found along the mountain streams and waterways, places where rhododendron creates immense thickets below black birch, tulip trees, and maple. Here grow the incredible displays of wildflowers, reflecting a cornucopia of color—purple dwarf crested iris, white trilliums, pink phlox, and red cardinal flower. On drier slopes rise hickory, oak, and mountain laurel. Cedars and pines thrive on rocky, sun-burnished slopes. Northern hardwood forests of yellow birch, beech, and cherry appear as you head higher in the mountains. Higher still are the rare spruce-fir forests that thrive above 5,000 feet, where northern red squirrels chatter and Turk's cap lilies color the late summer. It all adds up to vegetational variety of the first order that can be seen and experienced as spring climbs the mountains and autumn descends back to the valleys.

## Wilderness Restrictions/Regulations

The best hikes near Asheville primarily take place on federal lands of the Pisgah National Forest, Blue Ridge Parkway, and to a lesser extent Great Smoky Mountains National Park, as well as DuPont State Forest, Mount Mitchell State Park, and Conserving Carolina property. To enjoy the federal lands entrance is mostly free, and users of the national forest and national parks are expected to monitor their own behavior in backcountry areas, though you may see a ranger in designated wildernesses. Developed recreation areas with campgrounds and trails are more closely supervised.

Detailed trail and road maps of the Pisgah National Forest, Blue Ridge Parkway, and Great Smoky Mountains National Park are available. They come in handy in helping you get around. Backcountry camping is restricted to designated sites inside Great Smoky Mountains National Park but is generally more freewheeling in the Pisgah National Forest. Backcountry camping opportunities are limited in Blue Ridge Parkway lands and prohibited in the state parks included in this guide.

Then there are the nature preserves. Conserving Carolina protects the Trombatore Trail, Bearwallow Trail, and the Florence Nature Preserve, while the Bailey Mountain

Preserve is owned by the town of Mars Hill, but all other trails are located on publicly held lands.

# Getting Around

### Area Codes

The greater Asheville area code is 828, while the area code in upper East Tennessee is 423.

### Roads

For the purposes of this guide, the best hikes near Asheville are confined to a 1-hour drive from the greater metro region, which includes Hendersonville. Northerly, this stretches to the state of Tennessee and west to Hot Springs and the easternmost North Carolina Smokies. Southward, hikes extend to the Brevard area, DuPont State Forest, and Flat Rock. Hikes are located easterly as far as Lake James State Park near Nebo.

Two major interstates converge in the greater Asheville region: I-26 and I-40. Directions to trailheads are given from these arteries, and sometimes from I-240—the alternate interstate through Asheville. Other major roads are US 74A and US 25/70. The Blue Ridge Parkway is an important route to hikes in this guide.

### By Air

Asheville Regional Airport (AVL) is located off NC 280, roughly halfway between Asheville and Hendersonville. To book reservations online, check out your favorite airline's website or search one of the following travel sites for the best price: www. cheaptickets.com, www.expedia.com, www.orbitz.com, www.priceline.com, www. travelocity.com, or www.trip.com—just to name a few.

### By Bus

Asheville Redefines Transportation (known as "ART") operates bus services through-out Asheville, though it won't do you much good for this book, since the best hikes near Asheville are mostly in adjacent wild public lands not served by mass transit. Visit www.ashevillenc.gov or call (828) 253-5691. In addition to ART, Henderson County has Apple Country Public Transit. Their phone number is (828) 698-8571. Greyhound serves many towns in the region; visit www.greyhound.com for more information.

### Visitor Information

For general information on Asheville, visit North Carolina's official website for the area, www.visitnc.com/asheville-the-foothills, or call (800) VISITNC. This site links you to the varied western Carolina community tourism sites.

# How to Use This Guide

Take a close-enough look, and you'll find that this guide contains just about everything you'll ever need to choose, plan for, enjoy, and survive a hike near Asheville, North Carolina. Stuffed with useful western North Carolina area information, *Best Hikes Asheville, North Carolina* features forty mapped and cued hikes. I grouped the hikes into three units. "Northwest" covers hikes in the eastern Smokies, Pisgah National Forest near the Tennessee state line, and into the Volunteer State. "Southwest" harbors hikes along the Blue Ridge Parkway southwest of Asheville, and in the Pisgah National Forest toward Brevard and DuPont State Forest. "Southeast and Northeast" details hikes along the Blue Ridge Parkway east of Asheville, Mount Mitchell State Park as well as Pisgah National Forest hikes, and eastward to Lake James.

Here's an outline of the book's major components: Each hike starts with a short summary of the hike's highlights. This quick overview gives you a taste of the hiking adventures to follow. You'll learn about the trail terrain and what surprises each route has to offer. Following the overview you'll find the hike specs: quick, nitty-gritty details of the hike. Most are self-explanatory, but here are some details on others:

**Distance**: The total distance of the recommended route—one way for loop hikes, round-trip on a there-and-back or lollipop hike, point-to-point for a shuttle. Options are additional.

**Difficulty**: Each hike has been assigned a level of difficulty. The rating system was developed from several sources and personal experience. These levels are meant to be a guideline only, and hikes may prove easier or harder for different people depending on ability and physical fitness.

*Easy*—5 miles or less total trip distance in 1 day, with minimal elevation gain, and paved or smooth-surfaced dirt trail.

*Moderate*—Up to 10 miles total trip distance in 1 day, with moderate elevation gain and potentially rough terrain.

*Difficult*—More than 10 miles total trip distance in 1 day, strenuous elevation gains, and rough and/or rocky terrain.

**Elevation change**: This is the aggregate elevation gained and lost during a hike, whether it is a loop or a there-and-back. These numbers were found using GPS data obtained during the given hike loaded onto a mapping program.

**Maximum grade**: This details the steepest portion of the hike for a sustained distance, whether you will be going up or down that grade on the specific hike. The maximum grade is calculated by dividing the elevation gained or lost by the distance covered.

**Hiking time**: The average time it will take to cover the route. It is based on the total distance, elevation gain, and condition and difficulty of the trail. Your fitness level will also affect your time.

**Seasons/schedule**: General information on the best time of year to hike.

**Fees and permits**: Whether you need to carry any money with you for park entrance fees and permits.

**Dog friendly**: Know the trail regulations before you take your dog hiking with you.

**Trail surface**: General information about what to expect underfoot.

**Land status**: National park, national forest, state forest, etc.

**Other trail users**: Such as horseback riders, mountain bikers, inline skaters, etc.

**Maps to consult**: This is a list of other maps to supplement the maps in this book. USGS maps are the best source for accurate topographical information, but the local park map may show more recent trails. Use both.

**Amenities available**: Lets you know if restrooms, picnic areas, campgrounds, and other enhancements are at or near the trailhead. This way you can stop on the way to use the restroom if no restrooms are available at the trailhead, whether to bring a picnic to the trailhead, etc.

**Cell service**: This gives you an idea of whether or not your phone will get reception on the hike. In elevationally varied areas such as the highlands, you can have reception on a ridge but not down in the valley. Also, what carrier you use can have a lot to do with whether or not you have reception.

**Trail contacts**: This is the location, phone number, and website URL for the local land manager(s) in charge of all the trails within the selected hike. Before you head out, get trail access information, or contact the land manager after your visit if you see problems with trail erosion, damage, or misuse.

The **Finding the trailhead** section gives you dependable driving directions to where you'll want to park.

**The Hike** is the meat of the chapter. Detailed and honest, it's a carefully researched impression of the trail. It also often includes lots of area history, both natural and human. Under **Miles and Directions**, mileage cues identify all turns and trail name changes, as well as points of interest. Options are also given for many hikes to make your journey shorter or longer depending on the amount of time you have. Don't feel restricted to the routes and trails that are mapped here. Be adventurous and use this guide as a platform to discover new routes for yourself.

A **sidebar** is included with some hikes. This is simply interesting information about the area or trail that doesn't necessarily pertain to the specific hike but gives you some human or natural tidbit that may pique your interest to explore beyond the simple mechanics of the trek. Enjoy your time in the outdoors and remember to pack out what you pack in.

## How to Use the Maps

**Overview map**: This map shows the location of each hike in the area by hike number.

**Route map**: This is your primary guide to each hike. It shows all of the accessible roads and trails, points of interest, water, landmarks, and geographical features. It also distinguishes trails from roads, and paved roads from unpaved roads. The selected route is highlighted, and directional arrows point the way.

# Trail Finder

| Hike # | Hike Name | Best Hikes for Waterfalls | Best Hikes for Great Views | Best Hikes for Children | Best Hikes for Dogs | Best Hikes for Stream Lovers | Best Hikes for Back-packers | Best Hikes for Nature Lovers | Best Hikes for History Lovers |
|---|---|---|---|---|---|---|---|---|---|
| 1 | Hemphill Bald | | ● | | | | | ● | |
| 2 | Big Fork Ridge Circuit | | | | | ● | ● | ● | ● |
| 3 | Little Cataloochee Historic Hike | | | ● | | ● | | ● | ● |
| 4 | Mount Sterling Tower | | ● | ● | | | ● | ● | |
| 5 | Lovers Leap | | ● | ● | | | | | |
| 6 | Big Laurel Creek Hike | | | ● | ● | ● | ● | | ● |
| 7 | Falls of Hickey Fork | ● | | | ● | ● | | | |
| 8 | Jerry Miller Loop | ● | ● | | | ● | ● | ● | |
| 9 | Bailey Mountain Preserve | | ● | | | | | | |

| Hike # | Hike Name | Best Hikes for Waterfalls | Best Hikes for Great Views | Best Hikes for Children | Best Hikes for Dogs | Best Hikes for Stream Lovers | Best Hikes for Backpackers | Best Hikes for Nature Lovers | Best Hikes for History Lovers |
|---|---|---|---|---|---|---|---|---|---|
| 10 | High Rocks | | ● | | ● | | ● | ● | |
| 11 | Nolichucky Gorge Circuit | | ● | | | ● | | ● | |
| 12 | Unaka Mountain Wilderness | ● | | | | ● | | ● | |
| 13 | Flat Laurel Creek Loop | ● | ● | ● | ● | ● | | ● | |
| 14 | Art Loeb Loop | | ● | | | | ● | ● | |
| 15 | Falls of Yellowstone Prong | ● | ● | ● | ● | ● | | | |
| 16 | Cove Creek Falls Hike | ● | ● | ● | ● | ● | | | |
| 17 | John Rock Loop | ● | ● | | | | ● | ● | |
| 18 | Looking Glass Rock | ● | ● | | | | ● | ● | ● |
| 19 | Mount Pisgah | | ● | ● | | | ● | | ● |
| 20 | The Pink Beds | | | ● | ● | ● | ● | ● | ● |

| Hike # | Hike Name | Best Hikes for Waterfalls | Best Hikes for Great Views | Best Hikes for Children | Best Hikes for Dogs | Best Hikes for Stream Lovers | Best Hikes for Backpackers | Best Hikes for Nature Lovers | Best Hikes for History Lovers |
|---|---|---|---|---|---|---|---|---|---|
| 21 | High Falls Hike | ● | | | ● | ● | | ● | |
| 22 | Avery Creek Falls and Twin Falls Loop | ● | | ● | | ● | ● | ● | |
| 23 | Bradley Creek Circuit | | | | ● | ● | ● | | |
| 24 | Cantrell Creek Lodge Loop | | | | ● | ● | ● | ● | ● |
| 25 | Cedar Rock Bridal Veil Falls Hike | ● | ● | | | ● | | | |
| 26 | Waterfalls of DuPont Loop | ● | | | | ● | | ● | |
| 27 | Blue Ridge Pastures | | ● | ● | ● | | | | |
| 28 | Bearwallow Mountain | | ● | ● | ● | | | | |
| 29 | Florence Nature Preserve | ● | ● | ● | ● | | | | ● |
| 30 | Rattlesnake Lodge Hike | | ● | ● | ● | | | | ● |

| Hike # | Hike Name | Best Hikes for Waterfalls | Best Hikes for Great Views | Best Hikes for Children | Best Hikes for Dogs | Best Hikes for Stream Lovers | Best Hikes for Back-packers | Best Hikes for Nature Lovers | Best Hikes for History Lovers |
|---|---|---|---|---|---|---|---|---|---|
| 31 | Little Snowball Mountain | | ● | | ● | | | ● | |
| 32 | Cascade Falls and Douglas Falls | ● | ● | | ● | | ● | ● | ● |
| 33 | Point Lookout Trail | | ● | | | | | | |
| 34 | Mount Mitchell State Park Loop | | ● | | ● | | | ● | ● |
| 35 | Black Mountain High Country Hike | | ● | | | | ● | ● | ● |
| 36 | River Loop with Setrock Creek Falls | ● | | | ● | ● | | ● | |
| 37 | Crabtree Falls | ● | | ● | ● | ● | | | |
| 38 | Trails of Linville Falls | ● | ● | ● | ● | | | ● | |
| 39 | Linville Gorge Wilderness Hike | | ● | | | | ● | ● | |
| 40 | Lake James State Park Hike | | ● | ● | ● | | | | |

# Map Legend

## Transportation

⬢ 26 ⬢    Interstate

⬡ 276 ⬡    US Highway

○ 107 ○    State Highway

▭ 10 ▭    County/Forest/Local Road

= = = =    Unpaved Road

├───┼───┤    Railroad

- - - - -    State Border

## Trails

------    Featured Trail

- - - - -    Trail

## Water Features

⬭    Body of Water

∿    River or Creek

⌇    Intermittent Stream

ơ    Spring

≋    Waterfall

## Land Management

▭    National Forest/Park/
Wilderness Area

▭    State/County Park

▭    Preserve

## Symbols

⏝    Bridge

■    Building/Point of Interest

Ⱥ    Campground

†    Cemetery

○    City/Town

•─•    Gate

▲    Mountain/Peak

◪    Overlook/Viewpoint

🅿    Parking

⤫    Pass/Gap

⊞    Picnic Area

•─•─•    Pipeline

▣    Ranger Station

🛱    Tower

①    Trailhead

⊢───⊣    Tunnel

❓    Visitor/Information Center

# Northwest

# 1 Hemphill Bald

Take this Smoky Mountain gem of an adventure and experience high-country hiking en route to an open meadow and a fantastic panorama of western North Carolina. Start your hike on the Hemphill Bald Trail, trekking Balsam Mountain to join Cataloochee Divide among northern hardwoods and spruce. Ridge run along the national park boundary, staying above 5,000 feet the entire route, and make your way to Hemphill Knob, elevation 5,554 feet, where the open grasses of adjacent Cataloochee Ranch present spectacular vistas of mountains, meadows, and valleys, delivering the Southern Appalachians at their finest. Elevation changes are relatively minimal.

**Start:** Polls Gap trailhead
**Distance:** 9.4-mile there-and-back
**Difficulty:** Moderate-strenuous
**Elevation change:** +-1,121 feet
**Maximum grade:** 9 percent grade for 0.6 mile
**Hiking time:** About 4.7 hours
**Seasons/schedule:** Trailhead access road open early May through Oct; go when skies are clear
**Fees and permits:** Parking permit required
**Dog friendly:** Dogs prohibited

**Trail surface:** Forested natural surface
**Land status:** National park
**Other trail users:** A few equestrians
**Maps to consult:** National Geographic #229, Great Smoky Mountains National Park
**Amenities available:** None, campground, picnic area nearby
**Cell service:** Good
**Trail contacts:** Great Smoky Mountains National Park, www.nps.gov/grsm, (865) 436-1200

**Finding the trailhead:** From Asheville, take I-40 west to exit 31B and join US 74 west for 4 miles, then take exit 103 toward Maggie Valley on US 19 south and stay with US 19 south for 12 miles to exit onto the Blue Ridge Parkway. Once on the parkway, turn left, north, and follow it 2.4 miles to turn right onto Heintooga Ridge Road. Continue 6.1 miles to Polls Gap, on your right. The Hemphill Bald Trail leaves right. Trailhead GPS: 35.563299, -83.161650

## The Hike

The entirety of this hike stays above 5,000 feet, providing a bona fide high-country experience. Take note that the access road to reach the trailhead is open from early May through October. Hiking along the crest of Balsam Mountain then along Cataloochee Divide, trail adventurers will enjoy this upland splendor without excessive exertion, as elevation changes are not much while winding your way to a fantastic view at Hemphill Bald. Much of this hike travels along the Great Smoky Mountains National Park boundary, and by necessity the Hemphill Bald Trail bypasses knobs, making sure to stay on the park side of ridge crests. However, in several places, the trail straddles the national park boundary, where you will see fences. Upon approaching Hemphill Bald, the non-park side of the ridge opens to a meadow, part of

*The open meadow of Hemphill Bald gives way to Maggie Valley and beyond.*

Cataloochee Ranch. These meadows avail marvelous vistas and recall a time when open grassy meadows, known as balds, once covered ridges all through western North Carolina. Over time, the balds within the Smokies side of the boundary have reforested, while parts outside of the park have been kept open to grazing, providing insight into land use patterns over time and a reason why the balds of the Southern Appalachians have all but disappeared.

Your route is on well-maintained trail. From the Polls Gap trailhead, you pick up a wide old logging railroad grade, level as a plain. Mountain hiking doesn't get much easier than this. Overhead, yellow birch, maple, and other northern hardwoods rise over you and scattered red spruce provide an evergreen presence. After swinging through the interestingly named Sugartree Licks, the trek leaves Balsam Mountain and joins Cataloochee Divide, coming to the park boundary at Garretts Gap. Most of the hike the non-park side is wooded similar to the park, save for broken down wood fencing in places. After working around Buck Knob, you will climb Sheepback Knob, using well-designed switchbacks to ease the uptick, even at that only 320 feet of ascent. Next, work around Little Bald Knob. Trickling springs flow across the trail in places. At Pine Tree Gap, where there are no pine trees, you are straddling the park boundary. Pastures appear, along with a sturdy barbed wire fence, dividing the forested from the grassy. Views begin to open as you make the final uphill for Hemphill Bald. Gazing along the boundary, the trail takes you directly along the fence, where on the Smokies side vegetation stretches toward the sunlight, sometimes crowding the pathway.

Upon making the apex of Hemphill Bald at 5,554 feet, a meadow opens 180 degrees to the southeast, providing a panorama of the first order. A stone bench, with a picture pointing out the exact mountains before you, makes for an ideal stopping spot. A buckeye tree with widespread limbs provides shade, while below the grassy slopes of Hemphill Bald fall away, revealing ranges of ridges, deep valleys, as well as fields and woods in the distance. On your return trip contemplate what the scene would've looked like a century back, when balds cloaked many a ridgetop in western North Carolina, and also what the area would be like if Great Smoky Mountains National Park had never been established.

*Relax at this stone table while soaking in the view from Hemphill Bald.*

# Miles and Directions

**0.0**      From Polls Gap parking area, take the Hemphill Bald Trail east, joining an old railroad grade laid out by the Suncrest Lumber Company. Turn south on a level track, sometimes soggy after prolonged rains. A grassy understory expands along the slope under buckeye, yellow birch, maple, and spruce.

**0.6**      Reach the gap of Sugartree Licks after leaving the railroad grade, still on quality trail. Angle around the northeast slope of Whim Knob. Winter aspects open of Cataloochee Valley below, home to the Smokies' largest elk herd.

**1.3**      Come to Garretts Gap and Cataloochee Divide, leaving Balsam Mountain. Curve easterly, working along the north side of Buck Knob. Scads of stinging nettle will border the path in summer. Pass outcroppings among younger trees, growing where balds once were.

**2.2**      Circle past a small rock shelter that would come in handy during a thunderstorm.

**2.5**      Pass through Maggot Spring Gap. Below and to your left is Maggot Spring Branch, part of the upper Cataloochee Creek watershed. Climb away toward Sheepback Knob, using switchbacks winding among rhododendron groves.

**2.9**      Make a high point on wooded Sheepback Knob. Drop a little then hike along the north slope of Little Bald. Ahead, regain the crest and descend a sometimes rutted trail. Come along active pasture across the park boundary.

**4.0**      Reach Pine Tree Gap then ascend. From here on you will have open or partly wooded pasture across the park boundary, along which the Hemphill Bald Trail travels. Views open to the southeast. The trail hereabouts can be quite brushy during the warm season.

**4.7**      Top out on Hemphill Bald. An opening in the fence allows you to access a viewing area complete with a buckeye-shaded stone table and seats. Tremendous views open of Moody Top in the near, bordered by meadows, as well as Plott Balsam, Cold Mountain, and the Blue Ridge rising across Maggie Valley below. Backtrack.

**9.4**      Arrive at the trailhead, completing the circuit hike.

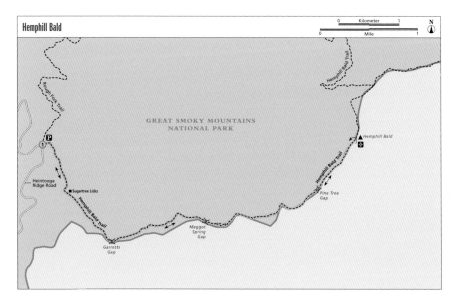

# 2 Big Fork Ridge Circuit

Old-growth trees highlight this loop hike that starts at lovely Cataloochee Valley in Great Smoky Mountains National Park. Add a visit to a pioneer homestead and you end up with a great day in the Smokies. The hike leaves Cataloochee on Rough Fork to see the Woody Place, then rambles under old growth, climbing up and over Big Fork Ridge to Caldwell Fork, a gorgeous stream. Visit the Big Poplars, massive tulip trees worthy of national park protection, then complete the circuit with a second climb of Big Fork Ridge.

**Start:** End of Cataloochee Road
**Distance:** 9.1-mile loop
**Difficulty:** Moderate to difficult due to distance
**Elevation change:** +-1,931 feet
**Maximum grade:** 13 percent grade for 1.4 miles
**Hiking time:** About 5 hours
**Seasons/schedule:** Winter to best see the big trees
**Fees and permits:** Parking permit required; fee and permit required for backpacking
**Dog friendly:** Dogs prohibited

**Trail surface:** Natural
**Land status:** National park
**Other trail users:** A few equestrians, some backpackers
**Maps to consult:** Great Smoky Mountains National Park; USGS Bunches Bald, Dellwood
**Amenities available:** Picnic area, seasonal campground within a few miles
**Cell service:** None
**Trail contacts:** Great Smoky Mountains National Park, (865) 436-1200, nps.gov/grsm

**Finding the trailhead:** From exit 20 on I-40 west of Asheville, head south a short distance on US 276. Turn right onto Cove Creek Road, which you follow nearly 6 miles to enter Great Smoky Mountains National Park. Two miles beyond the park boundary, turn left onto Cataloochee Road. Follow it to dead end at the Rough Fork Trail, which is at the end of the parking area. Trailhead GPS: 35.616209, -83.120841

## The Hike

This is one of those hikes that makes you realize how special Great Smoky Mountains National Park is, and what a blessing it is for Ashevillians to have the Smokies in their own backyard. This hike combines superlative human and natural history into one scenic package. You start in the Cataloochee Valley, home to a preserved mountain community nestled between towering mountains, now complemented with wild elk. Here, pre-park pioneer homes, ranging from log cabins to clapboard structures, along with churches and schools, have been preserved for all to see, set among woods and fields where families lived, loved, and died while calling the Cataloochee Valley home. However, this area is also home to crashing mountain streams, towering ridges, wild bears, and big woods, including massive old-growth tulip trees, some of which you

*Author admires a massive tulip tree on this hike.*

will see on this circuit hike that explores two of the primary streams—Rough Fork and Caldwell Fork—flowing through Cataloochee Valley.

Along the hike you will see the Woody Place, long the home of Cataloochee stalwarts. There is additional human history as well—for the hike takes you by a pair of graves leftover from the days when Civil War marauders on both sides crisscrossed this no-man's-land. The circuit hike does have challenges. It makes two climbs totaling around 2,000 feet of elevation change when looping from Rough Fork to Caldwell Fork and back again, surmounting Big Fork Ridge. However, despite being along water much of the way, there are no wet-footed fords. Hiker bridges conveniently carry you across creeks. That fact makes it a good winter hike, for then you can best see the old-growth trees and pioneer homesites, though the other seasons bring their delights, too. Backpackers be apprised that the circuit passes two fine designated backcountry campsites that can extend your adventure. A fee-based permit, accessible online, is required to camp overnight in the Smokies backcountry.

*The Woody Place adds a historical aspect to this trail adventure.*

The route starts on the Rough Fork Trail at the end of Cataloochee Road and its fields, which sometimes harbor elk. The path traces crystalline Rough Fork as the watercourse dashes around rocks under groves of rhododendron and lush hardwoods. Ironically, the Rough Fork Trail almost became a road in the 1960s. Park personnel wanted a route out of Cataloochee Valley, instead of the one way in, one way out setup, to alleviate anticipated traffic. And that was well before the arrival of the elk that have exponentially increased Cataloochee's popularity. However, the road was not built, and we can walk up still-wild Rough Fork valley.

Just a mile into the trek you can visit the Woody Place. By the way, the walk to the Woody Place makes a fine, short family-friendly there-and-back walk. Visit the wood clapboard structure fronted by a lone cedar in the front yard. The all-important springhouse stands nearby, while other outbuildings once dotted the locale. The garden was located in the level spot near the house. Pastures formerly extended well away from the structure.

Once inside the Woody Place, you will note the differing ceiling heights, giving away the fact that the home was built in stages over a long period, as most pioneer homes were back then. It started as a single-room log cabin. Moreover, they needed the extra room, for fourteen kids lived here at once, when Jonathan Woody wed a widower with her own children. Later, in the 1920s, when Cataloochee was discovered by tourists flocking to western North Carolina (as they have ever since), the Woody family hosted these visitors as they fished for trout and roamed the mountains. Steve Woody—Jonathan Woody's son—stocked Rough Fork with rainbow trout and charged fishermen by the number of fish they caught and kept.

Old-growth forests begin not far beyond the Woody Place, dominated by red oaks and sadly the skeletons of deceased hemlock trees fallen prey to the hemlock wooly adelgid. Then you come to Big Hemlock backcountry campsite #40, where some of the evergreens have been preserved. The campsite, nestled between Hurricane Creek and Rough Fork, is heavily cloaked in rhododendron and doghobble that form dividers between camps.

The hike then climbs a rocky, rooty path away from Hurricane Creek onto Little Ridge, shaded by big tulip trees as well as chestnut oak trees farther up. It is a little over 1,300 feet from the trailhead to the high point. The descent begins after the loop hike joins the Caldwell Fork Trail. Descend past the not-to-be-missed Big Poplars, huge tulip trees, some of which take several people linking outstretched arms to encircle. Caldwell Fork backcountry campsite #41 is not far from the Big Poplars. This camp is set in a hardwood flat along its namesake stream.

The circuit next passes a trail intersection then comes to a spur trail leading to the Civil War graves of three former Union soldiers, buried in two graves. They were killed just before the end of the Civil War by some fellow Northerners, who were terrorizing local residents in the wartime chaos. It isn't long before the second and final climb of the hike—gaining a little over 600 feet—leads you over Big Fork Ridge on a path carved out by Cataloochee residents and subsequently improved by the Park Service. After crossing Big Fork Ridge, the path descends past more pioneer homesites and the site of an elk enclosure where the beasts were acclimated before they were let loose into the wilds, where they have thrived ever since. Hopefully you will see some of these critters while in Cataloochee Valley.

## Miles and Directions

**0.0** Join the Rough Fork Trail as it leaves the uppermost end of Cataloochee Valley. Cruise a wide, nearly level track shaded by yellow birch, maple, and white pines. The valley shortly closes in. Span Rough Fork on a wooden hiker bridge, then cross the waterway again on a second hiker bridge. Walk a wet section of path before bridging Rough Fork a third time.

**1.0** Come to the Steve Woody Place after reaching a clearing.

**1.5** Reach Big Hemlock, backcountry campsite #40, after crossing Hurricane Creek. Climb to Little Ridge beyond the campsite.

**3.0** Come to a trail intersection. Turn left, joining the Caldwell Fork Trail, now heading downhill under more old-growth forest of northern hardwoods such as cherry and buckeye.

**4.1** Intersect the short spur trail to the Big Poplars, old-growth tulip trees, not poplars, as they were formerly known.

**4.4** Come to Caldwell Fork backcountry campsite #41, situated in a flat along Caldwell Fork. Cross Caldwell Fork on a hiker bridge, then pass a homesite on your right, now foresting over.

**4.5** Pass the Hemphill Bald Trail. Stay straight down the Caldwell Fork valley, often walking a hillside well above the stream.

**5.9** Reach a side trail leading right to a gravesite. Up the spur are two graves interring three Union soldiers. Meet the McKee Branch Trail not far beyond here. Keep straight still on the Caldwell Fork Trail in former farmland, now being reclaimed by fire cherry, locust, and tulip trees.

**6.0** Turn left on the Big Fork Ridge Trail. Span Caldwell Fork on a wooden hiker bridge then climb a pioneer-originated path in hardwoods. Soon make a big switchback, working up Rabbit Ridge.

**7.5** Bisect a gap in Big Fork Ridge. Your climb is over and the rest of the hike is downhill as you reenter the Rough Fork valley.

**9.1** Cross Rough Fork on a footbridge, then return to the Cataloochee Valley, completing the circuit hike.

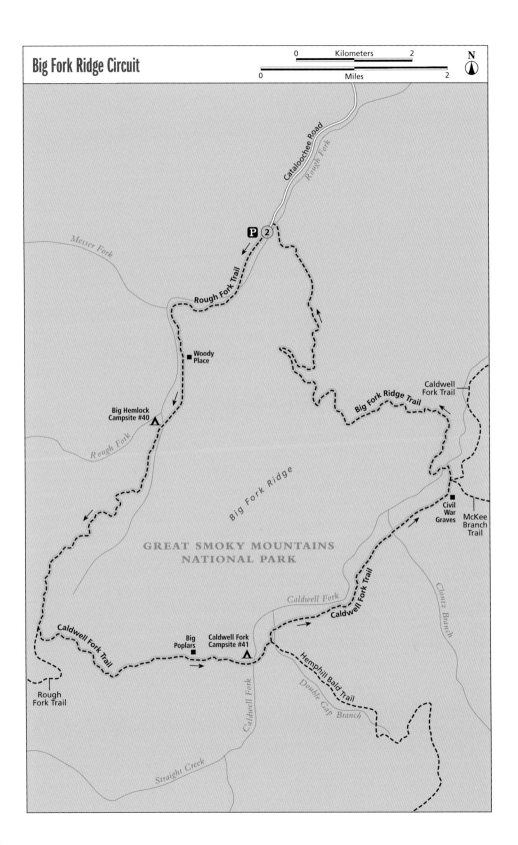

# Big Fork Ridge Circuit

0 Kilometers 2

0 Miles 2

N

Cataloochee Road

Rough Fork

Messer Fork

P 2

Rough Fork Trail

Woody Place

Big Hemlock Campsite #40

Rough Fork

Caldwell Fork Trail

Big Fork Ridge Trail

Caldwell Fork Trail

McKee Branch Trail

Civil War Graves

Big Fork Ridge

GREAT SMOKY MOUNTAINS NATIONAL PARK

Clontz Branch

Caldwell Fork

Caldwell Fork Trail

Caldwell Fork Trail

Big Poplars

Caldwell Fork Campsite #41

Rough Fork Trail

Hemphill Bald Trail

Caldwell Fork

Double Gap Branch

Straight Creek

# 3 Little Cataloochee Historic Hike

The secluded hike to Little Cataloochee Church is a trip back in time. Start at a remote trailhead, tracing an old road. Pass a preserved historic cabin on your undulating trek into the Little Cataloochee valley, where the pioneer community of Ola once stood. Explore Ola to see homesites and evidence of the past. Finally, climb a hill to bucolic Little Cataloochee Church, built in the 1800s and still maintained.

**Start:** Old NC 284
**Distance:** 4.0-mile there-and-back
**Difficulty:** Easy to moderate
**Elevation change:** +-532 feet
**Maximum grade:** 9 percent grade for 0.6 mile
**Hiking time:** About 2 hours
**Seasons/schedule:** Year-round, summer growth may make historic sights less visible
**Fees and permits:** Parking permit required
**Dog friendly:** Dogs prohibited

**Trail surface:** Natural
**Land status:** National park
**Other trail users:** A few equestrians
**Maps to consult:** Great Smoky Mountains National Park; USGS Cove Creek Gap
**Amenities available:** Picnic areas, campground in Cataloochee Valley
**Cell service:** None
**Trail contacts:** Great Smoky Mountains National Park, (865) 436-1200, nps.gov/grsm

**Finding the trailhead:** From exit 20 on I-40 west of Asheville, take NC 276 south a short distance to Cove Creek Road. Turn right on Cove Creek Road and follow it nearly 6 miles to enter the park. Two miles beyond the park boundary, reach paved Cataloochee Road. However, keep straight, looking for a sign for "Big Creek, Cosby," joining gravel Old NC 284. Follow it for 2.1 miles, then come to a split. Stay right, still on gravel Old NC 284 and follow it 3.5 miles to the Little Cataloochee Trail on your left. Do not block the gate at the trailhead. Trailhead GPS: 35.676169, -83.087304

## The Hike

Many parts of what later became Great Smoky Mountains National Park were settled and owned by ancestors of first pioneers who cleared off fertile valleys in this back of beyond, then established communities and cultivated a way of life that has long since faded away. However, the very establishment of the national park that threw these people off their land preserved relics of this North Carolina pioneer past. And in very few places is it better preserved than in the Smokies. This network of valleys draining mile-high mountains was first settled in the 1830s. The primary community that sprang up was known as Cataloochee. Not long after families named Caldwell, Hannah, and Palmer moved in and offspring were born, Cataloochee already seemed a mite crowded for some. Pioneers being the way they are, some of the offspring got a little restless and moved on. A fellow named Dan Cook led the way to this settlement a few ridges over on Little Cataloochee Creek, building his log cabin in the 1850s.

*A raw winter day frames Little Cataloochee Church standing perched on a hill.*

But things really got going when one Will Messer married Dan Cook's daughter Rachael and bought 100 acres on Little Cataloochee Creek. There, Will Messer established Ola, named after his daughter Viola. Messer built the all-encompassing general store, a post office bearing the name Ola, and a blacksmith shop along with his own rangy eleven-room house.

Others followed and Ola began to thrive. John Hannah built his cabin in 1864, and even used bricks in his chimney, a very unusual thing in this place at that time. This hike takes you past the John Hannah cabin and through Ola.

However, the highlight of the hike is the visit to Little Cataloochee Church. This white church sitting atop a hill is a vivid reminder of the simplicity of those days gone by. Also known as Ola Baptist Church, the rectangular structure was built in 1889, and the belfry you see was added in 1914. Even today, a rope connects to the bell and visitors to Little Cataloochee Church toll the bell much as they did a century back. A well-maintained, fenced cemetery filled with residents of Ola who attended this church stretches out on a hillside, below the white chapel. Inside, the whitewashed walls brighten the sunlit wooden floor, where simple bench pews and a pulpit stand in wait. An old-fashioned wood stove sits in the center of the house of worship.

Being very difficult to access from the outside, the community of Ola and Little Cataloochee Church were served by a circuit-riding preacher who visited various

*The John Hannah Cabin displays a Smokies way of life long gone.*

country churches on a rotating basis. He came about one Sunday a month, spending the night with different church member families. On the other Sundays, weekly gatherings were still held at the church. Members would have Sunday school and sing praise music. Other gatherings, including weddings and funerals, were held at Little Cataloochee Church.

Interestingly, when someone in the Ola community passed away, the 400-pound church bell was tolled to let residents within earshot know. The bell would be rung several times followed by extended silence. The toller of the bell would then ring the bell once for each year of the person's life. Locals would count the tolls to identify the deceased person.

In late fall, after the crops were harvested, Little Cataloochee Church would host a weeklong camp meeting and revival. Long services alternated with group meals and fellowship. The men would head in and out of the services, gathering outside to chew tobacco and shoot the breeze. To this day, descendants of those who lived in Cataloochee annually meet at the preserved church to worship, maintain the graves of their ancestors, and share a meal—and stories of the past—perhaps to see and appreciate the beauty of their ancestral home.

Life in Little Cataloochee happily crawled along as the world moved on by. It came as a great surprise when the residents heard the "feds" wanted to turn their quiet isolated valley into a national park. Some were glad to go, but most left their homeland with heavy hearts, bought out by the government using eminent domain. And today we can see the evidence of those days gone by.

I recommend making this hike from late fall through early spring, when the leaves are off the trees and you can best see the homesites, rock walls, and other evidence of pre-park settlers. You will also enjoy seclusion. This trek begins at a remote trailhead for the Smokies, and the few people who hike to Little Cataloochee Church usually start at more popular Cataloochee Valley. Be forewarned that the trail to Little Cataloochee Church has lots of ups and downs, though the undulations are never too long or too precipitous. However, the hike follows a roadbed, making it foot-friendly. After spanning Correll Branch, the Little Cataloochee Trail curves into the Little Cataloochee Creek valley on a hillside, well above the stream. The wide track travels under pines and oaks, then intersects the lesser-used Long Bunk Trail. Shortly after the junction, you come to the John Hannah Cabin, built in the 1860s, since restored by the Park Service. The distinctive red brick chimney adds color to the wood cabin, showing the effects of time. Explore uphill from the cabin to find rock piles adjacent to fields that were once striped with rows of green corn, now adorned with gray, straight-trunked tulip trees. While you are at it, imagine grassy hillsides dotted with apple trees that Hannah harvested.

It isn't long before you cross Little Cataloochee Creek on a bridge, arriving at Will Messer's community of Ola. Scan the area for relic apple trees. Ample evidence of homesites is scattered throughout the flats on the creek's south side. Any remains you find are part of Great Smoky Mountains National Park. Explore, enjoy, but then leave the remains behind.

From there, the trail leads up a ridge, where stands Little Cataloochee Church, atop a hill separating Little Cataloochee Creek from Coggins Branch. The fine, well-maintained, sturdy white sanctuary astonishes even more after seeing the older rustic cabin of John Hannah and other remnants of Ola in various stages of disrepair.

## Miles and Directions

**0.0**   Leave the Old NC 284 trailhead on a wide roadbed that is the Little Cataloochee Trail. (The trail is maintained this way to allow auto access to the graves at Little Cataloochee Church.) Drop to span Correll Branch under a thick forest.

**1.0**   Intersect the Long Bunk Trail after meandering in pine-oak woods with an understory of mountain laurel. It leaves right and climbs toward Mount Sterling Gap. Our hike stays straight with the wide Little Cataloochee Trail.

**1.2**   Meet the spur trail to the Hannah Cabin. Turn right here and soon come to the hillside cabin, notable for its brick "chimbley." Continue on the Little Cataloochee Church Trail.

**1.4**   Bridge Little Cataloochee Creek. You are now in the heart of what once was the community of Ola. Explorers can spot evidence of pre-park settlement, but leave all artifacts behind for others to discover.

**2.0**   Reach Little Cataloochee Church after topping the ridge dividing Little Cataloochee Creek from Coggins Branch. Respectfully explore the church and its grounds, then backtrack.

**4.0**   Return to Old NC 284, completing the historic hike.

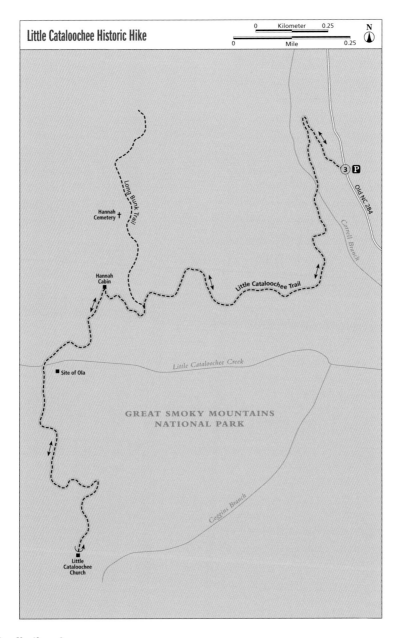

Little Cataloochee Historic Hike

Kilometer

Mile

N

Long Bunk Trail

Hannah Cemetery

Hannah Cabin

Little Cataloochee Trail

Old NC 284

Carrell Branch

Site of Ola

Little Cataloochee Creek

GREAT SMOKY MOUNTAINS NATIONAL PARK

Coggins Branch

Little Cataloochee Church

# 4  Mount Sterling Tower

This Great Smoky Mountains National Park hike begins at high and historic Mount Sterling Gap, then climbs higher to enter the rare spruce-fir forest that cloaks only the highest mantles of the Southern Appalachians. The ascent tops out at 5,842-foot Mount Sterling, where a preserved metal fire tower delivers unparalleled 360-degree views of the Smokies in the near and range after range in North Carolina and Tennessee.

**Start:** Mount Sterling Gap
**Distance:** 5.4-mile there-and-back
**Difficulty:** Moderate, does have steep sections
**Elevation change:** +-2,013 feet
**Maximum grade:** 15 percent grade for 1.9 miles
**Hiking time:** About 3 hours
**Seasons/schedule:** 24/7/365, whenever the skies are clear
**Fees and permits:** Parking permit required; fee and permit required for backpacking

**Dog friendly:** Dogs prohibited
**Trail surface:** Natural
**Land status:** National park
**Other trail users:** A few backpackers, occasional equestrian
**Maps to consult:** Great Smoky Mountains National Park; USGS Cove Creek Gap
**Amenities available:** None
**Cell service:** Decent up high
**Trail contacts:** Great Smoky Mountains National Park, (865) 436-1200, nps.gov/grsm

**Finding the trailhead:** From Asheville, take I-40 west to exit 451, just west of the North Carolina state line. Take the paved road and cross the Pigeon River. After the bridge, turn left to follow the Pigeon upstream. Come to an intersection 2.3 miles after crossing the Pigeon. Turn left here onto Old NC 284 and follow it 6.7 winding miles to Mount Sterling Gap. The trail starts on the west side of the gap. Trailhead GPS: 35.700173, -83.097491

## The Hike

This is a problematic hike to rate for difficulty. The hike is not long—5.4 miles. However, it is fairly steep—you gain a little over 1,900 feet in 2.7 miles. Yet, the trail is well graded and in good shape. Though sustained, the uptick does not stretch for miles and miles like other Smokies treks, so I give it a moderate rating—with an asterisk. The extraordinary view is worth the effort no matter the rating. The preserved metal tower stands at 5,842 feet, purportedly the highest true fire tower still standing east of the Mississippi River. This is just part of the panorama from atop Mount Sterling.

Constructed in 1935 by the Civilian Conservation Corps, the tower was designed for fire watching. A small cabin and outhouse were also constructed for the person manning the tower. Firewatchers generally stayed up here for 2-week stints during the spring and fall fire seasons. However, by the mid-1960s the tower was decommissioned when fire watching was done by airplane, though the firewatcher's cabin was left to deteriorate until the 1980s. The fire tower has been stabilized and its heights

*This is but part of the 360-degree view that can be had from Mount Sterling Tower.*

are used as a communications tower for Great Smoky Mountains National Park. This is one of two metal fire towers preserved in the Smokies, the other being Shuckstack Tower at the other—western—end of the park.

Mount Sterling Gap, at an elevation of 3,890 feet, lets you start high and get higher. Long before I-40 and the roads we have today, Mount Sterling Gap was a point of passage for travelers going between North Carolina and Tennessee. During the Civil War, the remote mountains around the state line became a no-man's-land, neither Confederate nor Union, loyal only to who controlled the passes, such as Mount Sterling Gap. Conscriptors from both armies sought deserters and draft dodgers to fill the ranks of their respective armies—or eliminate from the ranks of the opposition's armies. Conflicts occurred regularly here.

On April 10, 1865, a local named Albert Teague—part of the local Confederate home guard—intercepted three Union sympathizers at the gap and marched them along to the fiddle tunes played by one Harry Grooms. Mr. Grooms was carrying the fiddle and bow with him when he was captured along with his brother George and his brother-in-law Mitchell Caldwell. Teague shot Harry Grooms and the two others after one final song, allegedly "Bonaparte's Retreat," which was subsequently known also as "Grooms Tune." The three Union partisans were buried in a common grave by Harry's wife down in the community of Mount Sterling by Big Creek. The headstone above the freshly mounded dirt stated one word: "Murdered."

Though Mount Sterling is known for its spruce-fir forest, the hike begins among hardwoods—primarily oaks—cloaking the east-west ridge linking Mount Sterling and Mount Sterling Gap.

When the leaves are off the trees you can view the mantle of evergreen on the crown of Mount Sterling. Ironically, you are hiking the south side of the ridge where galax and mountain laurel belie the increasing elevation. Eventually, the path rises enough—and curves around to the north side of the ridge—to enter the spruce-fir zone, first starting with the red spruce, accompanied by fellow cool-climate specialists yellow birch and beech. Demonstrating how influential exposure is, mountain laurel, pines, and oaks are seen again when the trail enters southern exposure.

After angling onto the reaches of Mount Sterling Ridge, breaking 5,000 feet, the spruce-fir ecosystem takes over. Here, red spruce rise thick and high, creating a shady, moist environment, where springs trickle cool across the trail, a forest floor rich with mosses and an understory of Fraser fir.

Once atop Mount Sterling Ridge you will see a few grasses remaining from the days when this ridge was grazed by cattle, along with thickets of Fraser fir trees. The path is mostly level before rising to reach a little-used horse hitch post a little ways from the Mount Sterling summit. Just ahead, open onto a clearing and the top of Mount Sterling. This is also the location of backcountry campsite #38, also named Mount Sterling.

The tower stands at the very crest of the summit, where a USGS benchmark denotes the actual high point. Woe to those who reach the tower via the Baxter Creek Trail. It is a very tough climb from Big Creek ranger station. A few backpackers make their way here via Mount Sterling Ridge Trail; however, the vast majority of tower visitors come via Mount Sterling Gap.

The park's eastern swath is the featured view from the tower. The main crest of the Smokies runs to your north and west, mostly covered in spruce and fir as well. I-40 and its road cut in the Pigeon River gorge are easy to spot to the east. Look east also for the meadow of Max Patch. The hills of East Tennessee stretch to the west. At night, the lights of Newport, Tennessee, and Waynesville, North Carolina, are easily spotted. Backpackers overnighting at the campsite here climb the tower for these nocturnal vistas.

Mount Sterling backcountry campsite #38 is a desired site. The most popular camp spot is in the grassy area immediately below the tower. The campsite's claim to fame is being the highest backcountry campsite in the Smokies without a trail shelter. Other private wooded individual camps are set in the adjacent woods—and are good when the winds are howling. Looking for water? A spring is located a half-mile down the Baxter Creek Trail. Back during the firewatcher days, those manning the tower would use this spring as well as capture water from the cabin roof into a cistern.

*The view from Mount Sterling in winter*

# Miles and Directions

**0.0**   Join the Mount Sterling Trail as it ascends westerly from Mount Sterling Gap as a wide trail. Walk around a pole gate, and waste no time climbing on the jeep road built to haul men and materials up to the peak to construct the tower and cabin.

**0.5**   Level out and meet the Long Bunk Trail. It leaves left 3.6 miles to meet the Little Cataloochee Trail to the south. Our hike keeps straight, aiming ever higher.

**0.7**   The Mount Sterling Trail makes a sharp switchback to the right, leaving the southern exposure.

**1.3**   Switchback left, curving back into what is left of the oaks at this high elevation.

**2.3**   Meet the Mount Sterling Ridge Trail after cresting out on Mount Sterling Ridge. The Mount Sterling Ridge Trail leaves left 1.4 miles for Pretty Hollow Gap, but we go right on the Mount Sterling Ridge Trail, heading northeast for the peak of Mount Sterling on one of the more level segments of this hike.

**2.7**   Emerge onto the clearing atop Mount Sterling. You will see Mount Sterling Tower rising from the high point as well as the main camping area for campsite #38. Climb the tower for spectacular views. Backtrack.

**5.4**   Arrive at Mount Sterling Gap, completing the there-and-back hike.

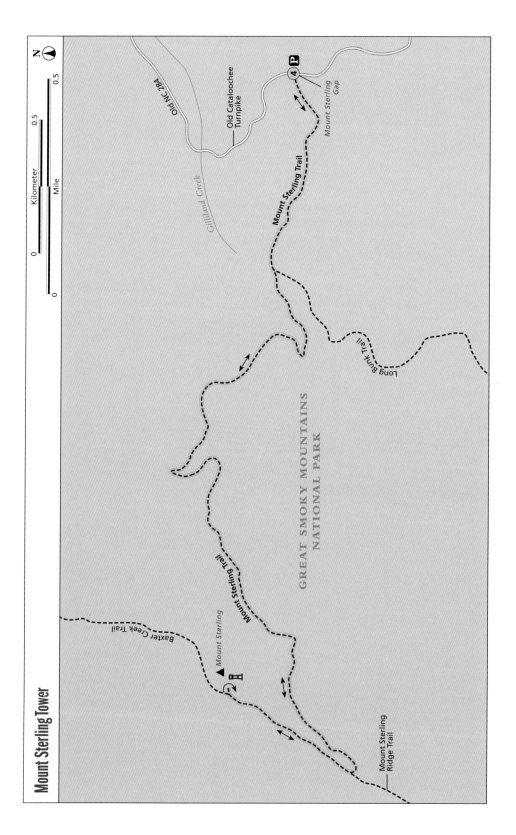

# Mount Sterling Tower

Kilometer

Mile

N

GREAT SMOKY MOUNTAINS
NATIONAL PARK

Old NC 284

Old Cataloochee
Turnpike

Gilliland Creek

Mount Sterling
Gap

Mount Sterling Trail

Long Bunk Trail

Baxter Creek Trail

Mount Sterling
Trail

Mount Sterling

Mount Sterling
Ridge Trail

# 5 Lovers Leap

This hike leaves the trail town of Hot Springs and makes a loop, passing cliffs above the French Broad River, where you can soak in an historic view from Lovers Leap. First, trek along a narrow mountain stream where spring flowers abound. Meet the famed Appalachian Trail (AT), then join Lovers Leap Ridge. Trace the AT atop this narrow spine as the brawny French Broad flows hundreds of feet below. As you near Hot Springs, you will come to a stone promontory presenting views of the town below and the mountains rising above the French Broad River valley. Enjoy an encore vista from the actual Lovers Leap before leaving the AT and returning to the parking area.

**Start:** Silvermine parking area
**Distance:** 3.9-mile loop
**Difficulty:** Moderate
**Elevation change:** +-1,160 feet
**Maximum grade:** 15 percent for 0.5 mile
**Hiking time:** About 2.5 hours
**Seasons/schedule:** 24/7/365, especially good in winter
**Fees and permits:** None
**Dog friendly:** Leashed dogs allowed
**Trail surface:** Forested natural surface
**Land status:** National forest

**Other trail users:** None
**Maps to consult:** National Geographic #782 French Broad & Nolichucky Rivers, Cherokee and Pisgah National Forests; USGS Hot Springs
**Amenities available:** Trail town with eateries, hot springs, and outfitters 0.2 mile from trailhead
**Cell service:** Good
**Trail contacts:** Pisgah National Forest, Appalachian Ranger District, (828) 689-9694, www.fs.usda.gov

**Finding the trailhead:** From Asheville, take I-26 north to exit 19A, Marshall. Join US 25/US 70 and drive 21 miles to Hot Springs. Before crossing the bridge over the French Broad River, just east of Hot Springs, turn right on River Road. Drive a very short distance to the river and turn left on a paved road, Silvermine Creek Road, following it under the US 25/US 70 bridge. Stay left again as it curves up Silvermine Creek past houses. Reach the signed Silvermine parking area on your left, 0.3 mile from US 25/US 70. Trailhead GPS: 35.892485, -82.818417

## The Hike

You can combine this fun trek with a trip to the trail town of Hot Springs, hemmed in by mountains on all sides, save for where the French Broad River fights its way west toward Tennessee. This hike is just across the river from this town built around and named for hot springs, a highlight among other area attractions such as rafting, kayaking, camping, and hiking. And did I mention eating? One of the perks of hiking is going to eat a big—and guiltless—meal after your hike. Hot Springs has dining options aplenty. And the outdoorsy tourist town is worth a day trip.

*Looking down at the French Broad River from Lovers Leap Ridge*

The Cherokee had found and used the thermal springs along the French Broad long before colonial settlers made their way to these mineral waters some thought had healing properties. By the time the United States had come to be, sick folk were soaking in the 100-degree aqua, hoping to heal.

One William Nelson saw an economic opportunity. He bought the springs and established a "resort" here, the first in what became a long line of hotels based around the springs. Back in those days, roads were rough and getting across the mountains wasn't easy. However, by 1828, the Buncombe Turnpike was routed along the French Broad River and passed beside the springs, raising the profile of the area for thousands of passersby who make their way from North Carolina into Tennessee and vice versa on the road.

The grand age of the springs began when Asheville's James Patten built a 350-room hotel in 1831. Times were good and for the next 8 decades the springs and the hotels beside them thrived. In 1882, a hot spring was discovered and the town of Warm Springs became Hot Springs. Despite the hotter water, the tourist trade declined until in 1917 the main hotel in town housed German merchant sailors at the height of World War I rather than tourists seeking the healing hot aqua. After the war, this last hotel burned, and only recently, with the rise of the AT in particular and outdoor tourism in general, has Hot Springs regained its swagger as a tourist destination.

It is not only the hot springs that made Hot Springs but also the French Broad River. It has already flowed through Asheville on its 100-mile journey to reach the mountain-rimmed Hot Springs. You will look down from Lovers Leap on the wide French Broad as it flows in shoals and sweeps through town. Even though this is a hike with a view, the trek is low elevation—a little over 2,400 feet at its highest point—and, therefore, is a good winter choice. Nevertheless, the elevations are not so low as to be hot and thus can be enjoyed year-round.

The hike starts at the parking area for the Silvermine Group Camp. A gated road takes you to the group camp, then joins the actual hiking trail, part of the Pump Gap Loop Trail. Traverse a wildflower-rich hollow pocked with rock outcroppings. Mosses and ferns are found in moist, shady spots.

The path keeps east, heading up along Pump Branch. The valley narrows as you parallel the shrinking stream. The trail then leaves Pump Branch behind, climbing steeply, aiming for Pump Gap amid rhododendron thickets from which rise straight-trunked tulip trees.

After making Pump Gap and intersecting the AT, take the master path of the East along Lovers Leap Ridge, now in dry-situation hardwoods such as chestnut oak, black gum, and pine. Occasional views can be had through the trees as the trail leads up and down along the craggy boulders of south-facing pine-clad slopes. You will pass a large campsite where northbound AT thru-hikers—their packs heavy with goodies after resupplying in Hot Springs—gorge.

Ahead, find a spur trail that noses out a rock spine for a fine view of the river valley for those who dare straddle the slender outcrop. Beyond this warmup view the AT continues a downgrade along Lovers Leap Ridge. Then you come to a trail junction with the Lovers Leap Trail but briefly stay with the AT and come to Lovers Leap. Here you can see the river, the railroad, the rapids, the town below, and the mountains beyond from the spot where an Indian princess leapt to her demise after learning the love of her life perished at the hands of an unwanted suitor. From here, it is all downhill back to Silvermine Group Camp and the trailhead. Be careful on the steep slope above Silver Mine Creek as you complete the circuit.

# Miles and Directions

**0.0**   Leave the Silvermine parking area at a trail signboard and walk the gated gravel access road heading up to the former Silvermine Group Camp. Walk the road along Silver Mine Creek. Buckeye, red bud, and other hardwoods shade the track.

**0.3**   Reach the Silvermine Group Campsite. Keep easterly on the Pump Gap Loop Trail, then walk around a pole gate at the upper end of the closed group camp. Hike past discarded Forest Service materials. Look for two old concrete explosives buildings. The trail narrows to a scenic singletrack path heading up the Silver Mine Creek hollow under widespread striped maple, regal white pines, and black birch, as well as rhododendron and doghobble. Pass through a productive spring wildflower area.

*The French Broad River flows past Lovers Leap Ridge, rising left from the water.*

**0.6** The Pump Gap Loop Trail climbs over an old roadbed as Silver Mine Creek flows under a culvert. Shortly come back alongside the creek and cross it. Leave Silver Mine Creek and start climbing along Pump Branch. The trail and waterway come together in spots.

**1.0** An arm of the Pump Gap Loop Trail leaves left, also heading for the AT. Stay right to meet the AT at Pump Gap.

**1.5** The Pump Gap Loop Trail reaches Pump Gap and the AT. Turn right, southbound on the AT. Climb a little as you head southwesterly, now on Lovers Leap Ridge.

**2.1** Top out on Lovers Leap Ridge after winding through side slope drainages. Listen for the sounds of the cascading French Broad River as you trace the rocky AT.

**2.8** Come near a large campsite on your left. Descend.

**3.1** Look for a user-created path leading acutely left. Walk out and join a narrow, tan-colored rock ridge extending out toward the French Broad River. Stand alongside a gnarled pine and scope out the river below, the town of Hot Springs downstream, and a host of mountains rising in the distance. Backtrack and rejoin the AT southbound.

**3.4** Come to a trail junction. Your return route, the Lovers Leap Trail, leaves right. However, first follow the AT to two overlooks, the first just past the intersection with the Lovers Leap Trail and the second a little farther down the AT at a switchback and an outcrop. This rock outcrop at the switchback is Lovers Leap. Enjoy the views, then join the Lovers Leap Trail.

**3.7** Make a sharp switchback left after heading steadily downhill on the Lovers Leap Trail.

**3.9** Emerge at the trailhead after cruising a bit at creek level, ending the adventure.

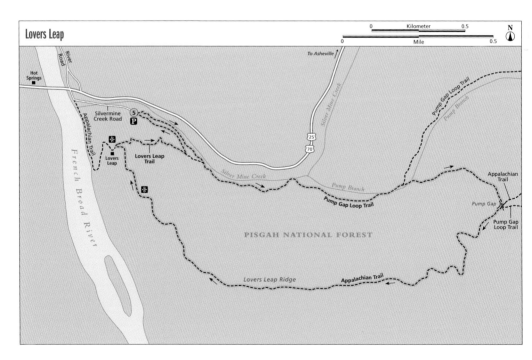

# 6 Big Laurel Creek Hike

This there-and-back trek traces an old railroad grade along Big Laurel Creek. Here, you follow the stream as it cuts a rugged gorge filled with geological wonders from steep cliffs to rock-constricted rapids below which deep pools form, to sun-splashed outcrops availing good watery views. The gentle grade reaches the former community of Runion, replete with relics, then cuts still deeper to reach the French Broad River and a turnaround point.

**Start:** Trailhead near intersection of US 25/70 and NC 208
**Distance:** 7.2-mile there-and-back
**Difficulty:** Moderate
**Elevation change:** +-190 feet
**Maximum grade:** 3 percent downhill grade for 0.2 mile
**Hiking time:** About 3.5 hours
**Seasons/schedule:** 24/7/365, year-round
**Fees and permits:** None
**Dog friendly:** Leashed dogs allowed
**Trail surface:** Natural, a little gravel

**Land status:** National forest, a little road right-of-way
**Other trail users:** Mountain bicyclers
**Maps to consult:** National Geographic #782 French Broad & Nolichucky Rivers, Cherokee and Pisgah National Forests; USGS Hot Springs
**Amenities available:** None
**Cell service:** Limited
**Trail contacts:** Pisgah National Forest, Appalachian Ranger District, (828) 689-9694, www.fs.usda.gov

**Finding the trailhead:** From Asheville, take I-26 north to exit 19A, Marshall. Then follow US 25/70 for 21 miles to the large roadside gravel parking area on your left just before US 25/70 curves left to bridge Big Laurel Creek. The Laurel River Trail starts at the south end of the gravel parking area, away from the bridge over Big Laurel Creek. Trailhead GPS: 35.913226, -82.756905

## The Hike

This hike explores the lowermost gorge of Big Laurel Creek, a scenic stream carving a canyon on its way to meet its mother stream, the French Broad River. Along the way you will see rock outcrops, crashing rapids, and deep pools, all while tracing a gentle trail that contrasts with the rugged terrain through which it travels. Along the trail Big Laurel Creek truly lives up to its name, since it is a sizable waterway, one of the bigger ones flowing through the national forest, and is regularly paddled by kayakers when Big Laurel Creek is up.

Of course, we will be hiking. Though you are traveling through a gorge, there is no need to ford the stream since the path stays on the east bank the entire route. The adventure is also good for hikers of all abilities since the trail grade is easy. Even though it is a 7.2-mile round-trip, hikers can turn around at any point they desire.

Furthermore, elevation changes are less than 200 feet, making it suitable for younger and older trail trekkers.

I recommend this hike for all seasons of the year. In spring, wildflowers abound and the crashing stream makes quite a sight. In summer, the slower waterway with its big pools and open sunning rocks fashion an ideal backcountry swimming destination. In fall, autumn's glory shines on the slopes of adjacent mountains rising hundreds of feet above. This is an especially good hike during the winter. The highest elevation of the hike is less than 1,700 feet, making it much warmer than the often frigid mile-high mountains around Asheville. And not having to ford the creek means you can follow a gorgeous waterway during the cold season without worrying about wetting your feet.

This hike traces an old logging railroad grade from the early 1900s. The Laurel River Logging Company ran a line along Big Laurel Creek to the French Broad River. The operation culminated at a sawmill operating what once was Runion, now a ghost town that you will see along the hike. Preceding the establishment of the logging railroad, a fellow named Amos Stackhouse had moved here from what is now the town of Hot Springs to form a new community. By 1883, Mr. Stackhouse had established a store and post office to serve local residents who were mining and processing an element known as barite for a company called Carolina Barytes. The lumber business followed, and the tracks were laid along Big Laurel Creek.

The mining and logging industry brought employees to the area that lived and worked here for decades. Thus grew Runion and the adjacent community of Stackhouse. Together, nearly 1,000 residents occupied this stretch of the French Broad. There was even a school for children of the lumbermen and barite processors. In 1916, a big flood damaged both the mill of Laurel River Logging Company and Carolina Barytes. Jobs were lost. Over time, residents began moving to larger communities, seeing better opportunity in places like Asheville. The industries shut down, and relics you will see on this hike are all that remains, from concrete forms to building foundations and unidentifiable metal objects, leftover from the days when work and life transpired along lowermost Big Laurel Creek.

Ultimately, this part of Big Laurel Creek valley was bought out and became part of the Pisgah National Forest. Today, we can hike the old railroad grade and see the scenic gorge that is Big Laurel Creek. The hike leaves a large gravel parking area and for the first 0.7 mile uses a right-of-way through private property to finally enter national forest. The blazed path cruises down the valley, mimicking the curves of Big Laurel Creek. The stream scenes form an ever-changing mix of moving waters and still pools as they cut through an incredible gorge. Waterside stopping spots continually beckon, whether they are gravel bars, rock outcrops, or simply tree-shaded boulders.

At one point, the creek is squeezed in a stony vise, forced to crash and tumble through rock-walled banks from which rise higher cliffs. There is no mistaking when you reach Runion, with its concrete walls and other reminders of industry now

*Big Laurel Creek crashes through a rocky basin.*

overtaken by woods. The final part of the hike leads through deeper canyon until you emerge at the confluence of the French Broad River and an active rail line. The return trip will be pleasant since the trail grades are minimal.

## Miles and Directions

**0.0**   Leave south from the large gravel parking along Big Laurel Creek, just south of the intersection of US 25/70 and NC 208. Follow a wide blazed path south, running parallel to US 25/70. Ignore a user-created angler trail dropping off to Big Laurel Creek. You are following a right-of-way through private land. Please respect the landowner's rights.

**0.1**   Pass a gate on your left, then drop off a hill, coming alongside Big Laurel Creek. Keep downstream, now on the old logging grade. Look at crashing rapids of the truly big creek to your right.

**0.2**   Meet a gravel driveway and rental cottage to your left. Stay with the trail downstream. A powerline parallels the trail. Enjoy good river views and water noise. Cedar bluffs rise ahead.

**0.3**   Walk under a high bluff. The lowermost segment was blasted to make way for the rail line.

**0.5**   Look left for a small, spring-fed stone fountain from days gone by. Pass a road heading left.

*Flowers rise from a gravelly beach beside Big Laurel Creek.*

**0.7** A final roadbed goes left. From here out you are following pure trail. Rhododendron and doghobble crowd the path while black birch and oaks form a canopy overhead. Springlets flow over the grade.

**1.0** Walk around a large conspicuous boulder in the middle of the trail. You have now entered the national forest. Pools and rapids fall ahead. From here downstream feel free to explore the river, rocks, and pools in national forest land. Keep hiking close to the stream.

**1.6** Come to a deep pool on your right. Here, the railroad grade was built up with a stone wall along the stream. The path is rocky for a bit.

**1.8** Pass a pair of big rapids with pools and sandbars. Just ahead, a flat opens. Beard cane covers the wooded flat that includes a campsite. The trail then makes a long curve to the right, mimicking a bend in the creek. Look for a long island forming in the waterway.

**2.2** Pass the lower end of the long island.

**2.4** Reach the most rugged part of the gorge. Here, the rock walls rise and constrict the creek, forcing it through a stone corridor. Parts of the grade were blasted to allow rail passage. Unfortunately, some of the exposed stone walls have proved irresistible for spray paint defacers.

**2.7** Leave the most rugged part of the gorge behind. Keep downriver in more typical Carolina mountain stream, a fine sight in and of itself.

**3.0** Reach the site of Runion. Concrete walls and other relics rise to your left. Here, a spur trail cuts left past machinery through a gap to the railroad tracks and the French Broad River.

The Laurel River Trail continues tracing Big Laurel Creek. Spot another island below. Turn northwest, following a stony gorge full of rapids and pools. A big flat forms between you and the waterway as Big Laurel Creek turns back south.

**3.6**   Emerge at the active Norfolk Southern rail line and the confluence with the big French Broad River. Backtrack.

**7.2**   Arrive at the trailhead, completing the hike.

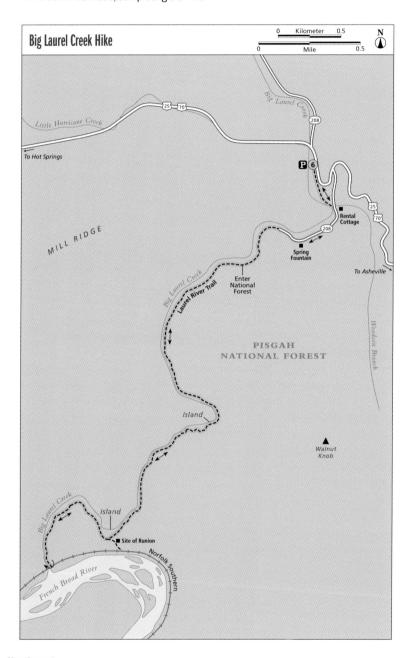

Big Laurel Creek Hike

# 7 Falls of Hickey Fork

This challenging waterfall hike makes a loop through remote terrain near the Tennessee state line. Explore the upper Hickey Fork valley in Pisgah National Forest's Shelton Laurel Backcountry. Cross a log hiker bridge, then turn up West Prong Hickey Fork, passing two significant waterfalls and other lesser shoals, before rising to Seng Gap. A mountainside climb commences before you descend to East Prong Hickey Fork. Reach an often-gated forest road and easy hiking to close the loop. Be apprised, there is a 1,950-foot elevation gain/loss and the trails can be brushy and faint in places.

**Start:** Hickey Fork Road/FR 465 Trailhead
**Distance:** 7.0-mile loop
**Difficulty:** Moderate to difficult, rough trail in places
**Elevation change:** +-1,953 feet
**Maximum grade:** 24 percent grade for 0.3 mile
**Hiking time:** About 4.5 hours
**Seasons/schedule:** 24/7/365
**Fees and permits:** None
**Dog friendly:** Leashed dogs allowed
**Trail surface:** Natural

**Land status:** National forest
**Other trail users:** None
**Maps to consult:** National Geographic #782 French Broad & Nolichucky Rivers, Cherokee and Pisgah National Forests; USGS White Rock, Greystone
**Amenities available:** None
**Cell service:** None
**Trail contacts:** Pisgah National Forest, Appalachian Ranger District, (828) 689-9694, www.fs.usda.gov

**Finding the trailhead:** From Asheville, take I-26 north to exit 19A, Marshall. Then follow US 25/70 for 21 miles to turn right on NC 208 west and follow it for 3.4 miles to NC 212. Turn right on NC 212 east and follow it for 6.9 miles, then turn left on Hickey Fork Road. There will be a sign indicating Shelton Laurel Backcountry. Follow Hickey Fork Road, which becomes FR 465 in the Pisgah National Forest, for 1.1 miles to reach a seasonally closed gate and parking area on your right. Trailhead GPS: 35.994563, -82.704761

## The Hike

This hike takes place in the Pisgah National Forest's Shelton Laurel Backcountry, a designated trail network banked against the North Carolina–Tennessee state line atop which runs the Appalachian Trail. The AT and the Shelton Laurel Backcountry trails also link with the Bald Mountain Scenic Area and Rocky Fork trails of Tennessee's Cherokee National Forest. Together, a pathway complex of over 100 miles adds myriad day hiking and backpacking possibilities. The Hickey Fork Loop is one of the fine adventurous hikes in this far-flung portion of western North Carolina. The 7-mile circuit hike has wild waterfalls and almost guaranteed solitude. However, the lesser use of the path means a fainter, sometimes-obscure trailbed, overgrown pathway sections, and occasional fallen trees across the path. This loop hike also has a 1,950-foot climb and subsequent descent, adding further challenge. However, the visual rewards and peaceful character of the loop overshadows the challenges.

The hike starts off in a fun fashion as you get to cross East Prong Hickey Fork on a log bridge. Luckily, it has handrails, thus minimizing potential peril. After spanning East Prong Hickey Fork, the narrow trail slithers through doghobble, ferns, and rhododendron before meeting West Prong Hickey Fork on a seemingly convoluted route that keeps the path on national forest property. After crossing West Prong, you head up the narrow, thickly vegetated and steep valley. The noisy falling waters of West Prong Hickey Fork testify to this steepness. Tiny tributaries cross over the trail, adding their waters to West Prong Hickey Fork.

The valley continues to narrow. Rock protrusions show their hard faces where unobscured by clouds of rhododendron. Ahead, the song of splashing water enters your ears—Hickey Fork Cascades. This first sizeable faucet-style spiller drops over 100 feet along a smooth, slender, mossy grooved rock face flanked by rhododendron and shaded by hardwoods. Continue climbing past more shoals, then come to Hickey Fork Falls. This spiller is more of a classic curtain-type cataract, sloping over a rock ledge, then diving down a tiered 35-foot-high stratified ledge. If this trail were busy at all, the path to the falls base would be well beaten down.

The climb continues and becomes very steep after leaving West Prong Hickey Fork and ascending one of its tributaries. Here, you huff and puff your way up 400 feet in a very steep 0.3 mile. Whew! Circle around an upland cove filled with tulip and magnolia trees.

You soon arrive at Seng Gap. Seng is mountain slang for the plant ginseng, often extracted from the Southern Appalachians due to its purported medicinal properties. Our hike joins the Pounding Mill Trail as it climbs further. However, off-trail hiking enthusiasts have additional options as the no-longer-maintained portion of the Pounding Mill Trail leaves left down Pounding Mill Creek for NC 208, while the abandoned Little Laurel Trail descends along Little Laurel Creek for NC 208.

The hike leaves the Pounding Mill Trail for the White Oak Trail. The south-facing slope along which the White Oak Trail travels reveals winter views of nearby peaks and faraway ridges. You then cross the headwaters of West Branch Hickey Fork. Here, a very wide spring dribbles through a boulder field, topped with trees. Trace the headwaters downstream on a slender trail.

Begin an easterly track on a lowering ridge that eventually leads you down to Big Rocky Branch and ultimately to FR 465. This seasonally closed forest road traces East Prong Hickey Fork downstream past its confluence with Little Prong and the trail connector to the Jerry Miller Trail. Walk with ease, bridging East Prong before completing the loop at the FR 465 gate and the trailhead parking area.

*Hickey Fork Falls is just one highlight on this solitude-filled circuit.*

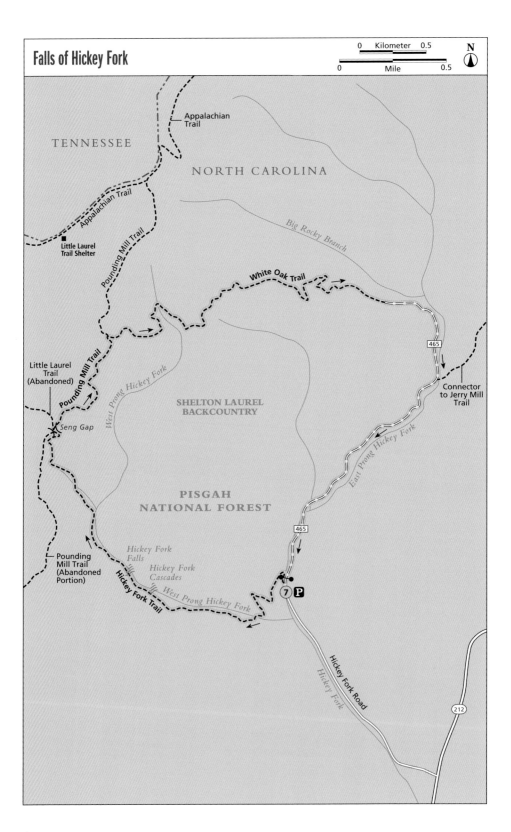

# Falls of Hickey Fork

0    Kilometer    0.5

0    Mile    0.5

N

TENNESSEE

NORTH CAROLINA

Appalachian Trail

Appalachian Trail

Big Rocky Branch

Little Laurel Trail Shelter

Pounding Mill Trail

White Oak Trail

Little Laurel Trail (Abandoned)

Pounding Mill Trail

West Prong Hickey Fork

SHELTON LAUREL BACKCOUNTRY

465

Connector to Jerry Mill Trail

Seng Gap

East Prong Hickey Fork

PISGAH NATIONAL FOREST

465

Pounding Mill Trail (Abandoned Portion)

Hickey Fork Falls

Hickey Fork Cascades

Hickey Fork Trail

West Prong Hickey Fork

7   P

Hickey Fork Road

Hickey Fork

212

# Miles and Directions

**0.0** From the parking area at the seasonally closed gate on FR 465, walk up FR 465, passing around the pole gate. Look left for the Hickey Fork Trail. Walk down stone steps, then cross East Prong Hickey Fork on a log bridge with handrails.

**0.1** Turn away from East Prong Hickey Fork. Start curving around the nose of a ridge dividing East Prong from West Prong.

**0.5** Cross West Prong Hickey Fork.

**0.9** The gradient steepens.

**1.1** Reach the first visible cataract—Hickey Fork Cascades. This long, sloping, sliding angled cascade dashes over a waterworn, smooth rock bed, spilling 100 feet or more. It is not easy to access but is worth the trouble.

**1.3** Reach Hickey Fork Falls, a classic curtain-type 35-foot waterfall. There is but a faint path to the base of this cataract.

**1.7** The Hickey Fork Trail leaves West Prong Hickey Fork, ascending along a feeder stream. Begin a very steep segment, gaining 400 feet in 0.3 mile! The trail opens into a wide hardwood cove after the climb, leaving the rhododendron behind.

**2.3** Come to flat Seng Gap. Look closely before continuing. To your left, the abandoned portion of the Pounding Mill Trail leaves left for Pounding Mill Creek. Straight ahead, the abandoned Little Laurel Trail drops into the headwaters of Little Laurel Creek. This loop hike leaves right on an old roadbed, joining the still-maintained segment of the Pounding Mill Trail. Ascend.

**2.6** The Pounding Mill Trail passes through a gap. Keep climbing.

**2.9** Reach a trail intersection. Here, the Pounding Mill Trail climbs left along Seng Ridge about a mile to the AT and the Tennessee–North Carolina state line. However, the Hickey Fork Loop turns right, joining an old logging grade. We are now heading easterly on the White Oak Trail.

**3.3** Turn into a hollow and abruptly leave right from the old logging grade you have been following.

**3.4** Cross a wide, shallow spring branch, the headwaters of Hickey Fork. Descend.

**3.6** The White Oak Trail makes a sudden left turn away from the headwaters. Begin cruising along the south-facing slope of piney Seng Ridge. Mountain laurel and chestnut oaks thrive here as well.

**3.7** Step over a trickling stream that when flowing well forms a long ribbon-like slide over a slender yet steep rock face.

**4.1** Join the nose of a ridge with dropoffs on both sides of the trail. Look for Baxter Cliff through the trees. Descend on a pine-shaded, needle-carpeted trail.

**4.4** Come to a gap. Pay attention as the White Oak Trail reaches a closed logging road. Don't be lured into following the wide logging road. Instead, the White Oak Trail makes a sharp left, diving toward Big Rocky Branch, still on singletrack, curving gently to reach the wider, lower valley of Big Rocky Branch.

**4.7** Pick up a partly eroded logging grade in the Big Rocky Branch valley.

**5.0** Emerge onto the end of FR 465. Begin descending FR 465 as it runs alongside the mountain stream of East Prong Hickey Fork. The walking is easy on the gravel track.

**5.8**   An old concrete road bridge to the left crosses rocky Little Prong. An unofficial connector crosses the bridge and surmounts a gap to meet the Jerry Miller Trail, also detailed in this guide.

**6.7**   FR 465 bridges East Prong. You are now on the left bank heading downstream.

**7.0**   Arrive at the FR 465 gate, completing the hike.

# 8 Jerry Miller Loop

This challenging circuit travels through the Pisgah National Forest's Shelton Laurel Backcountry. The Jerry Miller Trail first leads past the impressive and long 100-foot Whiteoak Flats Branch Cascade, then reaches the former meadow of Whiteoak Flats. A steady climb takes you near Baxter Cliff before joining the AT and Big Firescald Ridge, the protruding knife-edge rock rampart dividing North Carolina and Tennessee. Panoramic 360-degree views extend to distant horizons. The vistas continue for a half-mile before the AT enters wooded slopes. A final, very steep descent down Fork Ridge closes the loop.

**Start:** Jerry Miller trailhead on FR 111
**Distance:** 10.2-mile loop
**Difficulty:** Difficult
**Elevation change:** +-2,764 feet
**Maximum grade:** 19 percent downhill grade for 1.0 mile
**Hiking time:** About 6.5 hours
**Seasons/schedule:** 24/7/365
**Fees and permits:** None
**Dog friendly:** Leashed dogs allowed
**Trail surface:** Natural

**Land status:** National forest
**Other trail users:** None
**Maps to consult:** National Geographic #782 French Broad & Nolichucky Rivers, Cherokee and Pisgah National Forests; USGS Greystone
**Amenities available:** None
**Cell service:** Limited to ridgetops
**Trail contacts:** Pisgah National Forest, Appalachian Ranger District, (828) 689-9694, www.fs.usda.gov

**Finding the trailhead:** From Asheville, take I-26 north to exit 19A, Marshall. Then follow US 25/70 for 21 miles to turn right on NC 208 west and follow it for 3.4 miles to NC 212. Turn right on NC 212 east and follow it for 10.9 miles to turn left on Big Creek Road, at the Carmen Church of God. Follow Big Creek Road for 1.2 miles. The road seems to end near a barn. Here, angle left onto FR 111, taking the gravel road over a small creek. Enter the national forest. At 0.4 mile beyond the barn, veer left onto a short spur road to dead end at Jerry Miller trailhead. Trailhead GPS: 36.02372, -82.65277

## The Hike

This is a hike of superlatives, a big hike with big views from the ridgeline dividing North Carolina and Tennessee, lending open perspectives in all directions with the vistas continuing unabated for over a half-mile; a big 100-foot slide cascade waterfall; and big wildflower displays, from trillium in the creek bottoms to trout lilies up top. The hike also has big climbs—it is over 2,300 feet from low point to high point on this circuit. And you must go back down again. And during this downgrade, you will drop 1,000 feet in 1 mile! A part of the hike uses the most big-time trail in the

*Soak in dramatic winter views like this from Big Firescald Ridge.*

East—the Appalachian Trail. Finally, the Jerry Miller Trail was named after a big-time hero of America's national forests.

Furthermore, you can take side trips from this loop to attractions such as Baxter Cliff, Whiterock Cliff, the Blackstack Cliffs, and Jerry Cabin trail shelter. Even without these side trips, the hike can be long and arduous. Consider starting early or backpacking to maximize the possibilities. I have backpacked this loop on multiple occasions and consider it one of the best overnight circuits in western North Carolina.

The hike starts by bridging Big Creek, then climbs a ridge, keeping on national forest property to then turn up the steep-sided hollow of Whiteoak Flats Branch. It isn't long before you come to the 100-foot Whiteoak Flats Branch Cascade. This significant slide purges over a widening slope that steepens in a frothy climax into a shallow-plunge pool. Boughs of rhododendron escort Whiteoak Flats Branch during this sightly spill.

The Whiteoak Flats Branch valley closes after the falls and you cross the creek on a footbridge. You are now on the left-hand bank heading upstream. Shortly, enter the meadow of Whiteoak Flats undergoing succession where pines, tulip trees, and brush are overtaking the former homesite. Pass through more formerly farmed territory before rising via switchbacks toward the state line.

And then you come to the AT after bisecting Huckleberry Gap. The wild and stony ridgetop walk astounds once atop Big Firescald Knob. Views are nearly continuous into the mountains and valleys of Tennessee and North Carolina, and it is my favorite section on the AT in this area. If the leaves are off the trees, look down and spot the Jerry Miller Trail you just climbed.

Marvel at the trail construction here as a slow-moving path works through the stone backbone amid gnarled brush and trees. A pair of final overlooks delivers views and then you roll along the state line ridge, passing the Round Knob Trail before turning back into North Carolina on the often steep Fork Ridge Trail. Keep the brakes on as you dive for Big Creek and FR 111. The final part of the walk traces FR 111 back to the Jerry Miller trailhead and hike's end.

## Miles and Directions

**0.0**    From FR 111 parking area with the Jerry Miller Trail memorial plaque embedded into stone, join the Jerry Miller Trail and bridge Big Creek. Turn downstream into a flat known for its spring wildflower displays. Switchback up a ridge dividing Big Creek from Whiteoak Flats Branch, avoiding an old route that crossed Shelton property.

**0.3**    Enter Whiteoak Flats Branch valley. Turn west in a thick forest on a steep slope.

**0.9**    The trail takes you by Whiteoak Flats Branch Cascade, a 100-foot slide cataract. Continue up the narrowing valley.

**1.2**    Cross gurgling Whiteoak Flats Branch on a log bridge.

**1.3**    Step over a tributary, then enter Whiteoak Flats.

**1.6**    Leave Whiteoak Flats meadow.

**1.7**    Cut through a second, smaller shrinking clearing. Stay with the blazed trail and watch for old roadbeds spurring from the correct route.

**2.1**    Take a sharp left as an old road tempts you to keep straight. Climb a ridge forested in pine, black gum, and mountain laurel. Turn into the Chimney Creek valley, striding under tunnels of rhododendron. Ascend.

**4.0**    Reach a four-way trail intersection at grassy Huckleberry Gap. This is your first chance for a side trip. A short path leads right to a campsite. To your left, an unmarked trail surmounts a knob, then drops sharply down to Baxter Cliff after 0.4 mile, presenting a view of Whiterock Cliff and the Hickey Fork watershed. Our hike keeps straight on the Jerry Miller Trail, then crosses uppermost East Prong Hickey Fork.

**4.5**    Intersect the AT. A left turn will take you to nearby Whiterock Cliff and the Blackstack Cliffs. This loop turns right, northbound on the AT, to quickly find another trail junction. Here, the old AT, now dubbed "Bad Weather Route," stays left, while you stay right on the "Exposed Ridge Route," the relatively newer AT section. Join the Exposed Ridge Route. Snake over, around, and between whitish stone bluffs, boulders, and placed steps astride craggy windswept vegetation.

**5.1**    Top out on Big Firescald Knob and start relishing unobstructed views into Tennessee, including from signed Howard's Rock, where a steep dropoff reveals wooded hills, farm fields, and rolling mountains. Waves of ridges extend into the Tar Heel State as far as the horizon allows.

**5.6**    Leave the primary vista zone, entering woods.

**5.7**    Reach an open rock slab. Look north at Big Butt and Green Ridge Knob. Just ahead, you will come to another overlook into Tennessee.

| **6.0** | Intersect the Bad Weather Route. Keep straight in woods on the AT. |
|---|---|
| **6.7** | The Round Knob Trail leads left into Tennessee. |
| **7.4** | Come to the Fork Ridge Trail. Jerry Cabin trail shelter is a quarter-mile north on the AT. This hike heads right, south, on the Fork Ridge Trail. Descend over 1,000 feet in the next mile, despite a couple of short ascents. |
| **9.4** | Emerge at the Fork Ridge Trail parking area on FR 111. Walk south on FR 111. |
| **9.5** | Cross Chimney Creek at a road ford. |
| **9.8** | Cross Big Creek. |
| **10.2** | Arrive at the Jerry Miller trailhead, closing the loop. |

# WHO WAS JERRY MILLER?

Back in 1997, why was the Whiteoak Flats Trail rerouted and renamed the Jerry Miller Trail? The path was altered to keep it on national forest land, avoiding any potential trespassing problems. It formerly started on the property of the Shelton clan, which had occupied this parcel at the confluence of Whiteoak Flats Branch and Big Creek since the 1790s.

So what does that have to do with Jerry Miller and naming the trail after him? Well, Jerry Miller's mother was a Shelton from this very property. Jerry Miller was raised in both Madison and Buncombe Counties, becoming a US attorney for the Western District of North Carolina in the early 1980s. During his tenure, Mr. Miller prosecuted many a case arising from crimes perpetrated in the mountainous Pisgah and Nantahala National Forests.

However, it wasn't always so. Before Jerry Miller's tenure, the federal government didn't recognize federal jurisdiction in national forests, leaving enforcement to state and local authorities. National forests became havens for the lawless, threatening legitimate forest users. The locals charged with enforcing the law were already strapped, trying to maintain order in the rural areas where national forests are typically found.

However, a drunken driving case in the national forest prosecuted by Jerry Miller changed that. After many a legal tussle, the case went to the Supreme Court of the United States, where the robed ones recognized the federal government's role in patrolling, enforcing, and prosecuting the law in our national forests, adding a layer of protection as we enjoy those millions of acres of wildlands found throughout western North Carolina.

In appreciation of this change in law enforcement, the Pisgah National Forest renamed the Whiteoak Flats Trail for Jerry Miller. At the trail's beginning, there stands a plaque memorializing this man who fought to keep the Carolina mountains safe for hikers like us.

*Summer presents rewarding vistas as well.*

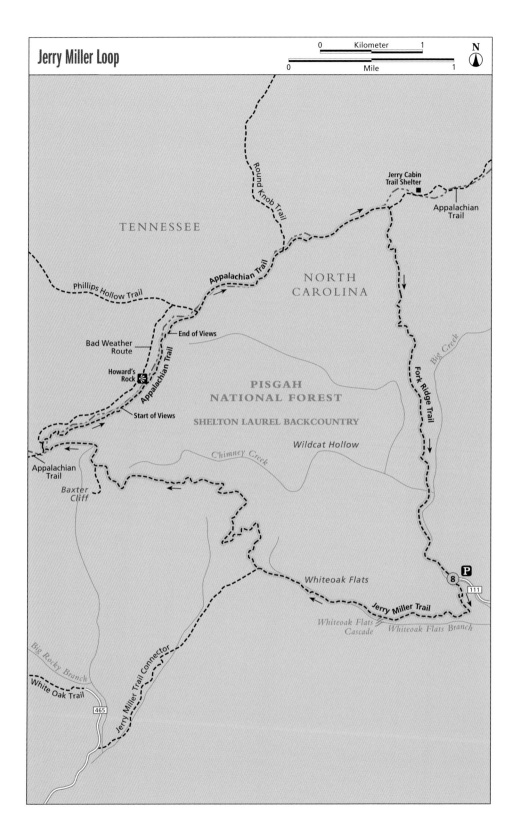

# Jerry Miller Loop

0 — Kilometer — 1

0 — Mile — 1

N

TENNESSEE

NORTH CAROLINA

Round Knob Trail

Jerry Cabin Trail Shelter

Appalachian Trail

Phillips Hollow Trail

Appalachian Trail

Bad Weather Route

End of Views

Howard's Rock

Appalachian Trail

Start of Views

Fork Ridge Trail

Big Creek

PISGAH NATIONAL FOREST

SHELTON LAUREL BACKCOUNTRY

Wildcat Hollow

Chimney Creek

Appalachian Trail

Baxter Cliff

Whiteoak Flats

P
8
111

Jerry Miller Trail

Whiteoak Flats Cascade

Whiteoak Flats Branch

Big Rocky Branch

Jerry Miller Trail Connector

White Oak Trail

465

# 9 Bailey Mountain Preserve

Explore Carolina highland farming history along with a trek to a mountaintop at the recently established Bailey Mountain Preserve, located near Mars Hill. First, explore safeguarded barns of the Smith Farm then trek through relic fields, garnering views to enter woods. From here, clamber up Connor Ridge to top out on Bailey Mountain. Your return trip skirts the upper reaches of Whiteoak Creek.

**Start:** Forest Street trailhead

**Distance:** 5.4-mile balloon loop

**Difficulty:** Moderate, does have significant elevation gain

**Elevation change:** +-1,485 feet over entire hike

**Maximum grade:** 10 percent grade for 2.2 miles

**Hiking time:** About 2.9 hours

**Seasons/schedule:** Year-round, dawn to dusk

**Fees and permits:** None

**Dog friendly:** Yes, on leash only

**Trail surface:** Forested natural surface, a little grass

**Land status:** Town of Mars Hill property

**Other trail users:** None

**Maps to consult:** Bailey Mountain Preserve

**Amenities available:** Restroom at trailhead

**Cell service:** Good

**Trail contacts:** Town of Mars Hill, townof marshill.org, (828) 689-2301

**Finding the trailhead:** From Asheville, take I-26 west to exit 11, Mars Hill, then take NC 213 west, Carl Eller Road, for 1 mile. Then turn right onto North Main Street and follow it for 0.1 mile. Turn left on Bailey Street and follow it for 0.3 mile and then veer left onto Hickory Drive. Stay with Hickory Drive for 0.3 mile, then turn right onto Forest Street and follow it 0.9 mile to reach the preserve trailhead on your left. Official preserve address: 889 Forest St., Mars Hill, NC. Trailhead GPS: 35.843129, -82.559664

## The Hike

The town of Mars Hill, nestled in mountain splendor north of Asheville, knows its mountain heritage, where farming has been a way of life for generations, a way of life that included planting corn, tobacco, and food gardens as well as ranging cattle, horses, and other livestock on slopes too steep to plant row crops. Farms continue to dot the mountainscape all around the Ivy Creek valley, itself a tributary of the mighty French Broad River.

One such place was the Smith Farm, situated on Banjo Branch, a tributary of Ivy Creek. From 1870 to the 2000s, the land was worked. Later, Bailey Mountain, located adjacent to and rising above the Smith Farm, with its signature knob peak and views of Mars Hill below, was eyed out by a group wanting to build mountainside homes like those that overlook much of the greater Asheville landscape. But this time the mountain was to be kept forested and houseless. Tracts were purchased and cobbled

*This view shows off the lower open Bailey Mountain Preserve valley.*

together and Bailey Mountain Preserve came to be, allowing the views of Bailey Mountain to remain natural. However, Bailey Mountain Preserve had no practical access for hiking and other passive recreation. Then the adjacent Smith Farm became available. The locale not only provided a fine access for those wanting to hike at Bailey Mountain Preserve, but the farm also provided a historic link to western North Carolina's agricultural legacy, especially considering the three distinct barns on the property, along with a small farmhouse. These barns are being preserved as examples of Southern Appalachian agricultural heritage for future generations to appreciate.

Work continues on the preserve, with exotic plant removal, erosion prevention, stabilization of the barns, and plans for continuing environmental education.

Opened in June 2022, the Smith Farm addition to the Bailey Mountain Preserve allows you to park your vehicle, explore the barns, then trek the trails of the park, a win, win, win situation. And the hike itself is a study in succession. Although part of Smith Farm remains field, the cleared lands were once much more extensive, and, today, the forest is reclaiming the slopes of Bailey Mountain. Leaving the old Smith farmhouse, you will ramble through fields past the barns on the Richard L. Hoffman Trail, to enjoy a view of the farm, the Banjo Branch valley, and hills beyond. Then, hand-built singletrack trail gently but steadily switchbacks up the steep slope of Connor Ridge. Once atop the ridge, begin the loop portion of the hike, making a detour to the top of Bailey Mountain along the way, standing proudly at 3,580 feet. Winter views open of the town of Mars Hill and Mars Hill University below. A ridge run leads down to Hamp Gap. A wider track continues the downgrade, circling past small spring-fed tributaries of Whiteoak Creek flowing from Bailey Mountain. After returning to Connor Ridge, it is a simple backtrack to the trailhead, allowing more views of the legacy that is the Smith Farm property and Bailey Mountain.

## Miles and Directions

**0.0**   From the parking area, take the Richard L. Hoffman Trail north, tracing a mown path up a grassy hill. The historic barns are to your left.

**0.1**   Enter woods and reach a swing hanging from an ancient oak. Views open south of the Smith Farm. Continue ascending on the yellow-blazed Hoffman Trail, avoiding any unmarked spur trails.

**0.3**   Reach a bench and cleared view overlooking the meadows and buildings of the Smith Farm, as well as the Banjo Creek valley. Continue in viney woods with young and old trees, as forest succession continues to transform what once were fields into pure forest. Note the pine, locust, and tulip trees, all pioneer species. Continue ascending via switchbacks up the east side of Connor Ridge.

**1.2**   Crest out on the nose of Connor Ridge. Head north among hardwoods, still rising.

**1.5**   Meet the Red Trail coming in from your left. This is your return route. Begin the loop portion of your hike by keeping straight on the Hoffman Trail, still on an uptick.

**1.7**   Pass a rock overhang on trail right.

**1.9**   Come to another intersection near large outcrops. Split right on the spur to the top of Bailey Mountain, ascending by switchbacks galore in rocky woods. Winter views open to your south of Mars Hill.

**2.2**   Top out on wooded Bailey Mountain, where a bench and trail register await. Backtrack.

**2.5**   Split right, joining the Blue Trail right, westerly. Descend an old roadbed.

**2.7**   Turn left at Hamp Gap, still descending in viney woods. Switchbacks ease the downgrade. Cross a few trickling branches, springheads of Whiteoak Creek.

**3.2**   Split left on the Red Trail. Your descent is over. Cruise by rock outcroppings.

**3.6**   The Red Trail splits abruptly left as a singletrack, while an old roadbed, the Blue Trail, keeps straight. *Note:* There is no public access at the bottom of the Blue Trail. Ascend.

**3.9**   Return to the Hoffman Trail, completing the loop portion of the hike. Head right on the Hoffman Trail, backtracking south.

**5.4**   Arrive at the trailhead, completing the circuit hike.

*This bench beckons you to soak in a bucolic view toward Mars Hill.*

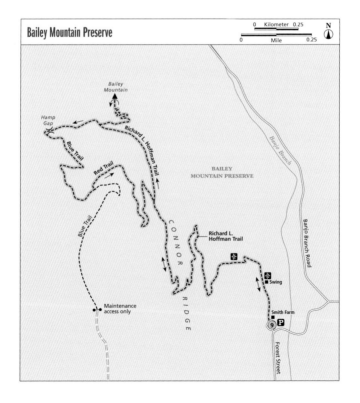

# 10 High Rocks

This fun little hike takes you to an outcropping known as High Rocks, a stony peak where the Bald Mountains meet Sugarloaf Mountain. Walk a lesser trod segment of the Appalachian Trail, first traipsing along a small stream before climbing a rib ridge of the Bald Mountain. Rise to the base of the High Rocks, then take a spur trail to an outcrop availing westerly views into the mountains of East Tennessee and the state line ridge dividing the Volunteer State from the Tar Heel State, upon which more of the Appalachian Trail travels.

**Start:** Spivey Gap trailhead
**Distance:** 3.8-mile there-and-back
**Difficulty:** Easy-moderate
**Elevation change:** +-1,114 feet
**Maximum grade:** About 9 percent grade for 1.9 miles
**Hiking time:** 2.3 hours
**Seasons/schedule:** 24/7/365, clear days recommended
**Fees and permits:** None
**Dog friendly:** Yes, on leash only

**Trail surface:** Forested natural surface
**Land status:** National forest
**Other trail users:** None
**Maps to consult:** National Geographic #782, French Broad & Nolichucky Rivers
**Amenities available:** None
**Cell service:** Limited
**Trail contacts:** Pisgah National Forest, Appalachian Ranger District, (828) 689-9694, www.fs.usda.gov/nfsnc

**Finding the trailhead:** From Asheville, take I-26 into Tennessee and exit 43. From there take US 19W south for 1.1 miles, then veer left, staying with 19W south. Enter North Carolina and after a total of 8.8 miles from I-26 you will come to the Appalachian Trail crossing and a parking area on your right. Trailhead GPS: 36.031781, -82.420153

## The Hike

Is there such thing as solitude on the Appalachian Trail? This hike may have it. However, the Appalachian Trail is America's most famous footpath. If you did a man-on-the-street interview and asked passersby to name a hiking trail, the Appalachian Trail would surely be the number one answer. And the AT is within the greater Asheville's hiking sphere, running northwest of the town, primarily along the North Carolina–Tennessee state line. The first 460 miles of the AT, the most southerly portion, lies within three states. Georgia has the first 76 miles of the Appalachian Trail, where it begins at famed Springer Mountain. The AT travels 96 miles exclusively in North Carolina, while North Carolina and Tennessee share 218 miles where the path traverses the state line, along the crest separating the two states. There are 70 miles of AT exclusively in Tennessee.

Completed in 1937, the Appalachian Trail is a privately managed unit of the national park system. On its journey from Georgia to Maine, the Appalachian Trail touches fourteen states and is maintained by over thirty trail clubs, including the Carolina Mountain Club, which oversees the section with High Rocks among the 92 trail miles it maintains. Established in 1923, the Carolina Mountain Club is the oldest such organization in western North Carolina.

The lowest elevation of the AT is 124 feet near Bear Mountain, New York. The highest elevation is 6,643 feet on Clingmans Dome in the Smokies, just over the Tennessee line from the Tar Heel State. The AT is marked by 2-inch by 6-inch white rectangular blazes, 165,000 of them on its entire length. Hikers that want to tackle the entire AT can expect to take approximately 5 million steps. Annually, around 4,000 trail trekkers attempt to hike the entire 2,190 miles of the AT, the exact mileage changing slightly year to year due to pathway reroutes. Most aspiring thru-hikers fail in their quest, with around a 25 percent success rate, dropping out for various reasons, namely injuries great and small, the relentless physical challenges, the mental trials of hiking day after day, as well as foreseen and unforeseen friend/family concerns, plus simply running out of money.

A thru-hike of the AT takes the average backpacker anywhere from 4 to 6 months to complete. This entails hiking miles and miles per day, day after day, and camping out most nights. It means trekking through temperatures ranging from 20 to 90 degrees and through an equally wide range of other weather, from snow to sleet to rain, to thunder and lightning.

Alternatively, some hikers trek the entire AT segment by segment, often taking many years to complete the entire trail. Then there are others who simply want to get back to nature for which the fabled Appalachian Trail is a major draw. After all, from a bragging standpoint it is easier to boast on social media of your hike on the AT— about which nearly everyone has heard—than a remote trek to nowhere without the panache of the heralded Appalachian Trail.

And that brings us back to High Rocks. This hike utilizes a lesser visited segment of the AT, as opposed to other Appalachian Trail sections within striking distance of Asheville, such as the Smokies, Roan Mountain, or where the AT makes its way through the town of Hot Springs, or perhaps along Big Firescald Ridge. The view from High Rocks is good, not great, but you are likely to have it to yourself, and that has value of its own.

## Miles and Directions

**0.0**      From the parking area just east of Spivey Gap, take the unnamed blue-blazed trail a short distance to meet the AT. Head left, southbound, and immediately span the upper reaches of Big Creek on a stone block bridge nestled in rhododendron thickets. Campsites are found to the right, just after the bridge. Follow the AT as it rises in woods of oak, white pine, and birch.

*Looking into the hills of East Tennessee from the High Rocks*

**0.2**    Pass a wildlife clearing on your right, kept open by the Forest Service (Pisgah National Forest) to enhance food for wildlife. Continue gently but steadily ascending up the wide vale of a small tributary of Big Creek.

**0.4**    Your climb steepens at a series of stone steps. Ahead, cross a small spring branch on footlogs. Circle through a cove.

**0.6**    Make a sharp switchback to the left and keep ascending. In places you will cross the old AT, which erosively ran straight up the mountain.

**0.8**    Cut through a boulder garden.

**1.3**    Look north toward big Flattop Mountain, across Spivey Gap. Turn south again toward High Rocks. Ahead, level off briefly, then resume the climb. The ridge becomes narrower and rockier.

**1.8**    Pass below High Rocks along a sheer stone monolith rising in the forest, then come to a trail intersection. Here, head left on the blue-blazed spur to the High Rocks.

**1.9**    Reach the open slab of the High Rocks. Vistas open primarily to the west into the mountains of East Tennessee, as well as Flattop Mountain to the north. Backtrack.

**3.8**    Arrive back at the Spivey Gap trailhead, completing the hike.

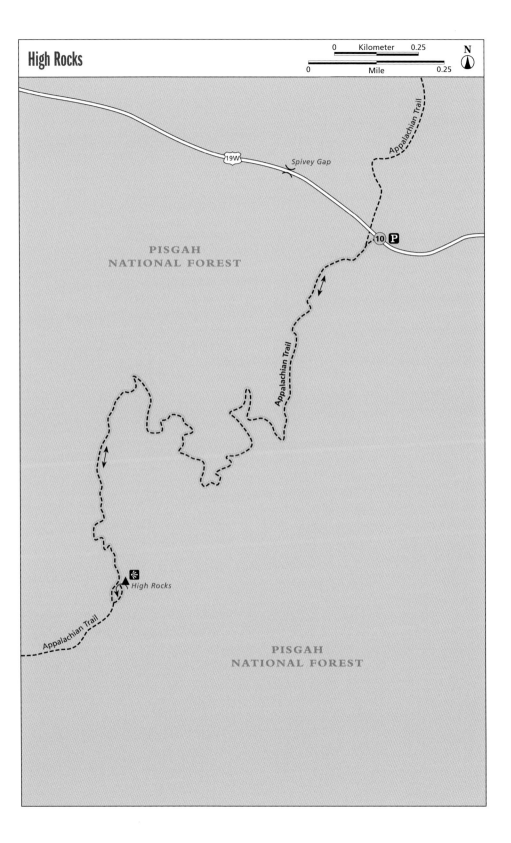

# High Rocks

0  Kilometer  0.25
0  Mile  0.25

N

19W    Spivey Gap

10  P

Appalachian Trail

PISGAH
NATIONAL FOREST

Appalachian Trail

High Rocks

Appalachian Trail

PISGAH
NATIONAL FOREST

# 11 Nolichucky Gorge Circuit

This solitude-filled hike starts at the crest of the North Carolina–Tennessee state line, then works out to the rim of the 1,000-foot-deep Nolichucky River Gorge, where hikers are rewarded with a magnificent panorama of this whitewater rafting destination and the ridges forming the foreboding defile. Cruise along the edge of the rim, passing occasional wildlife clearings, then ascend back to the state line trailhead. The hiking is easy on the feet, being a doubletrack path its entire distance.

**Start:** Ephraim Place Road
**Distance:** 10.5-mile balloon loop
**Difficulty:** Difficult due to distance
**Elevation change:** +-1,921 feet
**Maximum grade:** 11 percent grade for 1.9 miles
**Hiking time:** About 6 hours
**Seasons/schedule:** 24/7/365, best time early spring through late fall
**Fees and permits:** None
**Dog friendly:** Dogs on leash allowed
**Trail surface:** Natural

**Land status:** National forest
**Other trail users:** A few mountain bikers and equestrians
**Maps to consult:** National Geographic Trails Illustrated #783–Cherokee and Pisgah National Forests; USGS Huntdale, Chestoa
**Amenities available:** None
**Cell service:** None
**Trail contacts:** Pisgah National Forest, Appalachian Ranger District, (828) 682-6146, www.fs.usda.gov/nfsnc

**Finding the trailhead:** From Asheville, take I-26 west into Tennessee and exit 36, Main Street/Erwin. Take the access road leading to TN 107/Main Street and a traffic light. From the traffic light, turn right and join TN 107 west/Main Street for 0.4 mile to TN 395/Rock Creek Road. Turn left on TN 395 east and follow it 6.2 miles to the Tennessee/North Carolina line and Indian Grave Gap. At Indian Grave Gap, turn right on FR 5583, Ephraim Place Road. Follow it 0.9 mile to a road split. Here, a primitive private road leads right and uphill, while the gated forest road going left is the Shinbone Trail. Park here. Trailhead GPS: 36.106532, -82.372043

## The Hike

This is one of those "Why don't more people do this hike?" hikes. An added irony is the fact that the area's most popular path—the AT—passes within a quarter-mile (but does not connect). The hike deserves more attention by both North Carolinians and Tennesseans who live in accessible proximity of the path. The hike follows a doubletrack trail the entire route. The Forest Service uses the Shinbone Trail to access and maintain a series of wildlife clearings, enhancing the food prospects for nature's beasts that roam this highland on the edge of the Nolichucky River gorge—bear, deer, and wild turkey, among others.

The footing is easy on the doubletrack, allowing you to look around and appreciate nature rather than continually scanning the ground for the best place to drop your boot. Perhaps you may spot some wildlife, or a wildflower, or just immerse yourself in nature's glory. And you will likely be doing so in solitude. Not many folks make their way to this forgotten path, unlike many other greater Asheville hiking destinations.

The Shinbone Trail initially traces the old Ephraim Place Road, a wagon track used to access a homestead where the owner also appreciated solitude. The trail curves with the undulations of the state line but stays on the Tar Heel State side of the border and leads you to the first of many wildlife clearings, grassy meadows that provide contrast to the wooded hills.

The track then leaves the state line ridge and circles around the headwaters of Shinbone Creek. Despite the trail's name, this is as close as the path gets to Shinbone Creek. Then you will reach another wildlife clearing. Sometimes it is difficult to figure out which way to go in these clearings. Look for the main doubletrack leaving each meadow.

After a couple of miles, the loop portion of the hike begins. The track works its way to the edge of the Nolichucky Gorge. Along the way you get a glimpse of distant and lofty Roan Mountain, a signature Southern Appalachian peak, and when arriving closer you will see Flattop Mountain across the gorge.

The path then runs roughly parallel to the river crashing deep in the gorge. Pines and other trees cling to the sheer slope. A spur trail leads to a view of the Nolichucky Gorge. Here, the gulf opens below where the raucous river crashes. The scree slopes and outcrops of Flattop Mountain rise across the chasm. Upstream, the river curves into view, then exits from the panorama deeply nestled in montane splendor, bound for Tennessee. The CSX Railroad tracks turn with the river and apparent toy-sized trains roll over its tracks. On warm weekends you are sure to see seemingly little toy rafts challenging the cataracts along the Nolichucky. This is a spot to linger.

You reach the hike's low point shortly thereafter, crossing an unnamed creek diving down the gorge. The trek then works uphill from the gorge, visiting more wildlife clearings. Endure one steep stretch before completing the loop portion of the hike. From there it is a simple backtrack to the trailhead.

## Miles and Directions

**0.0**  Leave the trailhead and join the Shinbone Trail. Immediately pass around a pole gate on a doubletrack roadbed driven upon by Forest Service personnel only.

**0.6**  The softly rising Shinbone Trail descends and comes to the first wildlife clearing.

**1.2**  Come to a second wildlife clearing. The walking is more level than not.

**1.9**  Begin the loop portion of the hike, heading clockwise. Turn left, downhill under oaks and pines as the return route comes in from right and uphill through a pair of iron gateposts.

**2.4**  The Shinbone Trail turns easterly. Ahead, the dark green mantle of Roan Mountain stands tall and proud.

**2.8**  Step over a branch of the Nolichucky. Keep downhill.

| 3.3 | Making a sharp switchback to the right. |
|---|---|
| 3.5 | Curve along the edge of a wildlife clearing. The trail turns south. |
| 4.2 | Cross a small stream by culvert, then open onto a large wildlife clearing. |
| 4.7 | Cross another branch by culvert, then return to the gorge edge. |
| 5.1 | Work along the left side of a large wildlife clearing, with the wooded gorge to your left and the clearing rising to your right. |
| 5.2 | The trail splits. Here, a spur path angles left to another wildlife clearing, while the Shinbone Trail turns right and downhill. Stay left here, entering the clearing. Stay on the left-hand side of the meadow and after 0.1 mile look left for a footpath dropping to an outcrop and breathtaking panorama of the Nolichucky Gorge. Resume the Shinbone Trail. |
| 6.1 | Cross a steep stream by culvert, then curve back out to the gorge. |
| 6.4 | Bisect another wildlife clearing. |
| 7.2 | Make an elongated switchback around a pine-clad point. |
| 7.5 | Take a breath as the trail fleetingly levels off, then turns left, rising again. |
| 7.9 | Open onto another wildlife clearing. The uptick continues. |
| 8.2 | Open onto a wildlife clearing, ending a steep segment. |
| 8.6 | Complete the loop portion of the hike. Backtrack. |
| 10.5 | Arrive at the trailhead, finishing the balloon loop. |

*Autumn glory rises from the brawling Nolichucky River.*

# RAFTING THE NOLI

After looking into the deep chasm through which the Nolichucky River flows, you might be inspired to try a guided whitewater rafting trip down the Nolichucky River. It is a fun way to explore one of our outdoor treasures—the Nolichucky Gorge—while being led by experts who know the whitewater trade. As the guide saying goes, "It's better to watch the show than to be the show," meaning you don't want to be the one who has a rough time, flipping in the rapids. Outfitters operate in Erwin, Tennessee, on the way to this hike.

The mountain chasm of the Nolichucky slices right through the heart of the Appalachian Range, where the bordering mountains rise far above the boulder-strewn river. Many whitewater enthusiasts consider the Nolichucky Gorge the best combination of exciting rapids and superlative scenery in the entire eastern United States. And it is that combination of natural beauty and excitement that draws in rafters from states far beyond North Carolina and Tennessee.

The primary run goes from the put-in at Poplar, North Carolina, to emerge from the gorge at Erwin, Tennessee. This hike travels along the edge of the gorge above this segment. While rafting, both the riverside and mountaintop scenery, along with the cataracts, will vie for your attention. Above, the wooded walls of the gorge rise high into the sky. Craggy rock outcrops stand as sentinels hundreds of feet above the river. Beside the Nolichucky, imposing rock formations wall in rafters. Boulder gardens extend to and through the river. Sandbars form where the water stills. Songbirds flitter above the water, nary a care in the world.

And then there are the rapids. The Nolichucky features Class III and IV rapids in its upper stretches, with names such as Quarter Mile, Zig Zag, and the Souse Hole. At the more challenging rapids, guides line up in different positions in order to help any paddlers if they flip from the raft, as professionals should.

I highly recommend this backyard adventure that people from far away come to do. A trip through the Nolichucky Gorge delivers the unbeatable combination of superlative scenery with exciting whitewater.

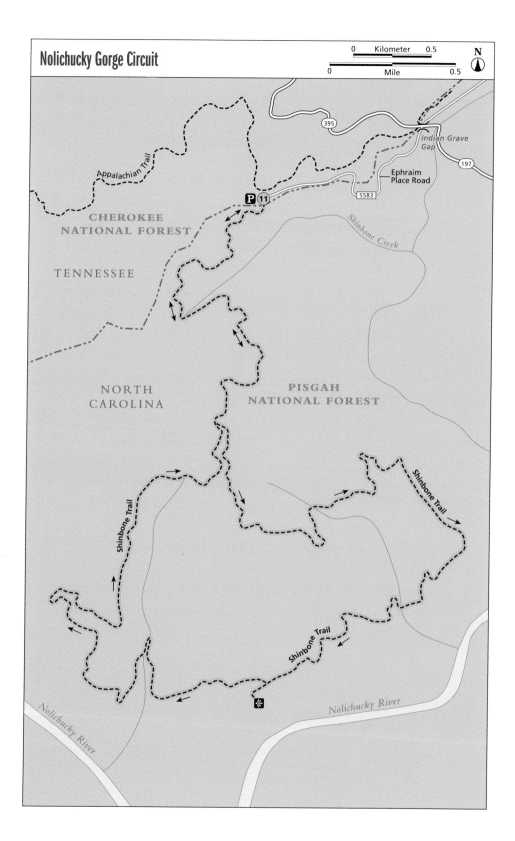

# Nolichucky Gorge Circuit

0    Kilometer    0.5

0    Mile    0.5

N

Appalachian Trail

395

Indian Grave Gap

Ephraim Place Road

197

5583

P 11

CHEROKEE NATIONAL FOREST

TENNESSEE

Shinbone Creek

NORTH CAROLINA

PISGAH NATIONAL FOREST

Shinbone Trail

Shinbone Trail

Shinbone Trail

Nolichucky River

Nolichucky River

# 12 Unaka Mountain Wilderness

This hike starts at an attractive and historic national forest recreation area, then enters the Unaka Mountain Wilderness. Here, hikers penetrate a deep, lush defile where aptly named Rock Creek cuts a mountain gorge. Trace a narrow path under rock bluffs interspersed in the wilderness. Crisscross Rock Creek several times without benefit of a bridge. Your efforts are rewarded upon reaching three waterfalls. The uppermost cataract, Rock Creek Falls, crashes 50 feet from on high into a sheer-walled curved stone amphitheater. The other two major spillers drop 12 and 30 feet respectively.

**Start:** Rock Creek Recreation Area
**Distance:** 4.2-mile there-and-back
**Difficulty:** Moderate
**Elevation change:** +-1,247 feet
**Maximum grade:** 20 percent grade for 0.4 mile
**Hiking time:** About 2.5 hours
**Seasons/schedule:** Spring for bold falls and wildflowers
**Fees and permits:** Parking fee required during warm season
**Dog friendly:** Leashed dogs allowed
**Trail surface:** Forested natural surface

**Land status:** National forest
**Other trail users:** Bicyclers on lowermost part of hike
**Maps to consult:** National Geographic #783 South Holston & Watauga Lakes, Cherokee and Pisgah National Forests; USGS Unicoi
**Amenities available:** Picnic area, restrooms, campground, swimming pool during warm season
**Cell service:** None
**Trail contacts:** Cherokee National Forest, Watauga Ranger District, (423) 735-1500, www.fs.usda.gov/cherokee

**Finding the trailhead:** From Asheville, take I-26 north into Tennessee and take exit 36, Main Street/Erwin, the access road leading to TN 107/Main Street and a traffic light. From the traffic light, turn right and join TN 107 west/Main Street for 0.4 mile to TN 395/Rock Creek Road. Turn left on TN 395 east and follow it 3.1 miles to Rock Creek Recreation Area. Turn left, enter the recreation area, and follow the entrance road past picnic areas to the swimming pool parking area, just before reaching the campground. Trailhead GPS: 36.138333, -82.350080

## The Hike

Unaka Mountain Wilderness comprises 4,700 acres along the slopes of its namesake mountain, where spruce trees cloak the crest, then hardwoods stretch down to Rock Creek and its rugged gorge and waterfall. The wilderness is best known for Rock Creek Falls, one of among over a dozen cataracts tumbling along Unaka Mountain's slopes. The wilderness was established in 1984.

This hike follows gorgeous Rock Creek the whole way to Rock Creek Falls, under a mantle of black birch, maple, and tulip trees. Cool-climate specialists yellow birch

Rock Creek Falls dives in stages from a stone cleft.

lord over ranks of rhododendron and doghobble rising thick from the stone-pocked forest floor. Rock bluffs rise on the slopes.

After passing alongside the recreation area campground, enter the closing gorge of Rock Creek shortly after leaving the trailhead. A sign indicates official entry into the Unaka Mountain Wilderness. Then you make your first of four unbridged crossings of bouldery Rock Creek, befitting a wilderness.

Nimble hikers can keep their feet dry at normal flows. However, in late winter, early spring, and after thunderstorms the crossings might increase in difficulty, but a bolder waterfall will reward your efforts. In still other places, Rock Creek will seem more rock than creek. Ahead, the winding trail and clear stream separate. Warmup cascades grace the valley. The deeply wooded vale closes and you come to what many think is the Rock Creek Falls. The 30-foot slide cascade is known as False Rock Creek Falls. A well-trod path drops left to this sliding spiller.

However, you will know when you reach Rock Creek Falls and the trail's end. There is nowhere else to go. First, you will walk beside a 12-foot unnamed slide fall. It flows over a tan stone tongue into a clear-as-air pool. The trail climbs and sheer cliffs rise on both sides of Rock Creek, then you come to the end of the line.

Here, 50-foot Rock Creek Falls dashes off the cliff lip dead ahead before crashing amid moss-covered stone, splashing into a gravel bed at the base of the semicircular amphitheater of stone, framing the two-tiered cataract.

The whole setting bespeaks wilderness—the white falls, the imposing, craggy walls, and the riot of vegetation. Sit back and feel the breeze blowing through the valley and the mist drifting from the falls. On your way back, contemplate what intrinsic values wilderness has and what it does for the mind and body to engage in untamed areas like this one on Unaka Mountain.

## Miles and Directions

**0.0**  Leave the parking area near the Rock Creek Recreation Area swimming pool, then walk up the paved road toward the campground, beyond the campground information station on your right. Walk the road a bit farther and turn left onto a gravel trail, just before you reach Loop A of Rock Creek Campground. Head up upper Rock Creek valley.

**0.1**  Part of Rock Creek's flow at this point has been drawn from upstream into the swimming pool of the recreation area where the trail starts. Look for a small concrete dam, the diversion to the natural swimming pool. Upstream, Rock Creek exhibits the full volume of its flow. Short spur trails link to the campground.

**0.4**  Come to a trail intersection. The Bicycle Trail and the Rattlesnake Ridge Trail head left across a wooden bridge over Rock Creek. Veer right, coming near the upper end of the campground beside the walk-in tent sites, then turn back left, continuing up the canyon of Rock Creek.

**0.7**  Reach another trail intersection. The other end of the Bicycle Trail comes in on your left over another bridge over Rock Creek. Keep straight on the wilderness-like Rock Creek Trail.

| 0.9 | Make the first rock-hop of Rock Creek. |
| 1.2 | Make the second crossing, then ascend higher into the gorge. |
| 1.5 | Make the third crossing. Hike up the left bank of Rock Creek. |
| 1.7 | Hike past a small slide cascade. |
| 1.8 | Make the fourth, and last, crossing of Rock Creek. Climb steeper. |
| 1.9 | "False Rock Creek Falls" drops 30 feet as a long slide cascade. |
| 2.1 | The path dead ends at 50-foot Rock Creek Falls. Backtrack. |
| 4.2 | Arrive back at the trailhead, completing the hike. |

# ADD CAMPING AT ROCK CREEK TO YOUR HIKE

Back in the 1930s, the Civilian Conservation Corps (CCC) developed the Rock Creek area for forest recreation. Though it was a tall order, the CCC introduced the works of man into the wilds of East Tennessee, making this part of the Cherokee National Forest more enjoyable for visitors. And they did a good job. Although Rock Creek campground and the stream-fed swimming pool have received a few makeovers over the last century, most of the original stonework remains, adding a rustic touch to the unimproved works of nature.

And to this day, we can enjoy overnighting in the cool, shady Rock Creek valley. Three loops divide the campground where regal trees rise above boulders and evergreens. Loops A and B cater more to pop-ups and recreational vehicles (RVs), with electrical hookups and a modern bathhouse with flush toilets and warm showers. Loop C is for tent campers. It is located higher in the valley, against the wilderness. Dense undergrowth avails maximum privacy. Consider overnighting at one of the five walk-in tent sites, where a little walk gets you even closer to nature.

The recreation area swimming pool is undoubtedly its signature feature. Built by the CCC, the pool is a concrete-and-rock-lined basin of clear stream water, lying behind a small dam. A diverted portion of Rock Creek flows into the head of the walkway-bordered pool. Big trout fin throughout the pool. A bathhouse with changing rooms, restrooms, and showers stands nearby.

For another hike, in addition to the trip to Rock Creek Falls, take the Rattlesnake Ridge Trail east uphill 3 miles to the Pleasant Garden Overlook, at 4,800 feet. Bicyclists have the 0.8-mile Rock Creek Bicycle Trail to enjoy as well. I highly recommend adding these other possibilities to your adventure here at Rock Creek Recreation Area.

*This unnamed slide fall is but one of several warmup cascades before Rock Falls.*

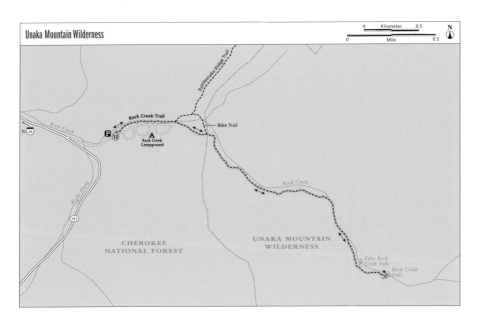

# Southwest

# 13 Flat Laurel Creek Loop

This is your opportunity to explore one of the highest mountain valleys in the East. But the mile-high hike is about more than the Flat Laurel Creek valley. It is also about extensive mountain vistas in the highlands of the Pisgah National Forest. Panoramas are immediate as you cross a meadow then take a side trip to rocky 6,000-foot Sam Knob, where first-rate views stretch in all directions. Rejoin the circuit to come along crystalline Flat Laurel Creek, sporting colorful rocks and cheerful cascades. Trek beyond uppermost Flat Laurel Creek, soaking in still more views of this highland wonderment.

**Start:** FR 816 trailhead off Blue Ridge Parkway
**Distance:** 3.9-mile loop with side trip
**Difficulty:** Moderate
**Elevation change:** +-831 feet
**Maximum grade:** 11 percent grade for 0.7 mile
**Hiking time:** About 2.5 hours
**Seasons/schedule:** 24/7/365, fall and spring for best views, weekdays for solitude
**Fees and permits:** None
**Dog friendly:** Leashed dogs allowed

**Trail surface:** Natural
**Land status:** National forest
**Other trail users:** None
**Maps to consult:** National Geographic #780 Pisgah Ranger District; USGS Sam Knob
**Amenities available:** None
**Cell service:** Iffy
**Trail contacts:** Pisgah National Forest, Pisgah Ranger District, (828) 877-3265, www.fs.usda .gov/nfsnc

**Finding the trailhead:** From the intersection of NC 280 and US 276 in Brevard, take US 276 north for 15 miles to the Blue Ridge Parkway. Follow the Blue Ridge Parkway southbound 8.4 miles to FR 816, on your right. Turn right on FR 816 and follow it for 1.2 miles to dead end at the Black Balsam trailhead. Trailhead GPS: 35.325820, -82.882051

## The Hike

Flat Laurel Creek, a tributary of the West Fork Pigeon River, is located just outside the busy but beautiful Shining Rock Wilderness. The gorgeous valley, covered in a mingling of grasses, meadows, wetlands, and forests, presents a continual canvas of Southern Appalachian highland beauty. Bordered by Pisgah Ridge to the south and Shining Rock Ledge to the east, Flat Laurel Creek drains Sam Knob and Little Sam Knob in a perched flat that ultimately dives off a mountainside to meet the West Fork Pigeon River.

No doubt, this area is a popular place, especially when you pull into the trailhead. However, remember that most of the trail traffic leaving the trailhead is bound for the adjacent Shining Rock Wilderness, not Sam Knob. At the same time, expect company unless you are here during colder times or during weekdays.

*A view of Shining Rock Ledge from Sam Knob*

The hardest part of the hike may be trying to find the correct path from the trailhead while still trying to look like the accomplished semi-pro hiker you are, as a multitude of unofficial and official paths stem from the large and often busy Black Balsam trailhead. The Sam Knob Summit Trail is the correct choice. It heads westerly through an assortment of trees, brush, and grasses, more open than not. Ahead, sally forth through a grassy gap, where late-summer wildflowers will be gently swaying in the wind, or where January's harsh gales will blast ice and snow, pummeling any hikers who dare this high-country hike in winter (assuming the Blue Ridge Parkway—which you must use to access this hike—is open). On a clear day you can see Little Sam Knob across Flat Laurel Creek and the rampart of Pisgah Ridge, atop which the Blue Ridge Parkway travels. The dark mantles of Fork Ridge rise westerly, across the West Fork Pigeon River.

The views are grand already and you haven't even reached Sam Knob yet! The opportunity soon arises and you begin switchbacking up the rocky east slope of Sam Knob in wind-stunted birch, maple, and rhododendron. More switchbacks work up the peak, and you curve to the south side of the mount where an outcrop reveals the valley of Flat Laurel Creek and the mountains beyond.

Look upon a land of highland meadows, wind-sculpted hardwoods, and evergreens rising among rock outcrops, upon dark spruce thickets adorning grassy slopes, and tannin-stained waterways emerging from mile-high wetlands. In addition to admiring the scenery, look below for tiny little hikers trekking the trails below. A practiced eye will soon discern the trails themselves, whether hikers are on them or not.

You shortly reach the crest of Sam Knob. Maintained trails go left and right. Explore vistas looking both south and north from the knob. The north view delivers distant looks at the Great Smoky Mountains National Park, the heights of which form the North Carolina–Tennessee border. In the near, look for the white quartz to the northeast and the glimmer of Shining Rock Ledge. The south view overlooks Black Balsam Knob, as well as the parking area below and the trail you used to reach Sam Knob. Speaking of white quartz outcrops, you will pass one while traipsing atop Sam Knob, the same type of white quartz visible in the distance.

After soaking in views aplenty, backtrack down Sam Knob, savoring still more panoramas. Look down upon where you will travel next. Rejoin the loop hike traveling through a successional area. Here, fire cherry trees and brush replace grass/brush meadows. Long after our lifetimes, red spruce and Fraser fir will have supplanted the hardwoods and brush that are slowly reclaiming the valley of Flat Laurel Creek.

Then you reach Flat Laurel Creek and the low point of the hike at 5,420 feet, a very high low point. What is more astonishing is the large size of the stream and its pools for this elevation. Here, the waters flow over an array of earth-toned stones, splashing in shallows and slowing in pools deep enough for an icy dunking downstream.

After crossing Flat Laurel Creek, the loop hike turns left and joins the Flat Laurel Creek Trail. The woods grow thick along the stream and astride the trail, a decidedly different experience than the first part of the hike. You will come to the Little Sam Knob Trail after crossing a gurgling tributary but will stay with Flat Laurel Creek Trail. The walk works around the upper watershed of Flat Laurel Creek, hopping over a collection of little feeder streams amid an often open and grassy area. Views clear west of Sam Knob and where you have been hiking. The path eventually turns north. Saunter through a mix of spruce and fir and open areas before completing the circuit.

## Miles and Directions

**0.0**   From the parking area on FR 816, as you face the parking area restrooms, look just right of the restrooms for a path leading west on a level grade. This is the Sam Knob Summit Trail. Join this trail, which immediately splits—a short path goes left to a campsite. Stay right, hiking among yellow birch, mountain ash, and Fraser fir all mixed in meadows. Rhododendron finds its place. Blackberries grow in season.

**0.3**   The Sam Knob Summit Trail opens to a field. A grassy gap sits below you. Sam Knob, which you will be climbing soon, rises as a backdrop. Keep west for Sam Knob in open grasses, descending for the gap, and beware of unofficial trails heading left.

**0.6**   Come to a trail junction. Turn right with the Sam Knob Summit Trail and begin your spur climb to Sam Knob. You will return here later, joining the Sam Knob Trail to continue the circuit hike.

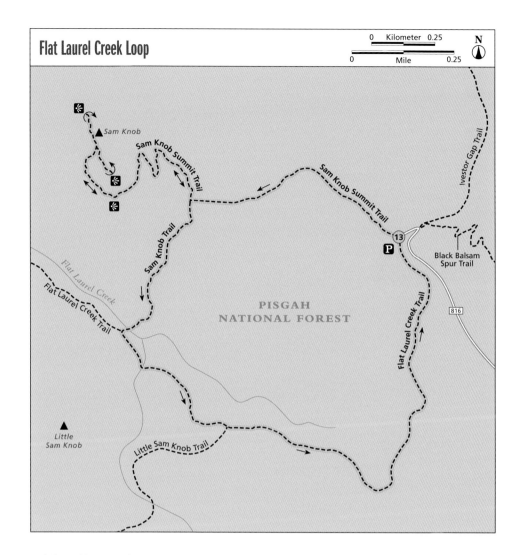

# Flat Laurel Creek Loop

0  Kilometer  0.25

0  Mile  0.25

N

Sam Knob

Sam Knob Summit Trail

Sam Knob Summit Trail

Sam Knob Trail

Ivestor Gap Trail

13

P

Black Balsam
Spur Trail

Flat Laurel Creek

Flat Laurel Creek Trail

PISGAH
NATIONAL FOREST

Flat Laurel Creek Trail

816

Little
Sam Knob

Little Sam Knob Trail

**0.8**    Make your first big switchback while ascending Sam Knob.

**1.0**    Reach a viewpoint from a stone ledge stretching westerly. Gaze down upon Flat Laurel Creek. Little Sam Knob, elevation 5,862 feet, is directly across the vale. Additional peaks circle around Flat Laurel Creek. Continue up Sam Knob.

**1.2**    Reach the crest of Sam Knob. You have broken the 6,000-foot barrier. Here, the path splits. Trails to views go left and right through a blend of rock outcrops and weather-stunted brush.

**2.0**    Turn right onto the Sam Knob Trail, after leaving Sam Knob. Hike south and downhill toward Flat Laurel Creek in a fusion of woods and meadows. Boardwalks and stepping stones have been placed over and among spring seeps, helping to keep your feet dry. Meander amid tree copses and grasses, keeping an eye out for dead-end paths leading to campsites.

**2.4** Wood steps lead to the banks of Flat Laurel Creek. Use big stepping stones to cross the stream. Gaze up Flat Laurel Creek as trees stretch over the golden waters flowing over and around rocks of all sizes. Immediately come to a trail junction. Turn left on the Flat Laurel Creek Trail, working up the watershed in thick woods.

**2.5** Rock-hop an unnamed tributary of Flat Laurel Creek, draining the high slopes of Pisgah Ridge.

**2.8** Intersect the Little Sam Knob Trail. It leaves right for Pisgah Ridge and the Mountains-to-Sea Trail. Our hike keeps straight on the Flat Laurel Creek Trail. Begin curving around the upper valley of Flat Laurel Creek. Grab looks at the ridges encircling Flat Laurel Creek, as well as the parking area.

**3.2** Cross the main headwater stream of Flat Laurel Creek. Curve north toward the parking area. Evergreens border the trail. Ahead, more trickling tributaries cross the pathway.

**3.9** Arrive at the FR 816 Black Balsam trailhead, completing the hike.

# 14 Art Loeb Loop

The Art Loeb Trail is a Carolina icon. This hike traces the famed path through its most lofty heights while traversing Shining Rock Ledge within the Shining Rock Wilderness. Begin the loop on the Ivestor Gap Trail, traveling a level railroad grade for 4 miles through meadows and spruce-fir forest. Your return route takes the famed Art Loeb Trail through a series of ridgetop undulations where the views are nearly nonstop, passing view after view from rocky points, grassy hillsides, and meadows. Expect heavy crowds on nice warm season weekends, and just about any time the weather is decent. Finally, the hike can be cut for shorter loops should the distance become too long.

**Start:** FR 816 trailhead off Blue Ridge Parkway
**Distance:** 8.8-mile loop
**Difficulty:** Moderate to difficult due to distance and navigation concerns
**Elevation change:** +-1,218 feet
**Maximum grade:** 11 percent grade for 0.5 mile
**Hiking time:** About 5 hours
**Seasons/schedule:** 24/7/365, fall and spring for best use, cold-weather weekdays for some
**Fees and permits:** None

**Dog friendly:** Leashed dogs allowed
**Trail surface:** Natural
**Land status:** National forest
**Other trail users:** None
**Maps to consult:** National Geographic #780 Pisgah Ranger District; USGS Sam Knob, Shining Rock
**Trail contacts:** Pisgah National Forest, Pisgah Ranger District, (828) 877-3265, www.fs.usda .gov/nfsnc

**Finding the trailhead:** From the intersection of NC 280 and US 276 take US 276 north for 15 miles to the Blue Ridge Parkway. Follow the Blue Ridge Parkway southbound for 8.4 miles to FR 816, on your right. Turn right on FR 816 and follow it for 1.2 miles to dead end at the Black Balsam trailhead. Trailhead GPS: 35.325820, -82.882051

## The Hike

The open meadows of Shining Rock Wilderness are not so natural as they seem. This mile-high series of clearings along Shining Rock Ledge—one of western North Carolina's most beautiful natural places—came about following the logging of the highland that later became part of the Pisgah National Forest, which was later designated as Shining Rock Wilderness.

A little over a century back in time, Pisgah Ridge, Shining Rock Ledge, and much of this high country was cloaked in a lush green blanket of red spruce and Fraser fir. Logging companies from the North swooped down on these untouched stands, laid railroads to speed a complete stripping of the forests, then shipped the wood to be processed. The denuded hillsides became repositories for unwanted trunks, limbs, and

*Turk's cap lilies color the highlands of Shining Rock Wilderness.*

brush that the loggers left to rot. However, before the cuttings could decompose they caught fire, spreading a conflagration that not only burned the logging remains but also roots, stumps, and soil down to bare rock. What soil remained was washed away by floods flowing unchecked down the hillsides.

The high country was a wasteland, a moonscape on Earth that contrasted greatly with the dense and ancient evergreen forests of before the logger's day. Nature always fills a void and slowly grasses begin to grow where soil accumulated despite recurring fires. And so it has been—brush coming in where grass once grew, then small hardwoods rising, leading ultimately to a return of the evergreens.

However, much of the area remains open to this day. This accidental landscape is a huge attraction to hikers who enjoy the views from its meadows and outcrops. The Shining Rock Wilderness encompasses over 18,000 acres of this highland terrain from which views extend miles in all directions.

No wonder this place is so popular! However, don't let this status keep you from making a well-timed hike on Art Loeb Trail. The hike starts on the Ivestor Gap Trail, following an old railroad grade. Instant panoramas stretch down the Little East Fork Pigeon River to your left and up to Shining Rock Ledge on your right. The Ivestor Gap Trail makes an easy ridge run along the west side of Shining Rock

Ledge. It works around knobs, availing shortcut opportunities, and passes through Ivestor Gap.

The walking remains easy and scenic all the way to Shining Rock Gap, where you join the Art Loeb Trail, now southbound. The circuit hike continues on a railroad grade to Flower Gap. Then the Art Loeb Trail ascends the crest of Shining Rock Ledge as a singletrack footpath, passing over knobs and through gaps. Views are extensive, culminating atop Tennent Mountain, elevation 6,046 feet. Keep rolling south to skirt the top of Black Balsam Knob. Vistas continue, and spur trails tempt you to explore the high point of Black Balsam Knob.

The Black Balsam Spur Trail takes you off Shining Rock Ledge and Black Balsam Knob via a series of switchbacks. Finally, you return to the parking area, completing the hike.

## Miles and Directions

**0.0**  Leave the Black Balsam trailhead, passing around a pole gate at the northeast end of the parking area on the Ivestor Gap Trail. Follow a wide railroad grade where trains and logs once traveled. Shortly pass a spring on your right. Additional springs flow across the path ahead. Willows, fire cherry, and rhododendron border the route.

**1.2**  Come to a gap between Tennent Mountain and Black Balsam Knob where a user-created spur trail leads right to Art Loeb Trail. This is your first shortcut opportunity. Stay left with the Ivestor Gap Trail.

**1.4**  Bisect a ridge amid a non-native red pine plantation.

**1.7**  Watch for the Fork Mountain Trail descending left for the Sunburst Campground trailhead.

**1.8**  Come to an unnamed gap, meeting the Art Loeb Trail, and your second shortcut opportunity. The Ivestor Gap Trail splits left, still on the wide railroad grade and stays on the west side of Shining Rock Ledge.

**2.2**  Reach Ivestor Gap and a five-way trail intersection. This is your third shortcut chance. The Art Loeb Trail heads north and south and the Grassy Cove Trail goes east. Stay left with the railroad bed and Ivestor Gap Trail on a narrower trail. More views lie ahead as you wind through open areas among springs and also tree copses and rhododendron thickets.

**3.9**  The Little East Fork Trail leaves left. Stay right, now easterly, for Shining Rock Gap.

**4.3**  Come to the small grassy flat of Shining Rock Gap and a nest of user-created and official trails. Meet the Art Loeb Trail and turn right, southbound, avoiding those user-created paths, walking a wide railroad. Ahead, log steps leave left, indicating the Shining Creek Trail. Stay straight with the Art Loeb Trail.

**4.9**  Enter grassy Flower Gap. The Art Loeb Trail leaves the railroad grade and ascends the crest of Shining Rock Ledge as a singletrack trail. Wind flagged trees rise above low-lying vegetation.

**5.2**  The Art Loeb Trail reaches an unnamed knob exceeding 6,000 feet. Views stretch in all directions. Beyond this knob, the Art Loeb Trail slips over to the east side of Grassy Cove Top.

**5.7**  Come to a trail junction. Here, a spur trail leads left to the Grassy Cove Trail. Stay with the Art Loeb Trail.

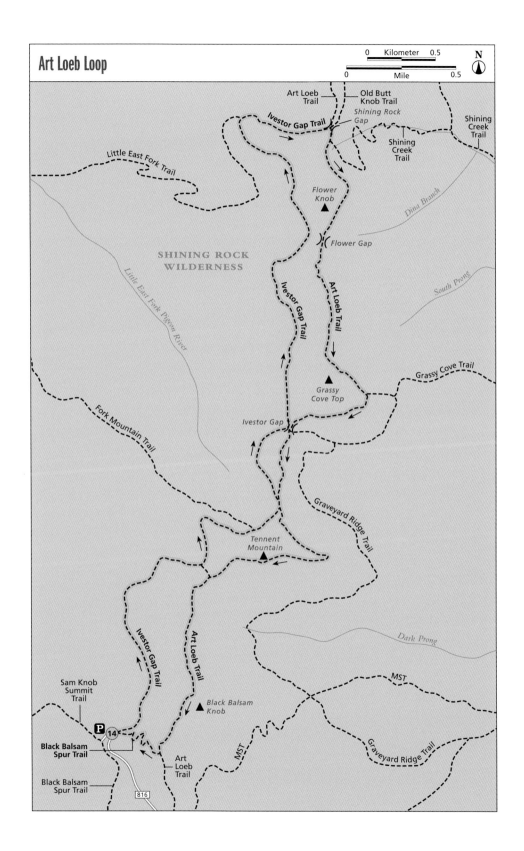

# Art Loeb Loop

0    Kilometer    0.5

0    Mile    0.5

N

Art Loeb Trail

Old Butt Knob Trail

Ivestor Gap Trail

Shining Rock Gap

Shining Creek Trail

Shining Creek Trail

Little East Fork Trail

Flower Knob

Dina Branch

Flower Gap

SHINING ROCK WILDERNESS

Ivestor Gap Trail

Art Loeb Trail

Little East Fork Pigeon River

South Prong

Grassy Cove Trail

Grassy Cove Top

Fork Mountain Trail

Ivestor Gap

Graveyard Ridge Trail

Tennent Mountain

Dark Prong

Ivestor Gap Trail

Art Loeb Trail

MST

Sam Knob Summit Trail

Black Balsam Knob

MST

Graveyard Ridge Trail

P 14

Black Balsam Spur Trail

Art Loeb Trail

Black Balsam Spur Trail

816

**6.1** Return to Ivestor Gap. Stay with the Art Loeb Trail as it cuts through a wooden stile, crosses a grassy clearing, and ascends into a stand of red pines. Tennent Mountain looms ahead as you work over a little knob.

**6.5** Descend to a gap, briefly run in conjunction with the Ivestor Gap Trail, then split left, ascending on the rutted Art Loeb Trail.

**7.2** Reach the peak of Tennent Mountain and its 360-degree landscapes. Look for landmarks in the near and the waves of mountains extending as far as the clarity of the sky allows.

**7.5** Drop off Tennent Mountain to reach a gap where a spur trail leaves right to Ivestor Gap Trail. Climb the slope of Black Balsam, peering west above windblown vegetation. Watch out for user-created trails going to the top of Black Balsam. The official path is equipped with water erosion bars and stays on the west side of Black Balsam Knob.

**8.4** Turn right on the signed Black Balsam Spur Trail. Soak in some final views as you descend switchbacks.

**8.8** Arrive at the FR 816 Black Balsam trailhead, completing the loop.

# ABOUT THE ART LOEB TRAIL

The 30-mile Art Loeb Trail, named for a Brevard resident who helped this trail come to be in 1969, starts down by Brevard at just above 2,300 feet, then climbs Shut-in Ridge and continues along the crest, topping Chestnut Mountain and Pilot Mountain, among other peaks. A pair of trail shelters enhances this lower section. Ultimately, the path rises to Pisgah Ridge and crosses the Blue Ridge Parkway. Here, the Art Loeb Trail enters Shining Rock Wilderness and is near where this hike begins. The path surmounts 6,000-foot-high knobs before nearing Cold Mountain. Finally, the path drops to the Little East Fork of the Pigeon River, and its other terminus. An end-to-end trek along the Art Loeb Trail is a backpacking adventure to remember. If overnighting is not for you, consider hiking the Art Loeb Trail in sections. It is worth the effort.

# 15 Falls of Yellowstone Prong

This hike visits two waterfalls situated in the nearly mile-high Yellowstone Prong valley along the Blue Ridge Parkway. The pair of cataracts each exceeds 40 feet. Along the hike you will experience a medley of landscapes, from meadows to hardwood forests to dense brush thickets to naked rock slabs. The busy and popular hike first leads to Lower Falls, accessed by stairs aplenty. From there, turn upstream, meandering through wetland bogs and meadows with views galore, along with woodland copses. Climb a bit to find Upper Falls, an impressive frothy ribbon dancing down a stone slope. After backtracking, pick up a new path, looping back to the trailhead.

**Start:** Graveyard Fields Overlook at milepost 418.8 of the Blue Ridge Parkway
**Distance:** 3.2-mile balloon loop
**Difficulty:** Moderate
**Elevation change:** +-459 feet
**Maximum grade:** 10 percent grade for 0.4 mile
**Hiking time:** About 2 hours
**Seasons/schedule:** 24/7/365, year-round
**Fees and permits:** None
**Dog friendly:** Leashed dogs allowed

**Trail surface:** Natural
**Land status:** National forest
**Other trail users:** None
**Maps to consult:** National Geographic #780 Pisgah Ranger District; USGS Shining Rock
**Amenities available:** Restroom in parking lot
**Cell service:** Not much
**Trail contacts:** Pisgah National Forest, Pisgah Ranger District, (828) 877-3265, www.fs.usda .gov/nfsnc

**Finding the trailhead:** From the intersection of NC 280 and US 276 in Brevard, take US 276 north for 15 miles to the Blue Ridge Parkway. Follow the Blue Ridge Parkway 7 miles south to the Graveyard Fields Overlook, on your right at milepost 418.8. Park only in the lot and not along the parkway. Trailhead GPS: 35.320364, -82.847077

## The Hike

The two cataracts on this hike—Lower Falls and Upper Falls—are part of the greater Graveyard Fields, a major attraction of the Pisgah National Forest, just off the Blue Ridge Parkway. I think Upper Falls is the more impressive of the two cataracts, despite being less visited, as Lower Falls is so close to the trailhead. Nevertheless, the entirety of the upper Yellowstone Prong valley is a continual visual cornucopia. Thus the area is popular, but this is simply one of those "must-do" well-loved treks. So swallow your pride and give this adventure a go—you will not be disappointed.

Situated where Yellowstone Prong and its tributaries flow down from 6,214-foot Black Balsam Knob, the waterfalls and the valley through which they flow present an array of highlights—the two falls, meadows delivering first-rate views, high-country hiking above 5,000 feet, and easy access.

*Lower Falls dashes over a naked rock ledge.*

With such an array of upsides, it is not surprising that the hike is popular. To that end, the Graveyard Fields Overlook parking area was expanded to forty spaces from the old fifteen-space lot and a restroom added. However, previously overflow parkers would leave their cars on the side of the parkway. Do not do that now—you will be ticketed. If the lot is full—as it can be on warm-weather weekend afternoons—then move on to another hike.

Avoiding the crowds is easy. Start early in the morning on a weekend, or arrive late in the afternoon. Things are always slower during the week. Spring is a good time to visit. However, the crowds are present during the fall color season. Winter can be iffy since trailhead access is dependent on the Blue Ridge Parkway being open or not, especially at this high elevation. By the way, the parkway website offers real-time road closure information, avoiding a wasted trip.

The hike leaves Graveyard Fields Overlook and descends to Yellowstone Prong through rhododendron thickets. The clear highland stream flows below the sturdy hiker bridge. Beyond the bridge, you head right for Lower Falls, avoiding user-created unofficial paths that can confuse hikers.

An elaborate wooden-tiered boardwalk leads to the base of Lower Falls, also known as Second Falls. Here, the wonderment of whitewater crashes over 50 feet in stages, each stage presenting a different slope delivering the froth of Yellowstone Prong in different ways. A substantial boulder pile jumbles at the fall's base. Waterfall fans use the boulders as impromptu seats.

From here, backtrack toward the trailhead, joining a new trail where you see a sign heading toward Upper Falls. Leave most other hikers now, and enter fast-changing landscape, sometimes meadows, sometimes forest, sometimes upland bogs, sometimes gravel bars banked along the creek.

The nearly level trail continues up the Yellowstone Prong Valley, still in a mosaic of growth—mountain laurel thickets, split-trunked maples, berry brambles, yellow birch copses, and plain old grass meadows. Watch for thick brush bordering highland bogs that reveal panoramas of the ridges surrounding Yellowstone Prong. Glance back toward the Graveyard Fields Overlook. Try to spot your vehicle in the parking area.

The last part of the trail climbs before reaching Upper Falls. Most hikers stop at a slide cascade below Upper Falls. This spiller runs over an open rock slab, usually along a channel to the right. Continue to 45-foot Upper Falls, a narrow cataract splashing on a tan rock base, widening out in fan fashion. But it is not over yet—Upper Falls then dives vertically, and continues over the wide rock slab, then eases up. Explore the falls, but be careful traversing the naked rock slab astride Upper Falls.

After backtracking down the Yellowstone Prong valley, cross Yellowstone Prong on a trail bridge. Enjoy the view of Yellowstone Prong from the bridge. Willow and rhododendron border the rocky clear waterway. From the bridge it is a half-mile back to the trailhead and Graveyard Fields Overlook on the Blue Ridge Parkway.

# Miles and Directions

**0.0** Leave the east side of the Graveyard Fields Overlook on stone steps, descending an asphalt trail. Enter Pisgah National Forest, winding through rhododendron thickets, black birch, and pin cherry, as well as fragrant galax.

**0.1** Cross noisy Yellowstone Prong on a sturdy hiker bridge. Turn right beyond the bridge toward Lower Falls. The trail uses boardwalks to escort hikers over rivulets.

**0.2** Come to a trail intersection. Here the Mountains-to-Sea Trail Connector leads left to the Mountains-to-Sea Trail. Keep straight to Lower Falls in spruce and maple. Watch for user-created trails leading down to the top of Lower Falls.

**0.3** Reach the base of Lower Falls after following a multilevel, curving boardwalk. Lower Falls, labeled as Second Falls on official USGS Survey maps, spills over 50 feet down a broken rock slope into a pool. Backtrack after enjoying the cataract, heading back to the lowermost Yellowstone Prong trail bridge. This time, keep straight up the right-hand bank of

*Upper Falls drops 45 feet over an angled rock face.*

Yellowstone Prong on the Lower Falls Trail in a mix of woods and meadows. Note how the trees are weather beaten, despite being in a valley.

**0.5**  The terrain opens and you cross a boardwalk with views of Graveyard Ridge, Black Balsam, and Pisgah Ridge.

**0.6**  Come to what seems to be an official trail intersection. A user-created trail leads left to Yellowstone Prong, but you turn right and immediately come to another intersection, this one official and signed. Our hike heads left on the Upper Falls Trail for Upper Falls. The Graveyard Ridge Connector Trail keeps straight to meet the Graveyard Ridge Trail. Ahead, traverse a boardwalk over a wet and fern-rich meadow.

**0.9**  Come to another trail junction. Your return route heads left to cross Yellowstone Prong, but you stay right, continuing up the Yellowstone Prong valley for Upper Falls. Stay with the most heavily used trail while coming near or through campsites. The official trails will have erosion bars and other structures to enhance or maintain the walking surface.

**1.3**  Step over the main tributary to Yellowstone Prong. Look for white quartz among the stones in the waterway.

**1.5**  Come along a hillside cloaked in yellow birch. Ascend along a stony slope.

**1.7**  The path splits. A trail leads left to a cataract. Many hikers think they have reached Upper Falls, but it is a warmup slide cascade. After exploring this slide fall, return to the main trail and climb further.

**1.8**  Reach Upper Falls. The 45-foot cataract dashes down a rock slope in myriad incarnations that change further under different flows. But no matter the season, the falls are worth the walk. Backtrack from Upper Falls.

**2.7**  Return to the trail junction where you were earlier. Turn right and span Yellowstone Prong, then head downstream bordered by evergreens.

**3.2**  Arrive at the Graveyard Fields Overlook after a final stretch of stone steps, completing the hike.

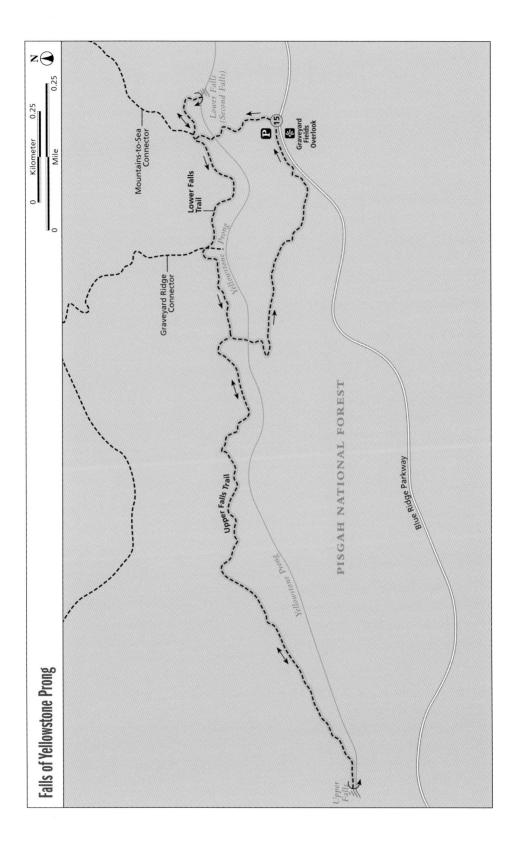

# Falls of Yellowstone Prong

Mountains-to-Sea Connector

Lower Falls Trail

Lower Falls (Second Falls)

Graveyard Ridge Connector

Yellowstone Prong

15

P

Graveyard Fields Overlook

Upper Falls Trail

PISGAH NATIONAL FOREST

Yellowstone Prong

Blue Ridge Parkway

Upper Falls

N

Kilometer

0        0.25

Mile

0        0.25

# 16 Cove Creek Falls Hike

Get a double waterfall dose on this circuit hike in the Pisgah National Forest. Start in the trail-rich Davidson River valley to trek up the valley of Cove Creek. Come near grassy Cove Creek Group Camp then angle up Caney Bottom Creek, where unheralded 55-foot Caney Bottom Falls awaits. From there, turn down Cove Creek to find rugged and splendiferous Cove Creek Falls making its 60-foot expansive drop before closing the loop.

**Start:** FR 475 trailhead
**Distance:** 5.1-mile balloon loop
**Difficulty:** Moderate
**Elevation change:** +-790 feet
**Maximum grade:** 6 percent downhill grade for 1.0 mile
**Hiking time:** About 2.8 hours
**Seasons/schedule:** 24/7/365, falls boldest winter through spring
**Fees and permits:** None
**Dog friendly:** Yes, on leash only

**Trail surface:** Forested natural surface
**Land status:** National forest
**Other trail users:** Mountain bikers, group campers
**Maps to consult:** National Geographic #780 Pisgah Ranger District
**Amenities available:** None at trailhead
**Cell service:** Limited
**Trail contacts:** Pisgah National Forest, Pisgah Ranger District, (828) 877-3265, www.fs.usda .gov/nfsnc

**Finding the trailhead:** From the intersection of NC 280 and US 276 on the northeast side of Brevard in the town of Pisgah Forest, take US 276 north for 5.2 miles, then turn left on FR 475 toward the Pisgah Center for Wildlife Education. Follow paved FR 475 for 3.0 miles to the Cove Creek Group Camp entrance on your right. Parking is on the left. Trailhead GPS: 35.283034, -82.816885

## The Hike

Transylvania County, down Brevard way, is often dubbed the waterfall capital of North Carolina, the land of waterfalls. Face it, the folks of that mountainous domain have a case. Exact numbers vary, but somewhere around 250 cataracts, cascades, and chutes can be found there, ranging from 400-plus-foot Whitewater Falls to overlooked spillers such as Caney Bottom Falls—found on this hike—tumbling their way off the Blue Ridge and in this case into the Davidson River then the French Broad River, which then flows through Asheville before punching through the spine of the Appalachians into Tennessee.

With other nearby non-waterfall attractions such as Looking Glass Rock, Cedar Rock, and the Cradle of Forestry, this circuit hike doesn't get too crowded. Elevation changes are under 1,000 feet and the trails are in good shape, together fashioning a rewarding hike that would be a fine outing for your friend who talks the hiking game but never seems to actually get out on the trail. Even Goldilocks would like this adventure—not too long, not too short, not too steep, and offers the promise of two tall waterfalls. The only potential trouble is the high number of user-created unblazed trails spurring off the official routes. Stay with the blazes and you will be fine.

The adventure starts by tracing gated FR 809. Cove Creek gurgles through thickets of doghobble, ferns, mountain laurel, and rhododendron underneath black birches. As you bridge Cove Creek ahead, note the varied colorful rocks on the creek bottom, from off-white to orange to brown, and every shade between. The changing light on the creek—from pure sunlight to muted skies—further intensifies the kaleidoscope of palettes presented on the streambed.

You'll spur onto hiking trail before reaching Cove Creek Group Campground (do not disturb campers if the site is occupied), then curve along a hill to the left of the group camp. Next comes your trip up Caney Bottom Creek. You are on a hillside well above the stream when Caney Bottom Falls comes into view. The long slide cataract drops off an angled slope, widening as it descends. The bottom of the pour-over is often cluttered with trees, limbs, and other natural detritus. A thick sea of brush stands between you and the base of the 55-foot falls, one reason why only ultradedicated, valiant waterfallers seek its base. Most hikers take their shots of the spiller from the trail.

The Caney Bottom Trail then takes you to the top of Caney Bottom Falls before charging into thickets of doghobble, mountain laurel, and rhododendron surrounding the now narrow, upper Caney Bottom Creek. Before long you join the Cove Creek Trail, gently climbing, aiming for Cove Creek. The upper valley of Cove Creek is wide and shallow, the very essence of a cove, replete with tulip trees. Eventually the creek valley steepens and you reach the spur down to Cove Creek Falls.

Exercise caution on this steep downgrade, but you will be rewarded with a bottom-up view of this majestic 60-foot cascade, pouring at a uniform rate over a widening slope then slowing before making a raucous concluding tumble into a shallow, gravelly pool. Note the small rockhouse near the falls base. The stone shelter has kept me dry during a summer thunderstorm. After making your way back up to the main trail, it is a short piece before you have completed the loop. From here, make a backtrack, perhaps checking out the group camp if it isn't occupied.

## Miles and Directions

**0.0**   From the parking area on FR 475, pass around a pole gate and start walking up FR 809, which leads to Cove Creek Group Campground.

**0.1**   Bridge clear Cove Creek on the forest road. Continue up FR 809.

**0.3**   Cove Creek plummets to your right in an angled multistage cascade with a large pool that attracts hikers to swim its depths.

**0.4**   The Cove Creek Trail splits left from the forest road before entering the clearing of the group camp. Continue up the Cove Creek valley, avoiding numerous user-created spurs.

**0.8** Come to an official, signed trail intersection. Here, the Cove Creek Trail, your return route, heads left but we turn right here, joining the Caney Bottom Trail as it descends right then turns down Cove Creek before bridging the stream on a footlog with handrail. Next, curve into the Caney Bottom Creek watershed after coming near the group camp restrooms. Beware additional unblazed trails.

**1.2** Pass under a small rockhouse with a cataract off to your right.

**1.4** Come to a viewing point of Caney Bottom Falls, situated well below the trail.

**2.0** Cross Caney Bottom Creek twice in quick succession then enter a big wooded flat.

*An upstream view of many-faceted Cove Creek Falls*

**2.1**      Meet and join the Cove Creek Trail, heading left, westerly. Immediately span a little tributary on a footbridge, then cross a second stream ahead.

**2.8**      Bridge Cove Creek. Watch in places where one path will ford the creek and another will lead to a hiker bridge.

**3.6**      Drop left to 60-foot Cove Creek Falls. The trail to the falls base is steep and slippery. Be careful. Backtrack.

**4.3**      Complete the loop portion of the hike. Backtrack, still on the Cove Creek Trail.

**5.1**      Arrive at the trailhead, completing the circuit hike.

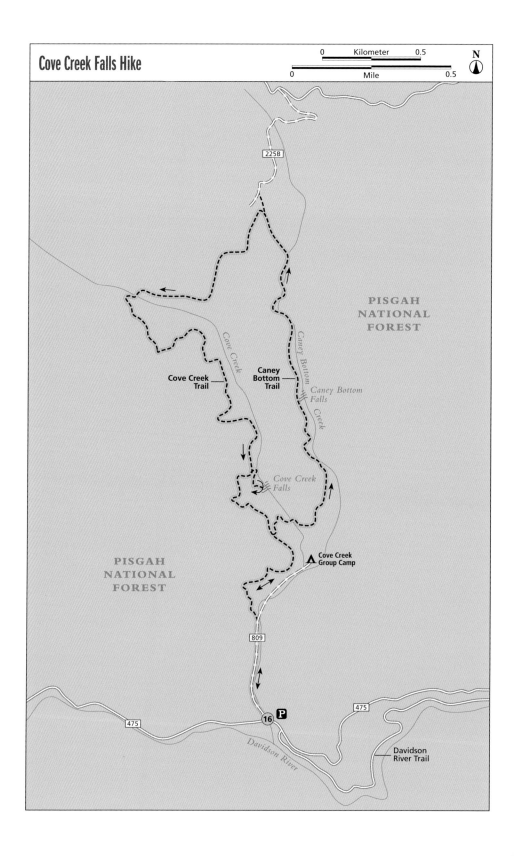

Cove Creek Falls Hike

0    Kilometer    0.5

0    Mile    0.5

N

225B

PISGAH
NATIONAL
FOREST

Cove Creek

Caney Bottom Creek

Cove Creek
Trail

Caney
Bottom
Trail

Caney Bottom
Falls

Cove Creek
Falls

Cove Creek
Group Camp

PISGAH
NATIONAL
FOREST

809

16    P

475

475

Davidson River

Davidson
River Trail

# 17 John Rock Loop

This hike takes you to the top of John Rock, a granite dome rising above the Pisgah National Forest. From John Rock you can see its more popular "big brother" Looking Glass Rock and mountains beyond. Begin by following the Davidson River. Turn up a tributary, then tackle an unbroken ascent to John Rock's naked top and a worthwhile panorama. The circuit drops off John Rock and descends along cascade-rich Cedar Rock Creek, where you can see Cedar Rock Creek Falls, adding to this already geologically fascinating trek.

**Start:** Bobby N. Setzer State Fish Hatchery parking lot
**Distance:** 5.4-mile loop
**Difficulty:** Moderate, does have 1,000-foot climb
**Elevation change:** +-1,118 feet
**Maximum grade:** 11 percent downhill grade for 0.2 mile
**Hiking time:** About 3.5 hours
**Seasons/schedule:** 24/7/365, spring for bold cascades along Cedar Rock Creek

**Fees and permits:** None
**Dog friendly:** Leashed dogs allowed (see caution below)
**Trail surface:** Natural
**Land status:** National forest
**Other trail users:** None
**Maps to consult:** National Geographic #780 Pisgah Ranger District; USGS Shining Rock
**Trail contacts:** Pisgah National Forest, Pisgah Ranger District, (828) 877-3265, www.fs.usda .gov/nfsnc

**Finding the trailhead:** From the intersection of NC 280 and US 276 in Brevard, take US 276 north for 5.2 miles, then turn left on FR 475 toward the Bobby N. Setzer State Fish Hatchery. Follow FR 475 for 1.4 miles, then turn left across the bridge over the Davidson River to the fish hatchery. The hike starts at the lower end of the parking area, away from the fish hatchery. Trailhead GPS: 35.284166, -82.790903

## The Hike

John Rock is a worthy destination in its own right but being literally in the shadow of one of the most famous mountains in the Southeast—Looking Glass Rock—leaves it as second fiddle, despite the fact it offers views similar to Looking Glass Rock and has a loop opportunity that also passes by 20-foot Cedar Rock Creek Falls.

My answer is to hike both, thus the two are included in this guide. Asheville and greater western North Carolina residents almost have to hike Looking Glass Rock as a rite of passage. Avid hikers can then take on John Rock for its own deserving qualities and additional bragging rights. John Rock has fewer visitors, despite being a viewing point for Looking Glass Rock in the near and the Blue Ridge rising a mile high in the background. And then there is 20-foot-high Cedar Rock Creek Falls.

*Mist swirls above the fish hatchery, Looking Glass Rock, the Blue Ridge Parkway, and David-son River as seen from John Rock.*

Finally, the trailhead is at the Bobby N. Setzer State Fish Hatchery, with a potential visit to the adjacent fish hatchery where trout are raised.

This is a good winter hike, since it is low elevation, but dog owners should beware of spring seeps atop John Rock, which especially when frozen have led to dogs slipping off the rock face. Pets have fallen even on the dry surface of the sloping rock. Keep Fido leashed up there!

After leaving the fish hatchery, the hike wanders down the Davidson River, a popular angling venue, especially since it is regularly stocked with fish raised at the adjacent hatchery. Expect to see wader-clad anglers plying the pools and riffles of the translucent mountain stream. Cedar Rock Creek flows into the Davidson River, adding volume as you head downstream. Other streams that you also bridge increase flow too. Pines grow thick.

The Cat Gap Loop leaves the Davidson River and turns up wide Horse Cove. This formerly settled and tilled terrain has now reverted to forest dominated by tulip trees. After joining the John Rock Trail, the hike exchanges streamside scenes for granite, stunted pines, and eye-popping views. Of course, you have to earn those views with a climb, but that is to be expected in these majestic highlands of western North Carolina. And from this granite dome that is John Rock, you can gaze north across the Davidson River valley to see Looking Glass Rock showing off its

*Walk by the Davidson River on this hike.*

own granite skin. And in the distance the Blue Ridge forms a rolling rampart over a mile high. Below, the fish-filled raceways and buildings of the trout hatchery fill the streamside flats.

A second worthy view lies ahead, then you turn south along a ridge. Your climbing isn't over, though you are now in classic hickory-oak woods. Beyond the high point the trail descends to a gap and trail intersection. Here, this loop turns right on the Cat Gap Bypass. However, you can extend the trek about 0.4 mile by heading to Cat Gap and staying with the Cat Gap Loop Trail. This does involve additional climbing however.

The bypass wanders through richly vegetated coves before meeting the Cat Gap Loop. Here, the circuit hike dives toward Cedar Rock Creek. However, switchbacks mitigate the steep ridge down that the trail travels. This ridge divides John Rock Branch from Cedar Rock Creek.

Then you saddle alongside Cedar Rock Creek and enjoy the beauty of falling water, pines, and the Picklesimer Fields, former meadows and cultivated land now transitioning to full-fledged forest. As you descend, Cedar Rock Creek picks up steam until it pours off a 20-foot ledge as Cedar Rock Creek Falls. These falls can be accessed from the main trail via a user-created manway.

The path then unexpectedly comes along the fish hatchery fence. The trail bridges Cedar Rock Creek twice before coming to the parking lot and trail's end.

## Miles and Directions

**0.0**  Leave the lower end of the large trailhead parking area near a big sycamore tree, walking east on the Cat Gap Loop Trail. Hike along the Davidson River bordered by a fence. Ahead, the official trail veers right and bridges Cedar Rock Creek, while an angler's access path continues downriver. Walk through wooded flats along the Davidson River after bridging Cedar Rock Creek amid doghobble and rhododendron, where several big campsites lie.

**0.3**  Bridge a little tributary of the Davidson River, then bridge another tributary 0.1 mile ahead.

**0.5**  The wide Cat Gap Loop Trail turns south up Horse Cove, through which flows an unnamed tributary of the Davidson River. In spring, wildflowers grow rich in Horse Cove.

**0.8**  The stream of Horse Cove enters into view as the trail comes along the foot of a little cascade.

**0.9**  Step over the stream of Horse Cove where the valley narrows. The trail crosses long-closed old FR 475C. Continue working up a now steep-sided valley.

**1.1**  Bridge a tributary, continuing uphill.

**1.2**  Intersect the John Rock Trail. Turn right as the John Rock Trail curves around an upland cove. The Cat Gap Loop Trail keeps straight and you will rejoin it after climbing John Rock. The John Rock Trail alternates between small, rhododendron-choked rivulets in hollows and dry oak woods on ridges.

**1.9**  Level out on the crest of John Rock. Shrubby trees and mountain laurel form a tightly knit forest. Step over a little spring rivulet. Curve onto the north slope of John Rock, where the granite face extends forth. Hike among black gum, sourwood, and other dry situation trees, along with leg-brushing blueberry bushes.

*Cedar Rock Falls is yet one more highlight on this rewarding trek.*

**2.1**   Turn right on a spur trail heading onto the granite face of John Rock. Enjoy immediate and remarkable vistas. First, find the fish hatchery below. The granite slab of Looking Glass Rock points north toward the Blue Ridge, and the Blue Ridge Parkway. Be careful on the rock, as water seeps over the granite, creating a slip hazard, especially while frozen.

**2.2**   A second spur trail heads to another granite slope and lookout. From there, turn south, away from the granite slope, ascending in the shade of classic hickory-oak woods.

**2.8**   Reach the high point of the hike. You are 1,000 feet above your starting point on the Davidson River. Drop sharply.

**2.9**   Come to a four-way trail intersection. Turn right here, picking up the Cat Gap Bypass Trail. The Cat Gap Loop Trail keeps straight for Cat Gap and an intersection with the Art Loeb Trail. The narrow bypass leads through holly and magnolia-rich north-facing coves.

**3.6**   Reunite with the Cat Gap Loop after hopping over the upper reaches of John Rock Branch. Begin descending by switchbacks toward Cedar Rock Creek.

**4.1**   Rock-hop Cedar Rock Creek. Turn downstream under an evergreen canopy.

**4.3**   Cross over to the right-hand bank of Cedar Rock Creek after passing beneath a planted pine grove. Enter the Picklesimer Fields.

**4.5**   Bridge Cedar Rock Creek and reach an intersection. Here, the Butter Gap Trail heads left up along Grogan Creek, which adds significant flow to Cedar Rock Creek. User-created trails lead downstream to a series of cataracts below highlighted by Cedar Rock Creek Falls. Stay right with the Cat Gap Loop Trail, descending.

**5.1** Bridge Cedar Rock Creek again.

**5.4** Finish the circuit after bridging Cedar Rock Creek a final time, ending the adventure at the fish hatchery parking lot.

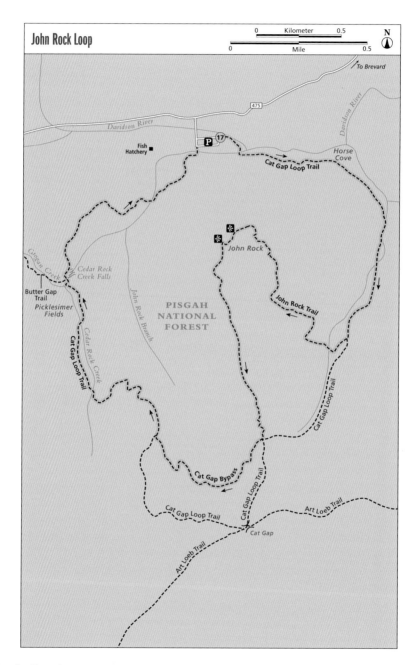

# 18 Looking Glass Rock

This hike leads to one of the area's most notable peaks—Looking Glass Rock. Here, you can rise to a granite grandstand rising above the Davidson River valley, where vistas of the Blue Ridge await. A first-rate but busy path switchbacks from the river through woods, passing occasional rock slabs before opening onto a colossal stone slab availing panoramas of the Blue Ridge rising in the distance as well as greater Davidson River valley stretching out below.

**Start:** Trailhead on FR 475
**Distance:** 5.6-mile there-and-back
**Difficulty:** Moderate to difficult due to ascent
**Elevation change:** +-1,665 feet
**Maximum grade:** 16 percent grade for 0.4 mile
**Hiking time:** About 3.5 hours
**Seasons/schedule:** 24/7/365, fall through spring for best views, weekdays for less traffic
**Fees and permits:** None
**Dog friendly:** Leashed dogs allowed

**Trail surface:** Natural
**Land status:** National forest
**Other trail users:** None
**Maps to consult:** National Geographic #780 Pisgah Ranger District; USGS Shining Rock
**Amenities available:** None
**Cell service:** Better up high
**Trail contacts:** Pisgah National Forest, Pisgah Ranger District, (828) 877-3265, www.fs.usda .gov/nfsnc

**Finding the trailhead:** From the intersection of NC 280 and US 276 in Brevard, take US 276 north for 5.2 miles, then turn left on FR 475 toward the Pisgah Center for Wildlife Education. Follow FR 475 for 0.3 mile and the trailhead will be on your right. Trailhead GPS: 35.291094, -82.776604

## The Hike

Spend any time in western North Carolina and you will hear about Looking Glass Rock. After seeing this unusual stone monument rising almost 2,000 feet above the Davidson River valley, you will agree it is a distinctive peak. Standing proud at 3,969 feet with expansive, sheer granite walls curving around three sides of the dome lends it an unmistakable appearance. The open rock delivers vistas of the Blue Ridge rising to the west as well as nearby ridges and valleys. If you think there's a good view from looking out from Looking Glass Rock, views of Looking Glass Rock are rewarding as well, whether you see this signature peak from the Blue Ridge Parkway or John Rock, a similar dome nearby. Seeing the open rock faces of Looking Glass Rock reflecting the sun purportedly inspired the name. Others contend it is the thin sheets of reflecting ice that cover the exposed rock after freezing rains or in some instances where water dribbles from thin soils atop the rock then flows over the rock and freezes, creating the reflecting surface.

*Looking Glass Rock as seen from the Blue Ridge Parkway*

Open rock expanses this large are unusual in the eastern United States. The origin of Looking Glass Rock is volcanic. At one time, molten magma rose toward the Earth's crust but did not quite break through before cooling, creating a dome. The dome never erupted and became a volcano. Instead, the resultant hardened granite formed what is known as a pluton, which is a body of rock below the surface of the Earth. Eventually, the body of rock was revealed following erosion by softer strata, leaving the granite-exposed dome we see today.

Looking Glass Rock is an icon to not only hikers but also climbers. Known in climbing circles as "The Glass," six primary routes are used by climbers, with *The Nose* being the classic route. Therefore, if you see intrepid athletes wearing those funny climbing shoes, draped in ropes and carabiners, they are likely using routes that cloak Looking Glass Rock. The first ascent of *The Nose* was made in 1966, and ever since then climbers have flocked to this arguably best-known climbing peak in the entire Southeast, especially since Looking Glass Rock offers climbing routes to entertain novice, intermediate, and expert climbers, whether they are free climbing or using ropes.

Most of us use the trail to reach the top of Looking Glass Rock. Though not as dangerous or challenging as rock climbing, the hike to the peak is a nearly continuous ascent from the parking area. You gain almost 1,600 feet from bottom to top. However, due to the hike's popularity, the Looking Glass Rock Trail is a near continual work in progress and its formerly steep gradient has been moderated by numerous switchbacks, in fact enough of them to practically make a hiker wobbly from the back and forth trail turns.

When you reach the top, be very careful and do not take the open slopes for granted. If you fall, it is a long way down with nothing to stop you. Be especially careful after rains or in subfreezing conditions, when water flows over the rock and freezes, potentially making a minor slip a big deal.

The trek starts by climbing along a stream, then the Looking Glass Rock Trail begins its festival of switchbacks. The higher you climb the more frequent the switchbacks become. Once away from the lowlands the trailside vegetation morphs to a more xeric variety—sourwood, pine, black gum, mountain laurel, and the unusual Carolina hemlock. Fragrant galax flanks the pathway. Eventually the trail leads to the ridge crest, but keep climbing. Look for views of adjacent mountains through the trees. Rock slabs start to appear along the sandy, rooty path, including a large one used as a helicopter pad. Stone and log steps aid your footing.

You reach a wooded high point a little before opening onto your destination, a huge sloped naked granite slab bordered by tenacious cedars and pines gripping with shallow roots onto thin soils among cracks in the granite. Depending on recent rainfall, you will see varying flows of water seeping over the bare rock. The farther down you go the steeper the granite slope becomes, until it is the domain of climbers only. Above you, the crest of the Blue Ridge stands over 6,000 feet in places, with many mile-high peaks extending across the landscape. Look for overlooks on the Blue Ridge Parkway, which is running on the crest of the mountains in front of you. To your left, southwest, layers of mountains stretch along the horizon to Georgia and South Carolina. This overlook on Looking Glass Rock is the most popular one on the mountain, but with a little searching you can find other vista points. Just remember it is a long way down the open slabs. Finally, it is worth the drive on the Blue Ridge Parkway to get the view of Looking Glass Rock from the parkway overlooks.

## Miles and Directions

**0.0**   Leave the parking area on the Looking Glass Rock Trail, a wider-than-average, hiker-only track designed for heavy traffic. Immediately bridge a little creek, then ascend under magnolia, black birch, and tulip trees. Turn up at an unnamed little streamlet flowing off the southeast side of Looking Glass Rock. Look for a rerouted former pathway while avoiding user-created shortcuts. Climb steadily above the spilling streamlet.

**0.5**   Make the first switchback. They come more frequently the higher you climb the mountain.

**0.8**   The path turns away from the creek it has been tracing. Keep climbing.

**1.0**   Reach the nose of the ridge atop Looking Glass Rock. If the leaves are off the trees you can look southwest at the Art Loeb Trail, wandering the ridge along Pilot Mountain among other peaks. Keep heading uphill.

**1.5**   Come along a small trickle of water, then turn away. The uptick continues.

**1.9**   A few rock slabs are exposed among the trees.

**2.1**   Reach the first wide-open rock slab along the trail to your left. Head out onto it and look for the painted H, a helicopter landing. Return to the Looking Glass Rock Trail, keeping straight beyond the helicopter landing.

**2.4**   A short spur trail takes you to a large rock slab on your right. Here, the main trail turns northwest, still atop the ridge crest. Watch for dead-end and user-created trails leading to campsites and harder-to-reach vistas.

**2.7**   Reach the high point of Looking Glass Rock, though you are in woods. Begin heading downhill under tree cover.

**2.8**   Open onto a huge sloped granite slab, your destination. The crest of the Blue Ridge extends across the horizon while lesser ridges and streams fall below. Explore, looking for other views. Backtrack.

**5.6**   Arrive at the trailhead, completing the hike.

*Another distant view of Looking Glass Rock*

# CAROLINA HEMLOCKS

Along parts of the trail you will find a tree known as Carolina hemlock. This is an often compact, conical evergreen with needles spreading in all directions along its branches versus the needles of an Eastern hemlock, which spread in two rows on either side of the branch. Carolina hemlock occurs—not surprisingly—in western North Carolina, as well as East Tennessee, southwest Virginia, and in limited areas of Georgia and South Carolina. It grows on dry slopes, usually between 2,000 and 4,000 feet, like those found on the slopes of Looking Glass Rock, unlike the moisture-loving Eastern hemlock. Western North Carolina is the heart of the Carolina hemlock's range. The evergreen also seems to be less susceptible to the hemlock wooly adelgid, which is decimating Eastern hemlocks throughout the Appalachians. However, since Carolina hemlocks are listed as rare in the wild, protective measures such as spraying a soapy insecticide for the hemlock wooly adelgid are undertaken in important and accessible stands of Carolina hemlock.

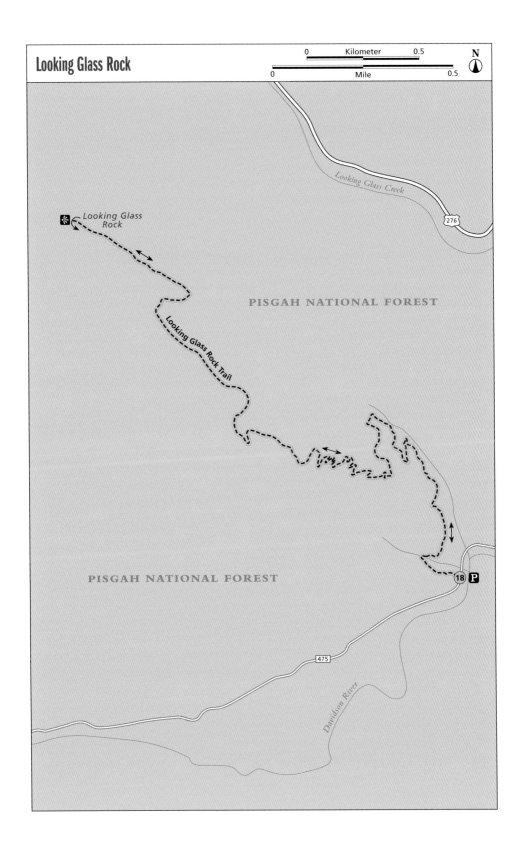

Looking Glass Rock

Kilometer

Mile

N

Looking Glass Creek

276

Looking Glass Rock

Looking Glass Rock Trail

PISGAH NATIONAL FOREST

PISGAH NATIONAL FOREST

18 P

475

Davidson River

# 19 Mount Pisgah

This hike is the walking centerpiece of plentiful recreation opportunities along a lofty stretch of the Blue Ridge Parkway. From near the parkway's Pisgah Inn, you will join a well-maintained trail past the headwaters of Pisgah Creek, then work up the slope of Mount Pisgah on a rocky track, eventually reaching a platform and tower where a veritable land of milk and honey stretches out in all directions. Other trails spur from this locale, adding more hiking opportunities. You can also picnic, camp, or stay at the venerable Pisgah Inn.

**Start:** End of Buck Spring Overlook Road
**Distance:** 2.4-mile there-and-back
**Difficulty:** Easy, does have 700-foot ascent
**Elevation change:** +-720 feet
**Maximum grade:** 22 percent grade for 0.4 mile
**Hiking time:** About 1.5 hours
**Seasons/schedule:** 24/7/365, whenever the skies are clear
**Fees and permits:** None
**Dog friendly:** Leashed dogs allowed
**Trail surface:** Natural

**Land status:** National park
**Other trail users:** None
**Maps to consult:** National Geographic #780 Pisgah Ranger District; USGS Dunsmore Mountain, Cruso
**Amenities available:** None at trailhead, picnic area and Pisgah Inn nearby
**Cell service:** Decent
**Trail contacts:** Blue Ridge Parkway, (828) 348-3400, www.nps.gov/blri

**Finding the trailhead:** From exit 33 on I-26 south of downtown Asheville, take NC 191 south for 2.4 miles, then turn right onto the short signed spur road to the Blue Ridge Parkway. Follow the parkway right, southbound, for 13.9 miles to milepost 407.7, turning left at the sign for Mount Pisgah parking area, which is Buck Spring Overlook Road. Follow Buck Spring Overlook Road for 0.3 mile to its dead end, passing the Buck Spring Overlook along the way. The Mount Pisgah Trail starts at the end of the road in a large parking area. Trailhead GPS: 35.418604, -82.747962

## The Hike

Taken from the Bible's book of Deuteronomy, the name Mount Pisgah comes from the mountain Moses climbed to view the Israelites' Promised Land—a "land of milk and honey." Fast forward a few thousand years to 1776, where Griffith Rutherford—who lent his name to several North Carolina places—is battling the Cherokee for control of the French Broad River valley. Noting the richness of the valley where Asheville is located today, one of Rutherford's soldiers, a preacher by the name of John Hall, thought the French Broad River valley also a land of milk and honey and a certain high peak with its commanding panorama of this bountiful terrain should be named after the biblical crag upon which Moses stood.

*Mount Pisgah was named after the peak where Moses stood looking out on "a land of milk and honey."*

Thus, Mount Pisgah entered North Carolina history and lore, where it has remained ever since. Former North Carolina senator and Confederate general Thomas Clingman (for whom the Smokies park highest point of Clingmans Dome is named) owned Mount Pisgah before selling off to George Vanderbilt, later to build the famous Biltmore Estate, along with 125,000 adjacent acres, much of what later became today's Pisgah National Forest and Blue Ridge Parkway.

After selling Mount Pisgah to the Forest Service, the Vanderbilt family kept a 400-acre parcel of land near the current trailhead for this hike, at Buck Spring. Mr. Vanderbilt had constructed a hunting lodge on the property around 1900, starting a tradition of coming to this parcel of the Blue Ridge for rest, refurbishment, and recreation. The first Pisgah Inn followed in 1918, where wealthy patrons of the pre–air conditioning South spent their summers. The current Pisgah Inn was built in 1964, after the state of North Carolina bought the 400 acres of what once was Mr. Vanderbilt's hunting lodge.

When the Blue Ridge Parkway became a reality, the Park Service made Mount Pisgah and its adjacent lands a recreation hub for the scenic road and the lands under its domain. They built trails, a campground, overlooks, picnic areas, and more. Today, we can soak in the views from this storied mount and look out on our own promised land, and then enjoy the amenities of the Blue Ridge Parkway.

The hike leaves from near Buck Spring Overlook, a place with its own rewarding vistas, including a good gander at Mount Pisgah and lands stretching to the east. Several trails emanate from the area, causing potential confusion for those looking for the proper trailhead. The Mount Pisgah Trail starts at the end of the spur road leading past Buck Springs Overlook. Interestingly, this spur road is routed atop the Buck Springs Tunnel, through which the Blue Ridge Parkway travels.

The trailhead is high, a shade under 5,000 feet. The heavily used but sturdy path circles around a high south-facing cove from which emanates the headwater of Pisgah Creek (which ironically feeds into the Pigeon River as opposed to the streams flowing east from the Blue Ridge feeding the promised land of the French Broad River Valley). It then starts to climb, reaching a gap separating Mount Pisgah from Little Pisgah Mountain, standing 5,270 feet in elevation. The Mount Pisgah Trail then straddles a narrow rocky ridge, where stone steps and naturally occurring rock guide you ever upward. Views begin to open through the trees of the Pisgah Inn, Buck Springs Gap, and the Blue Ridge Parkway, as well as mountains near and far.

Trailside trees and brush become more gnarled the more you climb. Then you reach the 5,721-foot top. A communication tower commands the rock crest, but a wooden viewing deck stands there and awaits your final steps. From here, the land falls away in all directions. The Blue Ridge zigzags northeasterly toward Asheville. The Pigeon River flows west into Tennessee, while the verdant French Broad valley is to the east, and flows north to Asheville, visible in the distance, as is Mount Mitchell. To the south rises the rugged mountains of Shining Rock. Look for the Frying Pan Mountain tower, another worthy destination. In the near, you can see the parking area and trailhead. After looking out on a clear day, it is easy to draw comparisons with Moses's view from the first Mount Pisgah.

## Miles and Directions

**0.0** From the north end of Buck Springs Overlook Road, join the Mount Pisgah Trail as it leaves north on a wide-level track. After a short distance, the Picnic Area Connector leaves left to Mount Pisgah Campground, Pisgah Inn, picnic area, and Frying Pan Mountain. Stay straight with the Mount Pisgah Trail as you curve into a cove.

**0.1** Pass a broad open rock face rising to your right.

**0.4** Cross a spring branch feeding Pisgah Creek.

**0.6** Reach a gap dividing Mount Pisgah from Little Pisgah Mountain. Curve left, ascending under craggy windswept hardwoods.

**1.0** The trail makes a sharp switchback to the right. Views open to the parkway below.

**1.2** Arrive atop Mount Pisgah, from which a transmission tower rises. A wooden observation deck stands a few feet above the ground and offers incredible panoramas in all directions.

**2.4** Arrive at the trailhead, completing the hike.

*A summertime view of the "Land of Milk and Honey"*

# OTHER ACTIVITIES AROUND MOUNT PISGAH

Just a short distance from this trailhead are overnighting opportunities, including the highest campground on the entire Blue Ridge Parkway at nearly 5,000 feet and Mount Pisgah Inn with its superlative views.

Mount Pisgah Inn is open from April through October. Its rooms feature inspiring panoramas of the surrounding mountains. The inn's restaurant is open for breakfast, lunch, and dinner by reservation. They are known for their fresh trout supper. Check for the latest rates and reservations at www.pisgahinn.com. Check out their live cam with the view from the mountain while you are at their site.

Mount Pisgah Campground is ideally incorporated into a wooded flat where wind-carved hardwoods shade campsites enveloped by mountain laurel and rhododendron, delivering exceptional campsite privacy. The eighty-five campsites are spread over four loops, primarily used by tent campers, vans, and popups as most modern-day RVs are too big to fit in this campground. Hot showers, flush toilets, and water are available. The campground is open from mid-May to October.

Campsites are available all but the major summer holiday weekends, but reservations can be made for any time. A campground host keeps things safe and orderly. Bear food storage regulations are in effect. Since this campsite is nearly a mile high, be prepared for cool conditions whenever you come.

The drive on the parkway to the trailhead delivers warmup views for your hike to Mount Pisgah. Once here at Mount Pisgah, a wide array of trails extends from this hub. One of my favorites in addition to Mount Pisgah is the 1.9-mile one-way hike from the campground to Frying Pan Mountain, where a 70-foot steel tower stands atop the Frying Pan Mountain, standing at 5,340 feet. You can climb this tower to an observation deck conveying fine views of the surrounding terrain. Interestingly, the towers of Mount Pisgah, at 5,721 feet, and Frying Pan Mountain are clearly visible from one another. What's more, you can hike from the campground to the Pisgah Inn, with its dining facilities and camp store, with souvenirs and supplies, enhancing your visit. Of course, if you stay at the Pisgah Inn, you can access the same trails system as do those staying at the campground. Don't forget a nice picnic area is located on the parkway just south of the Mount Pisgah trailhead.

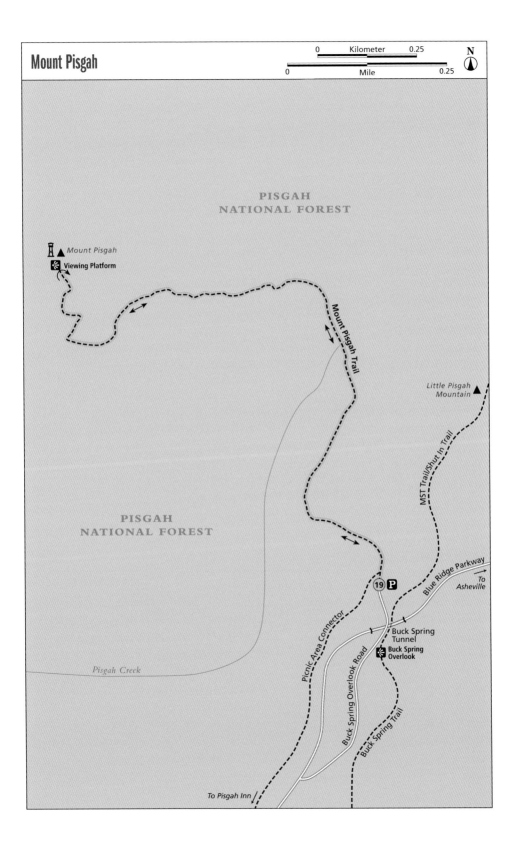

Mount Pisgah

0    Kilometer    0.25

0    Mile    0.25

N

PISGAH
NATIONAL FOREST

Mount Pisgah

Viewing Platform

Mount Pisgah Trail

Little Pisgah
Mountain

MST Trail/Shut In Trail

PISGAH
NATIONAL FOREST

Blue Ridge Parkway

To
Asheville

19  P

Buck Spring
Tunnel

Buck Spring
Overlook

Picnic Area Connector

Buck Spring Overlook Road

Buck Spring Trail

Pisgah Creek

To Pisgah Inn

# 20 The Pink Beds

Take a biologically, historically, and visually enriching hike at the Pink Beds, a highland bog entrenched in mountain ramparts. Walk the perched valley, sauntering through wetlands rich with plant and animal life. Hike down the upper South Fork Mills River valley using bridges and boardwalks aplenty. Circle back through the Pink Beds in a blend of wet and dry situations. Finally, travel through and near meadows, availing views and wildlife viewing opportunities. The walk is family friendly with a shortcut opportunity and minimal elevation variations for a mountain hike.

**Start:** Pink Beds Picnic Area
**Distance:** 5.3-mile loop
**Difficulty:** Moderate
**Elevation change:** +-418 feet over entire loop
**Maximum grade:** 3 percent grade for 0.7 mile
**Hiking time:** About 3 hours
**Seasons/schedule:** 24/7/365, late summer through early fall for driest trail, spring through fall for wildflowers
**Fees and permits:** None
**Dog friendly:** Leashed dogs allowed
**Trail surface:** Natural

**Land status:** National forest Other trail users: Mountain bikers during cold season
**Other trail users:** None
**Maps to consult:** National Geographic #780 Pisgah Ranger District; USGS Shining Rock, Pisgah Forest
**Amenities available:** Picnic shelter, restrooms at trailhead, Forest Discovery Center nearby
**Cell service:** Decent
**Trail contacts:** Pisgah National Forest, Pisgah Ranger District, (828) 877-3265, www.fs.usda.gov/nfsnc

**Finding the trailhead:** From the intersection of NC 280 and US 276 in Brevard, take US 276 north for 11.3 miles to the Pink Beds Picnic Area, on your right, 0.2 mile beyond the right turn to the Forest Discovery Center. Trailhead GPS: 35.353566, -82.778725

## The Hike

This is a fine family hike here in the highlands of the Pisgah National Forest. For starters, the trailhead is at an alluring picnic area with a shelter that is situated 3,200 feet in elevation. You can have a tasty mountain meal before or after your hike. In addition, the national forest's Forest Discovery Center is located less than a quarter-mile from the trailhead. You can stop in there and learn all sorts of things about these Carolina mountain lands and their history, including the story of the Cradle of Forestry. Additionally, the Blue Ridge Parkway is but a few miles distant and you can tool along on it while returning home. However, the hike itself may be the biggest draw—for starters, elevation changes a little over 400 feet for the entire loop, making it one of the flattest walks of 5 miles or more in the entire Pisgah National Forest. The trail wanders through highland bogs, beaver ponds, and other wetlands unusual for western North Carolina. The whole trek is 5.3 miles long; however, a shortcut trail about halfway through can significantly shorten the hike, making it doable by just about everyone.

The name Pink Beds derives from the plethora of blooming flowers that once dotted the valley when it was more open and not under today's heavy forest cover. However, despite the expansive tree growth, mountain laurel and rhododendron still conspire to color the forest pink during the warm season. From spring through fall, this perched wetland exhibits colorful flowering, albeit not pink but rather the complete palette of nature's hues.

Encircled by Pisgah Ridge, Dividing Ridge, and Soapstone Ridge, the relatively level valley of the Pink Beds creates a perched wetland. The adjacent highlands drain their waterways into the Pink Beds. These headwaters form the South Fork Mills River, a sluggish stream as it wanders through the Pink Beds and is part of the 1,500-acre biologically significant bog, harboring the rare plant swamp pink. Extensive beaver activity and dams add another lesser-seen component to the Pink Beds.

The Forest Service knows this is an important piece of the biological pie, and they are taking steps to preserve the resource, yet encourage visitation. To that end, additional trail boardwalks have been added in recent years, allowing visitors a chance to explore the area without damaging the wetlands. Furthermore, prescribed burns in the Pink Beds add biodiversity and help return the area to a more open state. These burns also reduce ground litter, keeping nearby historic buildings at the Cradle of Forestry from catching fire. Expect more burns in the future.

The hike starts at the Pink Beds Picnic Area, a fun place to dine. It offers tables in blends of sun and shade, picnic shelters, water, and restrooms in season. The counterclockwise loop soon begins after bridging Pigeon Branch. Then you roughly trace the uppermost reaches of South Fork Mills River. Boardwalks and bridges make the walking easier while traversing a forest in transition, as the hemlocks are being replaced. However, mountain laurel, doghobble, and rhododendron continue to thrive. Ferns rise along streamlets draining Soapstone Ridge.

Despite the Forest Service efforts, beaver dams threaten the trail. Don't be surprised if a stretch of trail may be underwater. As you continue downstream, more bridges help. The loop turns beyond the junction with the South Mills Trail and becomes a drier experience while rolling over hills dividing rills draining Pisgah Ridge. Even dry-site species vegetation such as sourwood can be found along this stretch. Cross streams and meet the other end of the Barnett Branch Trail—the shortcut opportunity. Ahead, an amalgamation of woods and meadows adds another ecological component to the hike. Suddenly you are back at Pink Beds picnic area, another Carolina hiking adventure notched on your belt.

# THE CRADLE OF FORESTRY

Just before reaching the Pink Beds Picnic Area and trailhead you will pass the Forest Discovery Center, a legacy offshoot of the original Cradle of Forestry, where the science of forestry began in the United States. It all started when George W. Vanderbilt begin purchasing land for the now famous Biltmore Estate in 1889. Not only did Mr. Vanderbilt purchase land for his immense manse and grounds, but he also acquired sizable chunks of mountain land that are now part of the Pisgah National Forest.

While developing the Biltmore Estate, Vanderbilt hired the famous landscape architect Frederick Law Olmsted to turn the grounds of the Biltmore estate into an outdoor showcase as visually exciting as the house itself. Seeing all the forestlands owned by Mr. Vanderbilt, Frederick Law Olmsted suggested a "forest manager" to oversee the vast woods under Mr. Vanderbilt's care. Initially, Gifford Pinchot took the job. He created a management plan for the forest and got things underway, but his calling was elsewhere (Mr. Pinchot was later named the first director of the US Forest Service).

In 1895, Carl Schenck was hired to succeed Pinchot. Mr. Schenck came from Germany where the science of forestry had already developed. For the next 14 years, Dr. Schenck—while managing Mr. Vanderbilt's holdings—established and ran the first school of forestry in America—the Cradle of Forestry. Much of Mr. Vanderbilt's land had been cut over, burned, or exhausted from overplanting at subsistence farms. The science of forestry worked at remedying these problems and restoring what later became the Pisgah National Forest to its current glory.

Today, the Forest Discovery Center carries on the tradition of forest education. You can stop by and learn more about the history of the Cradle of Forestry and the men involved. There are also historical buildings to visit, as well as informative videos and exhibits. So take time to incorporate a visit to the Forest Discovery Center when you hike the Pink Beds. For more information, visit www.cradleofforestry.org.

## Miles and Directions

**0.0**   Leave the upper end of the Pink Beds picnic area parking lot around a pole gate. Quickly bridge Pigeon Branch.

**0.1**   Come to the loop portion of the hike. Turn right away from a meadow into woods. White pines canopy a wildflower hotspot.

**0.3**   Come near South Fork Mills River and bridge an unnamed tributary.

**0.6**   Bridge another tributary.

**0.9**   Bridge the South Fork.

**1.3**      Span the tan-gold-colored South Fork on a bridge of standard lumber for its first half, which connects to a fallen tree trunk, also part of the bridge.

**1.4**      A sandy campsite lies on your left.

**1.6**      Intersect the Barnett Branch Trail. Even if you don't want to shortcut the loop, take the boardwalk over the wetlands and the South Fork Mills River for an opportunity to observe the mountain bog up close. Keep straight on the Pink Beds Loop, then meet the other end of the Barnett Branch Trail as it heads south to scale Rich Mountain. Turn away from the river for a bit, avoiding untenable wetlands.

**2.5**      Bridge the South Fork Mills River after spanning lesser tributaries.

**2.8**      Come to a trail junction, meeting the upper terminus of the South Mills River Trail. Turn left, staying with the Pink Beds Loop.

**3.8**      Hop over Barnett Branch amid scads of mountain laurel.

**3.9**      Bridge a tributary of Barnett Branch, then meet the other end of the Barnett Branch Trail. Keep straight on the Pink Beds Loop, passing through a meadow.

**4.4**      Cross Bearwallow Branch. Ahead, travel more meadows and woods.

**5.2**      Bridge Pigeon Branch, completing the loop portion of the hike.

**5.3**      Arrive at Pink Beds picnic area, finishing the hike.

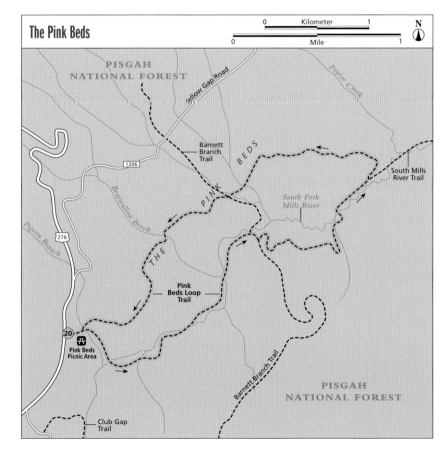

*This is but one of many bridges spanning streams of the Pink Beds.*

# 21 High Falls Hike

Grab two waterfalls for the price of one on this fun hike in the Pisgah National Forest. Follow the South Mills River as it descends through the mountains. First, check out the Otter Hole, a scenic swimming spot, on the wide and easy South Mills River Trail. Next, take a side trip along the way to lesser-visited 22-foot Billy Branch Falls. The hike then joins a narrower track before reaching the 18-foot High Falls, a picturesque cataract, enhanced with a huge swimming hole.

**Start:** End of FR 476
**Distance:** 4.2-mile there-and-back with short spur
**Difficulty:** Moderate, does have one sure ford
**Elevation change:** +-476
**Maximum grade:** 6 percent grade for 0.4 mile
**Hiking time:** 2.5–3.0 hours
**Seasons/schedule:** 24/7/365, spring through fall
**Fees and permits:** None
**Dog friendly:** Leashed dogs allowed

**Trail surface:** Natural
**Land status:** National forest
**Other trail users:** A few equestrians and bicyclists on first mile
**Maps to consult:** National Geographic #780 Pisgah Ranger District; USGS Pisgah Forest
**Amenities available:** None
**Cell service:** Weak
**Trail contacts:** Pisgah National Forest, Pisgah Ranger District, (828) 877-3265, www.fs.usda.gov/nfsnc

**Finding the trailhead:** From the intersection of NC 280 and US 276 in Pisgah Forest, take US 276 north for 12 miles to FR 1206, a little after the Pink Beds Picnic Area. Turn right on FR 1206 and follow it 3.2 miles to turn right on FR 476, near the Wolf Gap equestrian camping area. Follow FR 476 for 1.3 miles to dead end at the trailhead. Trailhead GPS: 35.366447, -82.738947

## The Hike

Western North Carolina—especially the mountainous areas near Brevard—has an abundance of waterfalls. Therefore, the hardest part of choosing a waterfall hike hereabouts is figuring out exactly which one to see! And if you can view two waterfalls on one hike, all the better. And that is what this particular trek presents—Billy Branch Cascades and the feature cataract High Falls.

The South Mills River, the location of the hike, begins a mile high in the shadow of the Blue Ridge, flowing south from Pisgah Ridge. Headwater tributaries like Bearwallow Brook, Pigeon Branch, and Thompson Creek merge to give aquatic vibrancy to the South Mills River. The river first flows slowly through the upland bog known as the Pink Beds before cutting through a water gap between Soapstone Ridge and Funneltop Mountain. The waterway's descent steepens. Dancing white swirls divide quiet pools and slower-moving sections.

*High Falls isn't really high but is a powerful cataract.*

High Falls, a multitiered, irregular cataract, is the most notable of several eye-catching cascades as the stream tortuously twists through national forest wildlands, exuding everywhere-you-look beauty, picking up still more tributaries as it curves northeasterly along Forge Mountain. Trails extend along the South Fork Mills River, nearly the entire portion of its journey through the Pisgah National Forest, allowing hikers to not only visit High Falls but also enjoy the stream in its multiple incarnations, whether they are waterfall hunting, trout fishing, day hiking, or backpacking. The South Fork Mills River leaves the forest just a few miles before it merges with the North Fork Mills River near the growing community of Mills River after having lost over 3,000 feet from its headwaters. That is a lot of falling water!

We explore the upper part of the South Mills River, beginning a little under 3,200-foot elevation. The trailhead features an old stone US Geological Survey (USGS) water gauging station. The South Mills River here is still smallish, averaging 15–20 feet wide and proudly displaying the superlative clarity expected of a Carolina mountain stream. A rock bottom underlies the waterway—some places flat slabs, other locales cobbled waterworn stones, other spots time-washed sands. Grayish outcrops overlook the moving water. At high flows daredevil kayakers ply this cavalcade of cataracts, but on any given day you are far more likely to see other hikers.

The hike then traces the waterway downstream, underneath a forest of black birch, maple, and oaks. Rhododendron finds its place in the shadows and along the cool reaches of the river. A small, unnamed stream adds its flow at the Otter Hole, a popular summertime swimming locale. Here, the South Fork Mills River bounces over a few low ledges, then settles into a wide, circular deep pool open to the sun overhead before turning and continuing its raucous ways. A small sandbar and a few rock outcrops provide sun-basking spots for those not splashing in the montane aqua.

Continuing on, the easy wide trail passes other ledges and pools and even a campsite or two before reaching the confluence with Billy Branch. Here, the hike changes. First, you follow an old roadbed up Billy Branch before scrambling downhill to reach the base of Billy Branch Falls, a 22-foot, curving cataract that spills down a rhododendron-bordered slick ledge into a correspondingly sized plunge pool. This waterfall is often overlooked by those concentrating on reaching High Falls. Still others do not even know it exists.

At this point, the South Mills River Trail crosses the South Fork Mills River on an old road bridge and climbs a hillside, well above the waterway. The gorge was just too rough downstream for loggers to construct the onetime logging road. However, the primitive High Falls Trail continues down the left bank of the river toward High Falls. The slender pathway irregularly works down the side slope of the valley, scooting around rocks, along outcrops, underneath rhododendron thickets, and over logs. However, the High Falls Trail is tramped enough to keep an easily followable footbed.

The weaving way leads to a mandatory ford a little before reaching High Falls. The crossing is not deep, yet it is never shallow enough at this crossing to rock-hop.

You can simply grab a stick and cross barefoot, bring sandals for the crossing or simply wade with your shoes on. Still working downstream and downhill, make your way past some seeping rock slabs and a long unnamed cascade before the unmistakable roar of 18-foot High Falls drifts to your ears. A short spur trail leads to the top of the falls but keep going beyond the cataract to find another spur dropping to the base of the white frothy force of water where a large pool slows, forming yet another swimming hole here on the South Mills River. Though not high enough to deserve the name High Falls, the spiller is still a backcountry sight to behold.

## Miles and Directions

**0.0**     Pass around the pole gate at the end of FR 476. Begin tracing a grown-over logging road directly alongside the South Fork Mills River. Trickling streamlets dribble over the trail. Descend at the same rate as the river.

**0.2**     Hike past your first significant shoal here. The waterway drops over a 4-foot ledge and creates a pool. Large rocks offer scenic sitting spots. Ahead, walk along a dripping bluff, blasted vertical when the former logging road was built.

**0.4**     Come to a small campsite on your right. A rising rank of rhododendron climbs the hill across the stream.

**0.7**     A spur trail drops right to the Otter Hole. Here, South Fork Mills River slows into a large circular pool open to the sun overhead.

**0.9**     South Fork Mills River makes a single 6-foot ledge drop into a big pool.

**1.0**     Come to a trail intersection. Here, the South Mills River Trail heads right across the river on a former road bridge. However, our hike heads left up Billy Branch. For now, ignore the trail crossing Billy Branch and stay left, ascending an old roadbed on the left side of Billy Branch.

**1.1**     Reach Billy Branch Falls after descending off the roadbed you've been following. Here, Billy Branch dives 22 feet into a plunge pool. Backtrack almost to the South Fork Mills River, then rock-hop Billy Branch, joining the High Falls Trail as it stays on the left bank of the river, heading downstream on a much narrower path used exclusively by hikers.

**1.5**     Top out on a ridge around which the South Fork Mills River curves, shortcutting a bend in the river. Descend back to the river's edge.

**1.9**     Reach the ford of South Fork Mills River just after passing a small campsite on your left. Angle downstream as you cross, avoiding the deeper portions of the pool. After crossing, work over seeping rock slabs, now on the right-hand bank. A long sloped cascade noisily spills on the other side of a screen of vegetation.

**2.2**     Pass the top of High Falls. A short spur trail leads down to this vantage. However, the best access is downtrail, where a primitive path leads down to the big pool at the base of High Falls. View the cataract as it spills in irregular fashion 18 feet over a slide. The pool far outsizes the volume of the river. Big rocks allow you to view the falls. Backtrack.

**4.2**     Arrive at the trailhead, completing the hike.

*High Falls is known for its huge swimming hole below the spiller.*

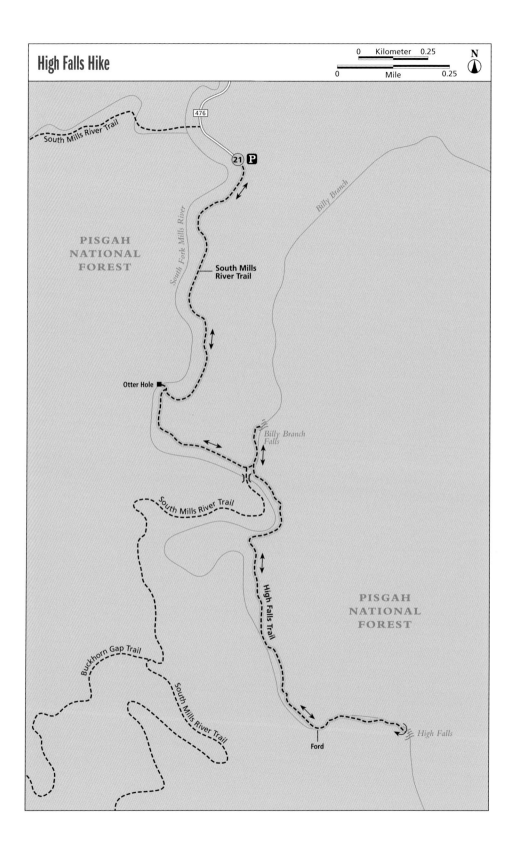

# High Falls Hike

0     Kilometer    0.25

0         Mile      0.25

**N**

476

21 P

South Mills River Trail

South Fork Mills River

Billy Branch

PISGAH
NATIONAL
FOREST

South Mills
River Trail

Otter Hole

Billy Branch
Falls

South Mills River Trail

High Falls Trail

PISGAH
NATIONAL
FOREST

Buckhorn Gap Trail

South Mills River Trail

Ford

High Falls

# 22 Avery Creek Falls and Twin Falls Loop

This circuit hike in the Pisgah National Forest near Brevard leads you to three fine waterfalls tucked deep in the hollows of the Davidson Creek Valley. Head up scenic Avery Creek and view warmup Avery Creek Falls, then cross numerous bridges before turning up Henry Branch. Find Twin Falls, a pair of 80-foot cataracts that merge at their base. This hike then winds along the slopes of Clawhammer Mountain before diving into narrow Clawhammer Cove to complete the circuit. Hiker bridges make this water-centric hike a dry-footed affair.

**Start:** FR 477 on Avery Creek
**Distance:** 5.8-mile loop
**Difficulty:** Moderate
**Elevation change:** +-1,020 feet
**Maximum grade:** 14 percent downhill grade for 0.3 mile
**Hiking time:** About 3.5 hours
**Seasons/schedule:** 24/7/365, late fall through spring for bolder waterfalls
**Fees and permits:** None
**Dog friendly:** Leashed dogs allowed

**Trail surface:** Natural
**Land status:** National forest
**Other trail users:** Mountain bikers, on some parts, a few equestrians
**Maps to consult:** National Geographic #780 Pisgah Ranger District; USGS Shining Rock, Pisgah Forest
**Amenities available:** None
**Cell service:** None
**Trail contacts:** Pisgah National Forest, (828) 877-3265, www.fs.usda.gov/nfsnc

**Finding the trailhead:** From the intersection of NC 280 and US 276 in Brevard, take US 276 north for 2.1 miles, then turn right on FR 477. You will see a sign here directing you toward Pisgah Riding Stables. Follow FR 477 for 2.5 miles and the trailhead will be on your right, 0.8 mile beyond the stables. Trailhead GPS: 35.316160, -82.752210

## The Hike

This is a rewarding and not too difficult loop hike that explores streams flowing off the slopes of Rich Mountain, highlighted by the visit to Twin Falls, a pair of 80-foot-high thrilling cataracts. These cascades make some heady spills, each showing off distinctive characteristics—dropping as narrow charging chutes, delicate curtain falls, splashing cascades, slaloming rapids, and just about everything in between.

Even if there were no waterfalls on this hike, the overall beauty of Avery Creek and its tributaries and the mountainsides that separate them would be worth the visit. Richly vegetated valleys create a temperate near jungle. The trails are never too far from water. A slew of hiker bridges not only allow dry passage but also provide close-up looks at Henry Branch and Avery Creek and other unnamed streams including the one cutting the vale known as Clawhammer Cove, an all-time Southern Appalachian name candidate. These bridges make doing this hike during the

*This waterfall on Henry Branch, one of the Twin Falls, makes several curtain-type drops.*

cold, leafless time of year very doable. Then, the streams are up and a lack of leaves allows you to simultaneously view the Twin Falls in all their glory. While looping around back to the trailhead, you do climb, but overall elevation changes are less than 600 feet, easing the strain.

The hike starts where the Buckhorn Gap Trail leaves FR 477. You will pass a per-haps better trailhead—the Avery Creek Trail starting point—just before reaching the Buckhorn Gap trailhead, but parking at the Avery Creek trailhead is limited to one or two cars beside a precarious slope, thus making the Buckhorn Gap Trail a superior embarkation. The Buckhorn Gap Trail soon comes alongside Avery Creek. The song of falling water sings into your ears—Avery Creek Falls. In their zeal to reach Twin Falls, many hikers bypass this initial cataract, as evidenced by the less-than-beaten-down spur to the two-tiered spiller that first descends as a 10-foot sloped cascade, gathers steam in a flat stretch before dropping in a 12-foot-high creek-wide sheet. Don't bypass Avery Creek Falls, especially if you are looking to play around in the creek. The Twin Falls lack plunge pools and big waters in which to wade or swim.

The Buckhorn Gap Trail is open to hikers, bicyclers, and equestrians, though horseback riders are the distinct minority. Hikers have to be on guard because the trail often splits at creek crossings—hikers go one way on log footbridges, while mountain bikers and equestrians go another way, crossing the streams via fords. Then the diverging paths reconverge.

Eventually, the Buckhorn Gap Trail leaves Avery Creek and heads up Henry Branch, a tributary of Avery Creek along which Twin Falls is found. Paths head up both sides of Henry Branch. Our hike heads up the left, west side of Henry Branch and passes a wet-weather fall spilling about 20 feet over a rock ledge just before com-ing to a steep cove, where the Twin Falls echo off the hillsides.

The first sight of these two tall cataracts is a thriller. You rush up the path ready to snap your best shots. The left-hand fall—Henry Branch—of the Twin Falls comes first. It pours white through rhododendron, then widens and rolls in four stages, the last of which is the grandest, descending in a regal curtain over bare rock, then slaloms in shoals over the trail. A spur leads to the base of the curtain.

Then it is on to the right-hand fall of the Twin Falls—the unnamed tributary of Henry Branch. This multilayer tumbler has a bit less flow and is narrower as it jumps off a ledge then squares itself, down, down, down, dashing over evergreen-shrouded rocks and crossing the trail before meeting Henry Branch. A spur heads up the right-hand side of this fall, where you can see a stage of the cataract lunge from an overhanging ledge.

The Twin Falls can both be seen from the confluence of Henry Branch and the unnamed tributary. Early morning and late afternoon present the best winter shade photography times. After shooting and admiring, take the trail heading down the east side of Henry Branch to meet a horse rack and trail intersection. Here, our hike makes its loop, skirting the slopes of Clawhammer Mountain, winding in and out of coves, joining quiet FR 5058 before meeting Clawhammer Cove Trail. This

*The right-hand branch of Twin Falls is a stair-stepping spiller.*

singletrack path wastes no time in making a downgrade into a slender valley. The cove cuts deep and you follow suit, diving into pines before finding Avery Creek and another hiker bridge. Pass alluring pools and noisy shoals along Avery Creek before climbing back to the trailhead, briefly joining FR 477 on the way.

## Miles and Directions

**0.0**   Leave the FR 477 parking area on the Buckhorn Gap Trail. The signed northbound path, flanked by mountain laurel and rhododendron, soon curves around coves above Avery Creek. Pass under a powerline twice.

**0.5**   Sidle along Avery Creek Falls, accessible by a spur trail leading right and downhill. Come to the lower part of the falls first, as it spills over a 12-foot ledge into a pool. To see the upper part of the spiller, walk upstream past a rock slab to see the angled 10-foot step fall. The rock slab at the top of the lower fall makes for a fine relaxation location. After resuming the hike, look for a low-flow waterfall tributary coming into the far side of Avery Creek. The Buckhorn Gap Trail then curves along a flat away from Avery Creek.

**0.9**   Meet the Avery Creek Trail, which has been running roughly parallel to the Buckhorn Gap Trail. Keep straight on the Buckhorn Gap Trail.

**1.0**   Cross Avery Creek on a hiker bridge near a powerline. Turn into the Henry Branch valley. Encounter several trail splits where hikers cross the stream on bridges and mountain bicyclers and equestrians use fords. Keep upstream along Henry Branch.

**1.6**   Reach a signed intersection. Here, the Twin Falls Trail crosses the hiker bridge across Henry Branch while the Buckhorn Gap Trail keeps straight up the right bank of Henry Branch. Cross the log bridge on the hiker-only Twin Falls Trail.

**1.9**   Pass an intermittent cascade on your left just before coming to a campsite and trail intersection. Here, the Buckhorn Gap Trail leads down Henry Branch. You will join this path later, but for now head up and explore the Twin Falls. Take the spur trails alongside the cataracts for additional photography opportunities.

**2.1**   Head down the Buckhorn Gap Trail after backtracking to the campsite below Twin Falls. This path quickly bridges Henry Branch. Hike downstream along the east side of Henry Branch.

**2.4**   Reach a trail intersection at some horse hitching posts. Head left on the Buckhorn Gap Trail, ascending into a maple-oak-beech cove.

**2.7**   Hop a small tributary of Henry Branch. Continue up the hardwood-rich cove with scattered grasses.

**2.8**   Come to a signed intersection. The Buckhorn Gap Trail splits into two arms. Turn right here, curving southeast along coves below Clawhammer Mountain on a doubletrack path toward FR 5058. The left arm goes also to FR 5058.

**3.6**   Meet gravel FR 5058 in a gap. Turn right here, descending through more coves.

**4.2**   Leave right from FR 5058 on the signed and blazed Clawhammer Cove Trail. Turn right here, descending a singletrack path.

**4.5**   Bridge the stream of Clawhammer Cove. Keep downhill.

**5.3**   Reach a trail intersection after reaching and turning up Avery Creek. Head left, crossing Avery Creek on a hiker bridge on the Avery Creek Trail. Briefly turn downstream on Avery Creek before climbing toward FR 477.

**5.6** Emerge at FR 477 and a very limited parking area at the Avery Creek trailhead. Turn right here, northbound up FR 477.

**5.8** Arrive at the Buckhorn Gap trailhead, completing the hike.

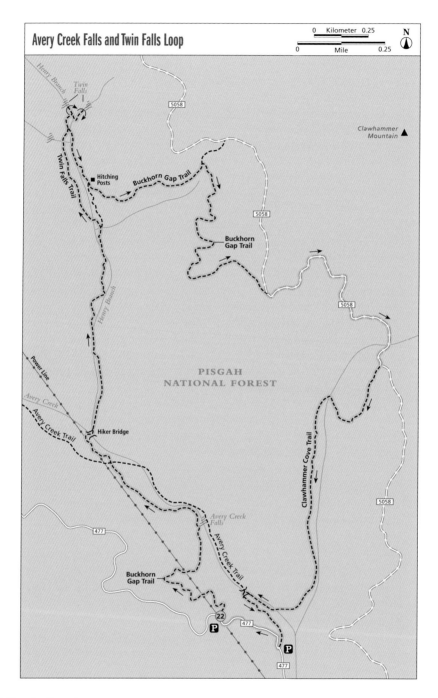

Avery Creek Falls and Twin Falls Loop

# 23 Bradley Creek Circuit

Looking for a fun watery hike with minimal elevation change? Look no further. This warm-weather loop hike circles Buck Mountain, first tracing South Mills River down a wildflower-filled valley, making many fords to then turn up smaller but no less scenic Bradley Creek. Enjoy more streamside backdrops and make more wet-footed crossings. Turn up still smaller Pea Branch, finally leaving the aquatic surroundings to cross a low ridge, then return to South Mills River. The final part of the hike traces an old forest road, adding new trail mileage.

**Start:** Turkeypen trailhead
**Distance:** 7.6-mile double loop
**Difficulty:** Moderate, does have numerous fords
**Elevation change:** +-810 feet
**Maximum grade:** 11 percent downhill grade for 0.4 mile
**Hiking time:** 4.5–5 hours
**Seasons/schedule:** Late spring through early fall
**Fees and permits:** None
**Dog friendly:** Leashed dogs allowed

**Trail surface:** Natural
**Land status:** National forest
**Other trail users:** A few equestrians
**Maps to consult:** National Geographic #780 Pisgah Ranger District; USGS Pisgah Forest
**Amenities available:** None
**Cell service:** Weak along the streams
**Trail contacts:** Pisgah National Forest, Pisgah Ranger District, (828) 877-3265, www.fs.usda .gov/nfsnc

**Finding the trailhead:** From exit 40 on I-26 south of Asheville, take NC 280 west for 10.2 miles to Turkeypen Road, on your right, just after Boylston Creek Church (Turkeypen Road is signed on the highway but the entrance looks like a gravel driveway). Follow Turkeypen Road for 1.2 miles to dead end at the trailhead. Trailhead GPS: 35.342792, -82.659369

## The Hike

An excellent, easily accessible trail network emanates from the Turkeypen trailhead, where this hike starts. So don't be surprised if the parking area is crowded, but there's room for everyone in the South Mills River valley, where a wealth of creekside and ridgetop paths form a pathway complex that presents multiple loop hike possibilities. I favor this particular circuit as it stays along mountain streams almost the whole hike, allowing you to maximize your aquatic experience. Strictly a warm season endeavor, multiple fords are required to complete the loop. So if you are going to get your feet wet, why not leave them wet and soak in streamside beauty of three waterways—South Fork Mills River, Bradley Creek, and Pea Branch? You'll see a cornucopia of wildflowers in spring, rushing cascades and silent pools, craggy waterside outcrops

*If you like fords, you will love this hike.*

and repose boulders, lushly wooded flats, and deep mountain scenes that transport you to the Carolina wildlands.

A little planning is in order, however. Since you will be fording repeatedly, wear sturdy soled shoes you don't mind getting wet. I do not recommend sandals since I don't favor the prospect of busting my toe on an underwater or aboveground rock. Low-top hiking shoes covering your entire foot that drain easily are my footwear of choice for this adventure. Additionally, a pair of trekking poles or a good old-fashioned hiking stick will aid your passage across the creeks. Finally, before coming to the trailhead, check the water level of the South Mills River to determine if the fords are passable for the day of your hike. Check the USGS water gauge, "Mills River near Mills River, NC," adding "USGS" to your search. This gauge is downstream of the trailhead, but will tell you whether the stream is at, above, or below normal levels for that given day.

Water levels will generally be higher in spring, then lower through the summer and be their lowest in autumn. However, heavy rains in spring, thunderstorms in summer, and tropical systems in autumn can each cause the watershed to be above normal. In spring, the waters can be quite chilly. The waters will be tolerable by June; and throughout the summer, the plentiful pools found along the circuit will become potential swimming holes. By September, the fords are downright easy and the water is still mild. The season for this hike is over by the end of October.

Since this is a backcountry area and not a designated wilderness, the trail network is signed and well maintained, making travel and navigation easy. Furthermore, elevation changes of only 800 feet make the loop more doable. Finally, consider making this an overnight adventure, as there are campsites aplenty.

The first part of the hike navigates through numerous trail intersections, then settles down as it descends the South Mills River on the Riverside Trail. The wide, road-like path is shaded by hornbeam, pine, and black birch, while the forest floor is carpeted in rhododendron, ferns, and doghobble. The South Mills runs around 30 to 40 feet wide, alternating in trouty stillwater and splashy shoals. You make your first ford a little less than a mile into the hike. Use this crossing as a rough gauge—if you feel comfortable making this crossing, then you can make the following fords. Begin soaking in the everywhere-you-look streamside aura in the form of mossy logs, sun-splashed pools, smooth gravel bars, irregular rock bars, and sparkling waters shooting past mute boulders. The fords continue as you head easterly downriver in first-rate western North Carolina beauty.

The hike turns up Bradley Creek. The riparian scenery—and the fords—continues. The only change is you are now heading upstream on a still gentle grade. At any given point, a streamside flat stretches wide while the other side of the stream rises hilly. After a final crossing of Bradley Creek, the jaunt on the Riverside Trail ends and you work your way up still smaller Pea Branch. Experience the first meaningful elevation change of the hike while surmounting Pea Gap, then return to the South

Fork Mills River. After a little backtracking you can take a closed forest road back up to the trailhead, completing the hike.

## Miles and Directions

**0.0**   Leave the Turkeypen trailhead on the South Mills River Trail, one of four trails emanating from the parking area. As you face north at the trail kiosk, you will have a gated trail to your right, your return route, and the singletrack South Mills River Trail to your left. The ridge-running Turkeypen Gap Trail and Vineyard Gap Trail leave behind you. Join the heavily trodden South Mills River Trail, descending toward the South Mills River, ensconced in rhododendron.

**0.4**   Reach the South Fork Mills River and a trail intersection. A trail bridge crosses the river here, and South Mills River Trail heads upstream with it. However, this hike stays right, on this side of the South Fork Mills River, heading downstream on the Bradley Creek Trail. Walk a short distance, then come to a four-way trail intersection. The road leading right is your return route to the trailhead. A horse ford goes left. You keep straight, still on the Bradley Creek Trail.

**0.8**   Make the first ford of the hike. If you can execute this stream crossing, then you can make the forthcoming fords. After crossing the stream, a hiker trail heads left back toward the trailhead.

**1.1**   Bend right, passing under a blasted bluff.

**1.3**   Come to a trail intersection. Here, the Bradley Creek Trail leaves left and is your return route. However, our counterclockwise circuit heads right, joining the Riverside Trail.

**1.4**   Ford South Fork Mills River. Sycamores are prevalent as you trace an old railroad grade. Look for embedded railroad ties.

**1.8**   Ford the river again.

**2.2**   Ford the river again. Enjoy a long walk on a level track. Admire the beautiful valley.

**2.9**   The Riverside Trail curves right, cutting across a long bend in the South Fork Mills River. Look for more railroad ties on the elevated bed pushing through a sea of evergreen.

**3.4**   Ford South Fork Mills River a last time. You are on the left-hand bank. The valley widens. Beard cane prevails in the flats.

**3.7**   Intersect the Vineyard Gap Trail. It has come from Turkeypen Gap.

**3.8**   Reach, then ford Bradley Creek in a huge flat. The Riverside Trail now turns up the rhododendron-heavy Bradley Creek valley, while an unmaintained path continues down South Fork Mills River. You and the Bradley Creek Trail are now heading upstream instead of downstream.

**4.0**   Ford Bradley Creek.

**4.2**   Ford Bradley Creek again. Watch for tall tulip trees.

**4.6**   Cut through a meadow. Keep up the Bradley Creek valley.

**4.8**   Make a final ford of Bradley Creek. Reach a trail junction and the end of the Riverside Trail. At this point, turn left on the Bradley Creek Trail, now following Bradley Creek downstream. Soon rock-hop Case Branch.

**5.0**   Come alongside Pea Branch. Ascend a slender valley.

**5.4**   Intersect the Squirrel Gap Trail. Turn left here, hop over Pea Branch, and stay with the Bradley Creek Trail.

**5.6** Cut through Pea Gap. Look at the mica in the sandy trailbed. Descend somewhat steeply from Pea Gap.

**5.9** Return to the South Mills River. Backtrack right, heading upriver.

**6.8** Come to a four-way intersection. Head sharply left up the gravel road, making a wide switchback.

**7.6** Arrive at the Turkeypen trailhead, completing the hike.

*Fording alluring Bradley Creek*

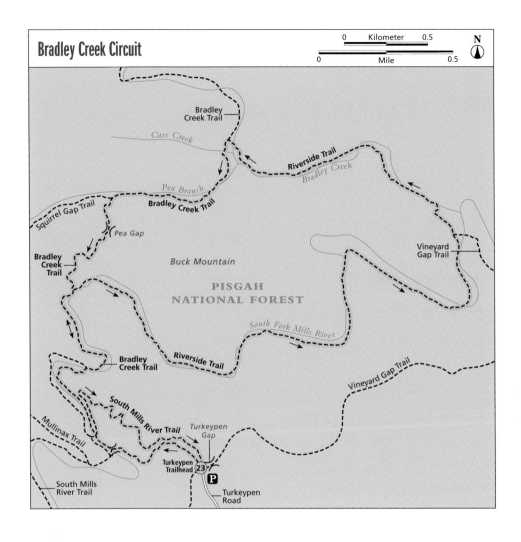

# Bradley Creek Circuit

Bradley
Creek Trail

Case Creek

Riverside Trail

Bradley Creek

Pea Branch

Squirrel Gap Trail

Bradley Creek Trail

Pea Gap

Vineyard
Gap Trail

Bradley
Creek
Trail

Buck Mountain

PISGAH
NATIONAL FOREST

South Fork Mills River

Riverside Trail

Bradley
Creek Trail

Vineyard Gap Trail

South Mills River Trail

Mullinax Trail

Turkeypen
Gap

South Mills
River Trail

Turkeypen
Trailhead 23
P

Turkeypen
Road

# 24 Cantrell Creek Lodge Loop

This long balloon loop, good for summertime, explores the gorgeous upper South Mills River valley, with a little side trip back in time. Head up South Mills River, crossing it on exciting swinging bridges to reach the site of Cantrell Creek Lodge, one of George Vanderbilt's early structures in his massive forest that later became part of the Pisgah National Forest. Continue up South Mills River, fording the stream to head for the hills, cutting through Squirrel Gap and Horse Cove Gap before dropping to Cantrell Creek, returning for a second look at the lodge site, with its still standing chimney.

**Start:** Turkeypen Gap trailhead
**Distance:** 17.6-mile balloon loop
**Difficulty:** Difficult due to distance and fords
**Elevation change:** +-1,430 feet
**Maximum grade:** 8 percent downhill grade for 1.4 miles
**Hiking time:** About 9.5 hours
**Seasons/schedule:** 24/7/365, July through Oct for low water fords
**Fees and permits:** None
**Dog friendly:** Yes, on leash only

**Trail surface:** Forested natural surface
**Land status:** National forest
**Other trail users:** Mountain bikers, equestrians
**Maps to consult:** National Geographic #780 Pisgah Ranger District
**Amenities available:** None at trailhead
**Cell service:** Decent
**Trail contacts:** Pisgah National Forest, Pisgah Ranger District, (828) 877-3265, www.fs.usda .gov/nfsnc

**Finding the trailhead:** From exit 40 on I-26 south of Asheville, take NC 280 west for 10.2 miles to Turkeypen Road, on your right, just after Boylston Creek Church (Turkeypen Road is signed on the highway but the entrance looks like a gravel driveway). Follow Turkeypen Road for 1.2 miles to dead end at the trailhead. Trailhead GPS: 35.342859, -82.659413

## The Hike

If you love hiking along, around—and through—Carolina mountain streams, this is the adventure for you. Done as a long summertime day hike or an overnight backpack, this balloon loop presents views aplenty of stunning South Mills River, especially from cool swinging bridges. Then you reach the site of Cantrell Creek Lodge, the small clearing centered with the remaining stone chimney of a lodge once used by George Vanderbilt, then forest rangers, and later moved to the Cradle of Forestry.

*Option:* Make an 8.4-mile dry-footed, year-round hike to Cantrell Creek Lodge site and back to the trailhead.

Conditions become more challenging beyond Cantrell Creek Lodge, but the beauty never wanes as you make several fords of pools and shoal-filled South Mills River, deep in a mountain valley in the shadow of the Blue Ridge, making your final crossing at a place called Wolf Ford, where there may or may not be an operational swinging bridge. After over 9 miles of streamside hiking, you've only climbed 500 feet. Water noises lessen and the scenery changes to oak-dominated xeric forest, bisecting Squirrel Gap. But even this climb is modest. Circle the headwaters of Laurel Brook, then make your way through Horse Cove Gap. Now comes the only "steep" part of the hike and it is downhill toward Cantrell Creek.

Once at Cantrell Creek, you crisscross the stream a few times before returning to the Cantrell Creek Lodge site. Your backtrack leads over those fine swinging bridges that offer views and safe passage over the South Mills River. The entire hike is recommended as a midsummer through early fall proposition. That is when the waters are at their lowest and the temperatures are warm, so you won't get cold feet fording. Bring hiking shoes you don't mind getting wet; and if backpacking, bring dry camp shoes. You may also consider fishing gear and perhaps bathing trunks. This area is a great place to spend a summer day—or night, too. Backcountry campsites can be found all along the South Mills River. *Note:* Beware unsigned user-created trails—they often lead along the river, to campsites or dead ends. However, the South Mills River Trail will split at the swinging bridges, one path leading to a ford and another to a swinging bridge.

## Miles and Directions

**0.0**    From Turkeypen Gap, take the South Mills River Trail westerly, downhill 0.4 mile to reach the South Mills River and an intersection. Here, the Bradley Creek Trail goes right, downstream, while we cross South Mills River on a swinging bridge. Once across the bridge, turn right, downstream, then reach an intersection. Here, stay left with the South Mills River Trail, now heading upstream along the right bank of the South Mills River.

**0.7**    Stay with the wide South Mills River Trail as the Mullinax Trail rises right. Climb well above the South Mills River among ferns, black birch, beech, rhododendron, and fire cherry, replacing hemlocks. Level trail sections may be muddy.

**2.0**    Pass a large outcrop extending left into the river. Just ahead the Poundingmill Trail splits right. Continue along the South Mills River.

**3.0**    The trail splits—stay left to span South Mills River on a swinging bridge while another trail leads to a ford on South Mills River.

**3.2**    The Wagon Road Gap Trail climbs left to the Turkeypen Gap Trail, providing an alternate return route. For now continue along flats of the South Mills River. Begin a large curve around Cat Ridge.

**3.9**    Cross a swinging bridge over to the right-hand bank heading upstream. Enter a big wooded flat. Ahead, bridge Cantrell Creek.

**4.2**    Come to the small clearing and chimney of Cantrell Creek Lodge. Just ahead, split left at the trail intersection, still on the South Mills River Trail, as your return route, the Cantrell Creek Trail, keeps straight. Climb over a small hill then resume up South Mills River. Look for evidence of a 2022 prescribed burn on tree trunks and other places. Shortly experience your first fords at 4.6, 4.8, 5.4, 5.5, and 5.7 miles. Yellow birches begin to appear. Watch for areas where blasted bluffs pinch the trail in by the river.

*Water lovers will soak in many views like this en route to the Cantrell Creek Lodge site.*

**6.9**    Make a short but potentially troublesome deep ford.

**7.1**    On the opposite bank from the trail, Brushy Branch makes a 10-foot waterfall as it dives into South Mill River.

**7.4**    Cross over to the left bank.

**7.8**    Ford over to the right-hand bank heading upstream near an immense overhanging bluff on the left-hand side of the river. Make more fords at 8.4, 8.8, and 9.2 miles. You are on the left-hand bank heading upstream.

**9.4**    Come to a major intersection at Wolf Ford. Here, head right across a swinging bridge that may or may not be in operation. Once across stay upstream then climb right away from South Mills River on the Squirrel Gap Trail. Other unmaintained trails can be found here, including one to High Falls, upstream. Climb by switchbacks easterly into oaks and mountain laurel. Ahead, hike along trickling Gladys Creek.

*A chimney marks the site of Cantrell Creek Lodge before the building was moved.*

**10.7** Bisect Squirrel Gap. Begin circling around upper Laurel Brook and its many tributaries.

**11.7** Reach Horse Cove Gap and multiple trail intersections. Stay right, descending on the Horse Cove Gap Trail among tulip trees. Begin the sharpest descent of the hike, and it is mild but steady.

**12.5** Turn down Cantrell Creek on rerouted trail. Cross the stream, sans bridges, a few times.

**13.2** Meet the rerouted Cantrell Creek Trail. Stay right, descending.

**13.4** Complete the loop portion of the hike. You are near Cantrell Creek Lodge site. Backtrack down the South Mills River Trail.

**17.6** Return to the trailhead, completing the long hike/backpack.

*South Mills River flows past an immense overhanging bluff.*

# Cantrell Creek Lodge Loop

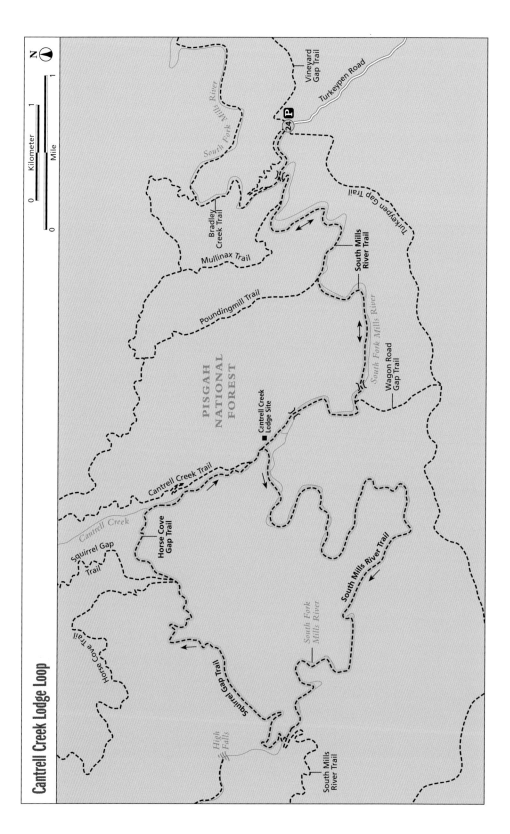

# 25 Cedar Rock Bridal Veil Falls Hike

This hiking adventure visits highlights high and low in the mountains and streams of DuPont State Recreational Forest. Leave the Corn Mill Shoals trailhead to ascend the granite side of Cedar Rock, where multiple views can be had in all directions. Descend stone and pine slopes to the Little River, which you cross at Corn Mill Shoals. Hike over hills to view incredible Bridal Veil Falls, first from a mountaintop vista, then from the base of the 120-foot inclined granite cascade. Backtrack a bit before joining a new trail to finish the adventurous trek.

**Start:** Corn Mill Shoals trailhead
**Distance:** 7.8-mile loop with spurs
**Difficulty:** Moderate to difficult due to distance
**Elevation change:** +-1,016 feet
**Maximum grade:** 9 percent downhill grade for 0.9 mile
**Hiking time:** About 4.5 hours
**Seasons/schedule:** 5 a.m. to 10 p.m., 365 days/year, winter for solitude
**Fees and permits:** None
**Dog friendly:** Leashed dogs allowed
**Trail surface:** Gravel, natural

**Land status:** State forest
**Other trail users:** Mountain bikers, equestrians
**Maps to consult:** National Geographic #504 DuPont State Recreational Forest, DuPont State Recreational Forest; USGS Standingstone Mountain
**Amenities available:** Restroom at trailhead
**Cell service:** Good
**Trail contacts:** DuPont State Recreational Forest, (828) 877-6527, www.dupontstaterecreationalforest.com

**Finding the trailhead:** From the intersection of NC 280 and US 276 in Pisgah Forest, just north of Brevard, take US 64 east for 3.7 miles to a traffic light at Crab Creek Road. Turn right on Crab Creek Road and follow it 4.2 miles to turn right on DuPont Road. Follow DuPont Road as it soon becomes Staton Road for a total of 4 miles to end at Cascade Lake Road. Turn left on Cascade Lake Road and follow it for 0.6 mile to the Corn Mill Shoals trailhead on your left. Trailhead GPS: 35.172904, -82.638783

## The Hike

Most hikers that visit DuPont State Recreational Forest include at least one of the six major waterfalls found in the 10,000-plus-acre preserve. This hike takes you not only to the most unusual—and to my personal favorite—waterfall at DuPont, Bridal Veil Falls, but you also get to enjoy some of the mountaintop scenery found among the granite-topped knobs towering above the aquatic features. These stone mountains often have limited vegetation and thus open views that include wide-ranging landscapes both near and far. Cedar Rock is one such place. This rolling trek leads over the granite and pine face of Cedar Rock, where extensive panoramas can be enjoyed for not just a glimpse or two but for extended segments while traversing

Cedar Rock. The hike then dives off the mount to course along the aquatic heart of DuPont State Recreational Forest—the Little River. This mountain waterway rushes clear and cold, collecting in pools where trout gather as well. Evergreens shroud the waterway, while large outcrops provide sunny spots to gather. You ford the waterway at an interestingly named place known as Corn Mill Shoals. This wet-footed crossing is unavoidable yet shouldn't deter hikers from making this trek. The ford is across a slick slab of stone, but at normal water levels the Little River shouldn't be over your knees. If the weather is cold, simply take off your shoes and socks and make your way across. No matter how you ford the Little River, you will have to do it again on your return trip to the trailhead.

However, the trip to Bridal Veil Falls is well worth it. Scenes from the two movies *The Last of the Mohicans* and *The Hunger Games* were filmed at this compelling site. Your first view of the formidable sliding cascade will be from an outcrop at the end of the Bridal Overlook Trail. There, spyglass northward down to the sloping cataract

*DuPont State Recreational Forest features panoramas like this and its legendary waterfalls.*

and beyond to rolling mountains and rushing rivers as well as a former industrial site in the heart of the property. From there, backtrack and work your way back down to the Little River and the base of big, bold, and brash Bridal Veil Falls. Here, the Little River begins this tumble with an 8-foot vertical drop over a ledge—the veil—then joins a long, widening granite slope, spilling and widening over bare naked rock, then crashing into a jumble of boulders from which visitors aplenty observe the aquatic marvel.

At this point you are a fair distance from the trailhead, thus a direct return is in order. Backtrack across Corn Mill Shoals—the only crossing of the Little River in this corner of the forest—then take the Corn Mill Shoals Trail back to the trailhead.

Allow plenty of time for this hike. You will be tied up taking pictures and shooting video along the way and will cover nearly 8 miles. Although a climb of Cedar Rock is involved and does require a rise of 300 feet from the trailhead to its apex, vertical variation is surprisingly limited for covering so many miles in the mountains. Nevertheless, there are ups and downs but no steep rises or descents. Trekking poles or a hiking stick will come in handy both on the bare granite slopes of Cedar Rock and on the ford at Corn Mill Shoals. DuPont State Recreational Forest is a busy place. Though much of the hike is off the beaten path, if you can avoid warm weekends you will experience more solitude. Be apprised the trail system is well marked and maintained and many pathways are doubletrack, therefore easy on the feet and eyes. Take note—DuPont State Recreational Forest is popular with mountain bikers and you will share the trail with them and equestrians. Be on the lookout and keep your ears open for fast-moving mountain bikers.

## Miles and Directions

**0.0**    Cross Cascade Lake Road, leaving the parking area to pass around a pole gate and join doubletrack Corn Mill Shoals Road, open only to vehicles of park personnel. Walk 160 feet, then stay right as the Longside Trail heads left.

**0.1**    Head left on the narrower Big Rock Trail. Ascend through tightly growing woods of pine, chestnut oak, and mountain laurel. The path quickly becomes very rocky and traverses stone slabs.

**0.5**    Enjoy your first views through the pines from a rock dome to the left.

**0.7**    Reach a very open granite dome. Wide views open to the west of the magnificent Blue Ridge in the distance and other lands in the near.

**0.8**    Descend, still in a mix of stone and pine.

**0.9**    Turn right onto the Cedar Rock Trail. You are atop Cedar Rock with many views extending on the horizon. Stone slabs beckon your footsteps. Follow the Cedar Rock Trail downhill, southbound over nearly continuous rock slabs, as broad views stretch to the south of Standingstone Mountain and other ridges. Reenter full-blown woods at the base of the hill.

**1.5**    Turn right onto the Little River Trail. This level path runs alongside the Little River, flowing through rich woods to your left.

**1.7**    Bridge Tom Creek. Keep parallel to the Little River, then turn away.

**2.1**    Meet the Corn Mill Shoals Trail. Join it heading left. Traverse deeply wooded flats.

*Bridal Veil Falls spills over a naked granite slope.*

**2.3**    Intersect the east end of the Burnt Mountain Trail. Stay left on the Corn Mill Shoals Trail.

**2.4**    Come to the ford at Corn Mill Shoals. The crossing is over a slick stone slab. Use caution.

**2.5**    Stay left with the Corn Mill Shoals Trail, as the Shoals Trail leaves right. Climb via switchbacks.

**2.7**    Reach a short spur trail leading left to a limited view from a rock promontory looking into the Little River valley. Resume the Corn Mill Shoals Trail.

**3.0**    Stay straight with the Corn Mill Shoals Trail as the Laurel Ridge Trail leaves right. Top out, then descend along an unnamed tributary of the Little River.

**3.5**    Come to a powerline and the Bridal Overlook Trail. Head left on the Bridal Overlook Trail, heading up the powerline clearing, then returning to woods, still climbing. Cross the clearing again.

**4.0**    Top out on a granite knob above Bridal Veil Falls. Descend just a bit to reach an outcrop with a view below of Bridal Veil Falls and a host of mountains in the distance. Backtrack.

**4.5**    Return to Corn Mill Shoals Road. Resume following the tributary of the Little River downhill.

**4.6**    Stay left with the Corn Mill Shoals Trail as the Shelter Rock Trail leaves right.

**5.0**    Head left on Bridal Veil Falls Road. The awesome cataract is audible from this juncture forward. Pass a viewing deck for a distant yet complete look at the huge cascade.

**5.1**    Reach the base of 120-foot Bridal Veil Falls. Here, you can scramble among the rocks at the falls' base and see the water sheeting over a wide rock slab. Backtrack toward the trailhead.

**6.8**    Make the repeat ford at Corn Mill Shoals. Continue backtracking.

**7.1**    Meet the Little River Trail, ending the backtracking. Here, stay left on the Corn Mill Shoals Trail, immediately passing the west end of the Burnt Mountain Trail. The walking is easy.

**7.4**    Cross Tom Creek by culvert. Surmount a gap and descend.

**7.7**    Pass the Big Rock Trail. Backtrack toward the trailhead.

**7.8**    Arrive at Cascade Lake Road and the trailhead, completing the trek.

# Cedar Rock Bridal Veil Falls Hike

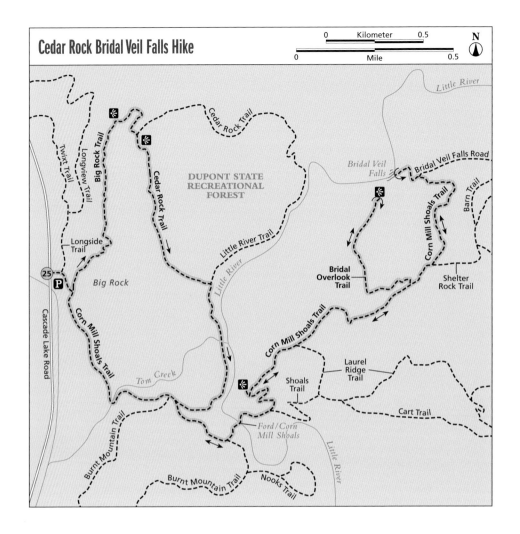

# 26 Waterfalls of DuPont Loop

This circuit hike at DuPont State Recreational Forest visits four of the six major waterfalls located at this preserve outside Brevard. Leave the Lake Imaging trailhead and trace mostly doubletrack paths to lesser-visited Grassy Creek Falls, then nearly circle around magnificent and popular High Falls, viewing it from multiple angles. Next, admire rollercoastering Triple Falls. Trace the Little River to wide, rumbling Hooker Falls. Finally, take a quiet path to return to the trailhead, closing the loop. Elevation changes are moderate on the well-marked and maintained and exceedingly popular trail system.

**Start:** Lake Imaging trailhead
**Distance:** 6.4-mile loop
**Difficulty:** Moderate
**Elevation change:** +-1,028 feet
**Maximum grade:** 6 percent grade for 0.6 mile
**Hiking time:** About 3.5 hours
**Seasons/schedule:** 5 a.m. to 10 p.m., 365 days/year, winter for more solitude
**Fees and permits:** None
**Dog friendly:** Leashed dogs allowed
**Trail surface:** Gravel, natural

**Land status:** State forest
**Other trail users:** Mountain bikers, equestrians
**Maps to consult:** National Geographic #504 DuPont State Recreational Forest, DuPont State Recreational Forest; USGS Standingstone Mountain
**Amenities available:** Restroom at trailhead
**Cell service:** Good
**Trail contacts:** DuPont State Recreational Forest, (828) 877-6527, www.dupontstaterecreationalforest.com

**Finding the trailhead:** From the intersection of NC 280 and US 276 in Pisgah Forest, just north of Brevard, take US 64 east for 3.5 miles to a light at Crab Creek Road. Turn right on Crab Creek Road and follow it 4.2 miles to turn right on DuPont Road. Follow DuPont Road as it soon becomes Staton Road for a total of 2.5 miles to the Lake Imaging trailhead on your left. Trailhead GPS: 35.209273, -82.615512'

## The Hike

This hike travels through extremely scenic DuPont State Recreational Forest, home of waterfalls, granite outcrops, wildlife aplenty, and an extensive trail system. DuPont came to be after lands ended up under state ownership following a tense time of land bidding whereupon key features of this particular hike—including High Falls and Triple Falls—nearly ended up being part of an upscale housing development. Ironically, some of the trails you hike on this feature-laden loop were actually roads laid out by the developer. The state forest now contains over 10,000 acres and is a magnet for hikers, mountain bikers, and equestrians who seek to enjoy nature and get some outdoor exercise on the 90 or so miles of pathways that course throughout the terrain. These trails can range from wide gravel gated roads—open only to forest personnel—to singletrack remote paths winding through the hills and hollows. Almost all the trails here are multiple-use trails, therefore expect to share the path with mountain bikers as well as equestrians.

The large Lake Imaging trailhead is popular with all three groups, with hikers being the largest assemblage, mountain bikers a close second, followed by equestrians. Be a defensive hiker and listen for mountain bikers—sometimes they will be traveling excessively fast and not give you time to jump out of the way. However, most of them are courteous to hikers. Both hikers and mountain bikers should yield to horses.

It is just a short distance from the trailhead until you see your first water feature— Lake Imaging. The peculiar name is derived from one of the corporate property owners by the name of Sterling Diagnostic Imaging. Name aside, the small 2-acre impoundment is more of a pond than a lake. However, a shelter stands astride Lake Imaging and makes for a fine picnic spot. Pathways circle the impoundment. This is one of five lakes located in DuPont State Recreational Forest. The largest is Lake Julia, coming in at 99 acres. Anglers vie for bream and largemouth bass on these lakes, but trout are found in the Little River, the primary watercourse in the forest, and its tributaries.

Beyond Lake Imaging the easy, undulating doubletrack takes you to a spur and Grassy Creek Falls—your first moving-water feature. Like many of the cataracts here, 50-foot Grassy Creek Falls sheets over a long, widening angled stone slab into a plunge pool. Unlike most other waterfalls here, this cataract is decidedly less crowded. Use caution at this and all the other falls here at DuPont. Unfortunately, aquatic accidents are a common occurrence among forest visitors.

Buck Forest Road leads you through the covered bridge above High Falls. Here you enter the busy but beautiful area where the three primary spillers of DuPont are situated together, concentrating the visitation. However, do not let this deter you as the three falls—High Falls, Triple Falls, and Hooker Falls—all deserve your attention. You can see the 120-foot High Falls from an elevated viewpoint near some picnic shelters as well as from the base. Here, the Little River positively roars in white froth over a solid granite face exuding power and majesty. No wonder it is so popular! Next comes Triple Falls, a three-tiered spellbinder also dropping 120 feet, dancing and dashing over granite in massive stages. Steps lead to the middle of the cataract but you can also see all three drops at once from a trailside vista.

After crossing Staton Road, trace the Little River past the large Hooker Falls parking area to visit Hooker Falls. This tumbler stands in complete contrast to all the other cascades at DuPont. Here, a wide wall of white uniformly spills 12 feet over a ledge into a gargantuan pool that is easily the most popular moving-water swimming spot in the forest.

Leave the crowds behind beyond Hooker Falls, joining quiet and little traveled Holly Road. This doubletrack path heads north, winding through hills of pine and oak, eventually leading back to the trailhead, completing a waterfall extravaganza worthy of the Carolina mountain region.

*High Falls is big and powerful.*

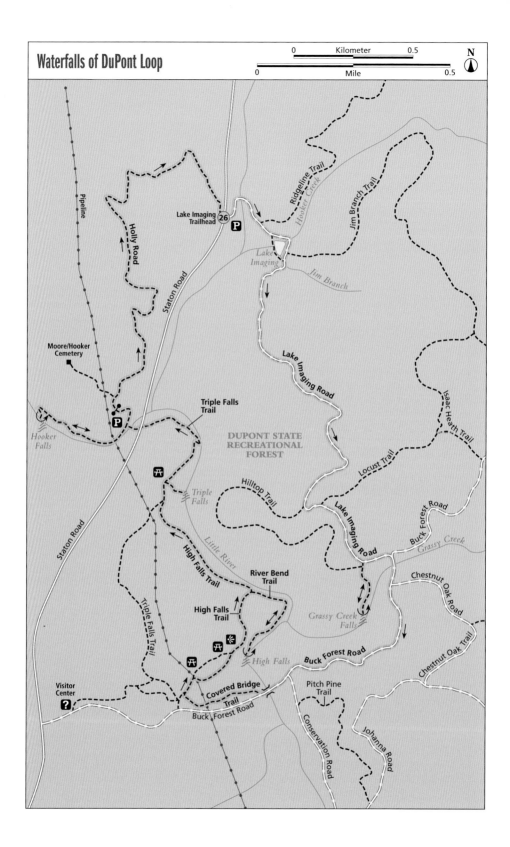

# Waterfalls of DuPont Loop

0       Kilometer       0.5

0       Mile       0.5

N

Pipeline

Holly Road

Lake Imaging Trailhead   26   P

Riddleline Trail

Hooker Creek

Jim Branch Trail

Lake Imaging

Jim Branch

Staton Road

Moore/Hooker Cemetery

Lake Imaging Road

Isaac Heath Trail

Triple Falls Trail

P

Hooker Falls

DUPONT STATE RECREATIONAL FOREST

Locust Trail

Triple Falls

Hilltop Trail

Lake Imaging Road

Buck Forest Road

Grassy Creek

Little River

High Falls Trail

River Bend Trail

Chestnut Oak Road

Staton Road

High Falls Trail

Grassy Creek Falls

Triple Falls Trail

High Falls

Buck Forest Road

Chestnut Oak Trail

Visitor Center

?

Covered Bridge Trail

Buck Forest Road

Pitch Pine Trail

Conservation Road

Johanna Road

# Miles and Directions

**0.0** Pass around the pole gate at the Lake Imaging trailhead. Head northeast on Lake Imaging Road, quickly spanning a stream by culvert.

**0.1** Keep straight on Lake Imaging Road as the Ridgeline Trail heads left.

**0.2** Come to 2-acre Lake Imaging. Stay left as a trail also goes around the right side of the pond. Just ahead, the Jim Branch Trail leaves left. Span small Hooker Creek by culvert, then ascend.

**0.7** Bisect a former clearing growing up in pines.

**1.2** Stay on Lake Imaging Road as the north end of the Hilltop Loop leaves right. Just ahead, the Locust Trail leaves left. Descend, passing a small quarry on trail left in pine-oak woods.

**1.4** Turn right onto the Grassy Creek Falls Trail. Just beyond here, the south end of the Hilltop Trail enters from the right. Descend toward Grassy Creek. Shortly reach an old stone barbecue pit and the top of Grassy Creek Falls. See the cascade sheet downward 50 feet. Backtrack, then resume Lake Imaging Road.

**1.8** Turn right onto Buck Forest Road. As mentioned, all these roads are open only to forest personnel vehicles. Immediately bridge Grassy Creek, then ascend a hill with partial wintertime views of the Blue Ridge to the west.

**1.9** Chestnut Oak Road leaves left. Stay straight with Buck Forest Road. Grassy Creek Falls noisily spills below.

**2.3** Conservation Road leaves left. Stay straight with Buck Forest Road, passing a mountain wetland to your left. Ahead, walk through the covered bridge above High Falls. Do not try to access the top of High Falls from here. Forest personnel have blocked the routes. After spanning the Little River via the covered bridge, split right on the Covered Bridge Trail.

**2.6** Turn right onto the High Falls Trail after crossing a pipeline clearing. Descend, crossing the pipeline clearing a second time.

**2.7** Split right toward High Falls as a spur trail goes straight to a pair of picnic shelters. Descend, then come to an astonishing vista of 120-foot High Falls. Continue dropping toward the Little River, passing a second access for the nearby picnic area.

**3.0** Turn right onto the dead-end River Bend Trail. Follow the Little River upstream, curving toward the base of High Falls.

**3.3** Reach High Falls base. A little rock scrambling is required to get close to the massive, misting roar of white. Backtrack.

**3.6** Rejoin the High Falls Trail, paralleling the Little River downstream.

**3.8** Stay right on the Triple Falls Trail. Descend.

**3.9** Split right, joining a wooden stairwell to the middle of Triple Falls, as a trail leads left to a huge picnic area. Backtrack up the stairs after viewing the falls, then rejoin the Triple Falls Trail, descending along the Little River.

**4.4** Pass under Staton Road.

**4.5** Cross the Little River on a trail bridge. Come to the large upper Hooker Falls parking area. Head left toward Hooker Falls.

**4.8** Reach low, wide Hooker Falls and its big pool. Backtrack.

**5.1** Return to Hooker Falls parking area, then join Holly Road after passing around a metal pole gate. Quickly pass the spur leading left to Moore/Hooker Cemetery. Ahead, enjoy the interpretive signage about woodland trail and road building along Holly Road.

**5.9** Bridge a small creek by culvert after ascending along a trickling branch.

**6.3** The trail devolves to singletrack and drops through pine-oak woods.

**6.4** Arrive at Staton Road. Turn right and come to the Lake Imaging parking area and the loop's end.

*This vista reveals a view of the three drops of Triple Falls.*

# Southeast and Northeast

# 27 Blue Ridge Pastures

Take a hike on protected conservation land, roughly paralleling the Blue Ridge, to a grassy mountaintop with stellar views of the Black Mountains, Hickory Nut Gorge, and other nearby peaks and valleys. The Trombatore Trail is your pathway to the open meadows. The path drops into a wildflower-heavy valley before making its way to Blue Ridge Pastures, where grand vistas will be your reward.

**Start:** Bearwallow Gap
**Distance:** 5.0-mile there-and-back
**Difficulty:** Moderate
**Elevation change:** +-685 feet
**Maximum grade:** 11 percent downhill grade for 0.9 mile
**Hiking time:** About 3 hours
**Seasons/schedule:** Daily sunrise to sunset; whenever the skies are clear
**Fees and permits:** None

**Dog friendly:** Leashed dogs allowed
**Trail surface:** Natural
**Land status:** Private preserve open to public
**Other trail users:** None
**Maps to consult:** Trombatore Trail; USGS Bat Cave
**Amenities available:** None
**Cell service:** Decent
**Trail contacts:** Conserving Carolina, (828) 697-5777, conservingcarolina.org

**Finding the trailhead:** From downtown Asheville, take I-240 east to exit 9, Blue Ridge Parkway/Bat Cave, joining US 74A. Take US 74A east for 12.7 miles to turn right on Bearwallow Mountain Road. (If you pass the Gerton post office you have gone a little too far.) Follow it for 2.1 miles to Bearwallow Gap. Park on the right-hand shoulder. There is limited parking, thus be mindful of the spots where parking is expressly forbidden. Trailhead GPS: 35.460724, -82.367916

## The Hike

Blue Ridge Pastures is a grassy grandstand from which you gain spectacular views of the Black Mountains to the north and the Hickory Nut Gorge to the east, as well as Bearwallow Mountain rising to the south and southeast. Thanks to Conserving Carolina, hikers like us can access these stellar panoramas. Not only did they purchase the land but the organization also worked to build the Trombatore Trail used to reach the mountain meadow that is Blue Ridge Pastures.

That being said, the hike itself does not always go where you think it will or should go. Starting at Bearwallow Gap and climbing to a mountaintop grassy meadow leads most hikers to expect an ascent. However, the Trombatore Trail does the unexpected and descends from the gap, switchbacking into the headwaters of Brush Creek. This wooded vale is rich with wildflowers in spring, from jack-in-the-pulpits to multiple varieties of trillium, Solomon seal, false Solomon seal, and many other plants. Interestingly, the valley harbors a host of yellow buckeye trees, far more than your average Carolina hollow.

The well-constructed singletrack path was built to last, as it wanders down the Brush Creek valley. After a series of foot-saving switchbacks, the trail bottoms out near its crossing of Brush Creek. Beyond here, the path begins to go on and off old logging and woods roads, some of them leading to private property as well as lands under conservation easement. These twists and turns do not always go where you think they will, either. Nevertheless, strategically placed signage and a distinctly worn footbed keep you on the right track. In places, the Trombatore Trail returns to singletrack path, as it does before crossing a stile and opening onto the grassy Blue Ridge Pastures. The meadow rises to your left and descends to your right. And as you climb to its top, a fantastic mountain scene opens before you. Here, the Black Mountains stretch across the horizon dead ahead, rolling from gap to peak and back down to a gap. And as you descend to the other side of the grassy clearing, look right, easterly through the chasm of the Hickory Nut Gorge and beyond into the lowlands and Piedmont of North Carolina. In the near, to the south and southeast, the forests, meadows, and antennas of Bearwallow Mountain rise beyond the elevation of Blue Ridge Pastures, where you stand. Enjoy the view and look forward to the day when the Trombatore Trail is extended and linked to other pathways of Conserving Carolina. Even now, hikers can access Bearwallow Mountain from the same trailhead as the Trombatore Trail. That hike is also detailed in this guide.

## Miles and Directions

**0.0** From Bearwallow Gap, join the Trombatore Trail leaving west from the saddle, the same side of the road as the main parking shoulder. The Trombatore Trail climbs a few steps, passes a trailside kiosk, then begins descending. The singletrack path works down the slope of Bearwallow Mountain, coming near a vertical rock slab before making the first of several switchbacks into the Brush Creek watershed.

**0.4** Make the last of the initial switchbacks. Rhododendron, ferns, and moss-covered boulders border the trail. Wildflowers are abundant in spring. Brush Creek gathers steam in the bottom of the hollow below, and its falling white noise rises to your ears.

**0.7** Enter a younger forest of spindly hardwoods.

**0.9** After a right turn, walk by piles of rocks, indicating land formerly under cultivation and/or grazing.

**1.0** Reach a low point. You have dropped about 500 feet. Join an old roadbed. Now, begin to watch for other tracks spurring off the primary Trombatore Trail. Signs are posted at potentially confusing spots.

**1.1** Step over Brush Creek by culvert, still in youngish forest.

**1.3** Pass under a transmission line.

**1.6** Top out, now along the ridge dividing Henderson County and Buncombe County.

**1.7** Split left with the Trombatore Trail in a gap. Climb, staying with the signs.

**1.9** Step over a little spring branch near a fast-disappearing clearing and former cabin site. Make a switchback, crossing the uppermost reach of the spring branch, which may not be flowing up here.

**2.3** Make a final uphill push through locust trees, cherry, and other pioneer species.

*The Black Mountains rise in the distance from the meadow at Blue Ridge Pastures.*

| 2.4 | Reach a stile and climb over a wire fence. Open onto the Blue Ridge Pastures. Head left, climbing toward the pasture high point. Views open to the southeast of Bearwallow Mountain and its tower and antennae. |
| 2.5 | Top out and open onto a panorama of the Black Mountains, ahead to your north, as well as Little Pisgah Mountain in the near. Explore and soak in more views ahead to the east of the Hickory Nut Gorge. Look back at Bearwallow Mountain, too. Backtrack. |
| 5.0 | Arrive at Bearwallow Gap, completing the hike. |

# ABOUT THE YELLOW BUCKEYE

Along the first part of this hike, look for the yellow buckeye tree, growing in above-average numbers for North Carolina. Yellow buckeyes, also referred to simply as buckeyes, are primarily found in mountain coves in the western part of the Tar Heel State, with Great Smoky Mountains National Park being a stronghold. Buckeyes are found from around 1,500 to 5,000 feet in elevation. The cove of Brush Creek is in the middle of the elevation range, around 3,200 feet. Other types of buckeyes grow in the Southeast, but in a more shrublike form.

The yellow buckeye is the largest of all the buckeye trees. Its fruit—the smooth brown orb with the singular lighter spot—the eye of the buckeye—is its most easily identifiable feature. Carrying a buckeye in your pocket is considered good luck. Leaves are usually found in clusters of five. The fruit does recall the eye of a deer. The bark is grayish brown and often mottled. In spring, clusters of large showy yellow flowers rise 2 to 3 inches from the leaves. Buckeyes are among the first trees to leaf out in spring and also one of the first trees to turn color in the fall.

Buckeyes range from southwestern Pennsylvania down to northern Alabama and west to extreme southern Illinois. The buckeyes growing in the cove of Brush Creek are among the most easterly in its range. Buckeye nuts are considered poisonous, and shoots of the tree can sicken cattle. Since animals do not eat the seeds of the buckeye, this limits its spread and reproduction.

Buckeye is a soft, light wood and is subject to rot, limiting its uses. Buckeye is, however, smoothly grained and it is occasionally used for furniture, but primarily for boxes, crates, and pulpwood. Moreover, yellow buckeye can also beautify a mountain cove such as the one found here along Brush Creek.

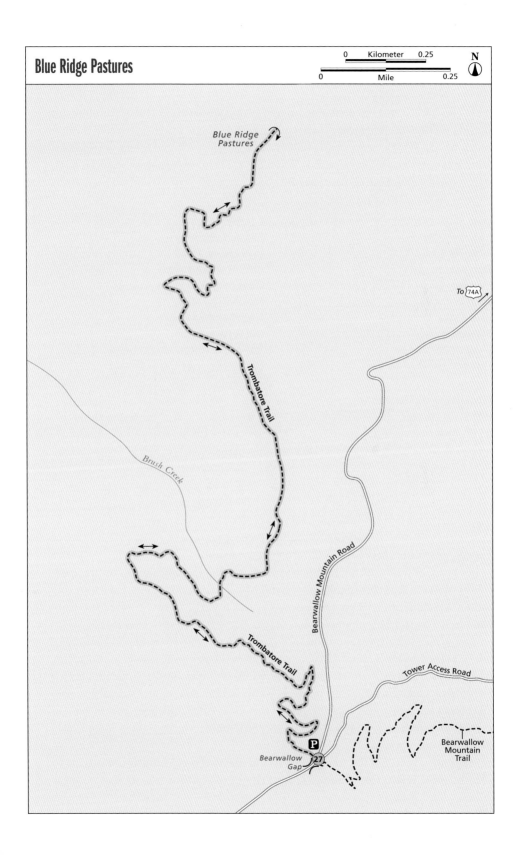

# Blue Ridge Pastures

Blue Ridge
Pastures

0    Kilometer    0.25

0    Mile    0.25

N

To 74A

Trombatore Trail

Brush Creek

Trombatore Trail

Bearwallow Mountain Road

Tower Access Road

Bearwallow
Mountain
Trail

P

27

Bearwallow
Gap

# 28 Bearwallow Mountain

This short but scenic hike climbs through rocky woods to an open meadow and historic mountaintop fire tower. Start high and trace a switchback-laden trail through rocky woods. Reach grassy Bearwallow Mountain, where views of the surrounding highlands will stun first-time visitors. From the 4,232-foot-high peak, you can backtrack or make a loop using the tower maintenance road.

**Start:** Bearwallow Gap
**Distance:** 2.0-mile loop
**Difficulty:** Easy
**Elevation change:** +-582 feet
**Maximum grade:** 11 percent grade for 1.0 mile
**Hiking time:** About 1 hour
**Seasons/schedule:** Daily sunrise to sunset, whenever the skies are clear
**Fees and permits:** None

**Dog friendly:** Leashed dogs allowed
**Trail surface:** Natural, gravel
**Land status:** Private preserve open to public
**Other trail users:** None
**Maps to consult:** Bearwallow Mountain; USGS Bat Cave
**Amenities available:** None
**Cell service:** Decent
**Trail contacts:** Conserving Carolina, (828) 697-5777, conservingcarolina.org

**Finding the trailhead:** From downtown Asheville, take I-240 east to exit 9, Blue Ridge Parkway/Bat Cave, joining US 74A. Take US 74A east for 12.7 miles to turn right on Bearwallow Mountain Road. (If you pass the Gerton post office, you have gone a little too far.) Follow it for 2.1 miles to Bearwallow Gap. Park on the right-hand shoulder. There is limited parking, thus be mindful of the spots where parking is expressly forbidden. Trailhead GPS: 35.460724, -82.367916

## The Hike

For decades, visitors have been coming up to the top of Bearwallow Mountain, despite its not being officially open to the public. However, the curious want to see the spectacular prospects from the mountaintop, where the Hickorynut Gorge, Lake Lure, and Mount Mitchell can be seen. On especially clear days the Great Smoky Mountains stand to the west. The buildings of downtown Asheville are easily identifiable.

Knowing what an attraction and special place Bearwallow Mountain had become, the Carolina Mountain Land Conservancy, as it was known then, sprang into action. In 2009, they garnered an 81-acre conservation easement on the peak, and built a hiking trail leading to the crest in 2011. Today, we can trek to the top as welcome hikers and soak in the spectacular landscapes that will fulfill even the highest of expectations. And you can return via the fire road upon which so many went before the conservancy built the Bearwallow Mountain Trail.

The fire tower on the grassy slopes atop Bearwallow Mountain was built in 1934 by the Civilian Conservation Corps. The steel structure rises 47 feet from the

*Early morning view from Bearwallow Mountain*

open bald where million-dollar views can be had. The tower was used to spot fires until it was decommissioned in 1994. A firewatcher lived on site first in a cabin and then later in the wood frame house. The weather was rough on the open meadow. The winds, snows, and thunderstorms were most punishing.

Today, the tower and old frame house are surrounded by a wire fence and off limits to visitors. Plans are in the works to restore the tower, enhancing already stellar panoramas from this mountain meadow. However, perhaps we are getting ahead of the story. And there is still more. From the trailhead the hike first works up a rocky slope, passing a wildflower-rich hillside, where white and other shades of trilliums bloom by the hundreds in spring. Come to a place where wind-pruned oaks testify to the harsh climate atop Bearwallow Mountain. Admire big boulders standing mute through the passage of time. Upon emerging onto the grassy bald, you can roam around, finding landmarks in the distance, feeling the almost constant cool breeze, and sometimes warm sun. Inspect the historic steel fire tower, where one day hikers will be able to scan the horizon from the very spot where rangers for a half-century cast an eye for conflagrations over the mountains and valleys of western North Carolina.

For now the views from the balds will do. And when you have explored and pho-tographed and walked around, and perhaps had a grassy picnic, complete a loop by descending the fire tower access road, today used by those who maintain the gaggle of antennae that rise from the tip-top of Bearwallow Mountain. While recalling the vistas up top, thank the Carolina Mountain Land Conservancy for their efforts.

## Miles and Directions

**0.0**   From Bearwallow Gap, pass around a road gate and take the Bearwallow Mountain Trail leaving east from the gap. The hiking trail going west—across Bearwallow Mountain Road—is the Trombatore Trail. The gravel road climbing is the tower access and is your return route. Begin switchbacking up the mountain slope on the Bearwallow Mountain Trail in rocky hardwoods such as hickory, oak, and buckeye. Much of the trail uses wood-and-earth stairs. This area presents an astounding display of trilliums in late April and early May.

**0.5**   Pass atop a bluff. The trees become more stunted as you gain elevation.

**0.7**   Come alongside a boulder garden, with huge stones upon which grow ferns and other plants.

**0.8**   Emerge onto the bald of Bearwallow Mountain. The peak and array of antennae rise in front of you. At this point, views will likely try to pull you south or north to identify the summits and valleys in the distance.

**0.9**   Come to the tower access road. Head right and curve left, climbing toward the apex and the historic tower, as the Wildcat Rock Trail heads east for Wildcat Rock. Easy views open south and north.

**1.1**   Reach the historic steel tower and adjacent outbuildings and more antennae than you think could be atop one mountain in western North Carolina. Backtrack down the gravel road.

**1.5**   Turn west down the mountain on the gravel road, leaving the open meadows of the bald.

**2.0**   Return to Bearwallow Gap, completing the view-laden hike.

# ABOUT CONSERVING CAROLINA

Conserving Carolina (before a 2017 merger with the Pacolet Area Conservancy, it was known as the Carolina Mountain Land Conservancy) was born from one woman's concern about protecting the natural resources of Henderson County. Lela McBride had moved to western North Carolina from the state of Illinois. She was taken with the beauty of the mountains and rural areas that comprised the county when she moved here, back in the 1980s. Simultaneously, she also saw many of these special places becoming another shopping center or mountain home community.

Lela stepped up and did something. She collaborated with the Hendersonville League of Women Voters and together they took stock of the remaining special natural areas in Henderson County, everything from mountain wetlands harboring rare plants, to old-growth forests, to mountain peaks and biologically diverse waterways.

After the inventory of special lands was completed, a group that came to be Conserving Carolina was formed to safeguard the unique locales. Their mission is "protecting and stewarding land and water resources vital to our natural heritage and quality of life and to fostering appreciation and understanding of the natural world."

To that end, the nationally accredited Conserving Carolina has protected over 48,000 acres over 30 years in parts of Henderson, Transylvania, Buncombe, Rutherford, Polk, and Jackson Counties. They not only purchase properties for preservation but also partner with private landowners to "conserve land and maximize financial benefits through the use of voluntary land protection agreements, land donations and purchases."

Nearly a dozen full-time staff members work for the conservancy, identifying special lands for protection and working with other groups. A protected property known as the "World's Edge" is an important example of Conserving Carolina in action. World's Edge not only harbored attractive features such as views from rock outcrops and waterfalls but perhaps more importantly was a wealth of biodiversity and a migratory stop for birds. The conservancy acquired the 1,568-acre tract, then conveyed it to the state of North Carolina, adding to the newly established Chimney Rock State Park. It is success stories like these that keep the conservancy on an upward track. For more information and how to join Conserving Carolina, please visit conservingcarolina.org.

# Bearwallow Mountain

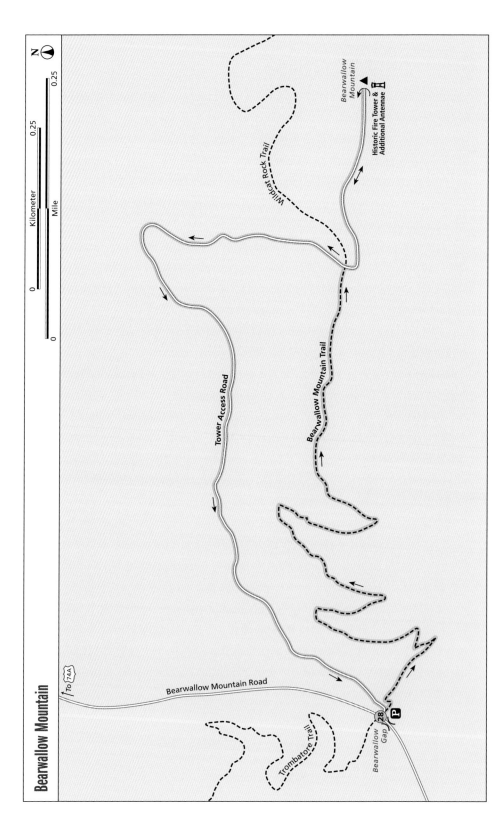

N

Kilometer
0    0.25    0.25

Mile
0    0.25

To 74A

Bearwallow Mountain Road

Tower Access Road

Bearwallow Mountain Trail

Wildcat Rock Trail

Bearwallow Mountain

Historic Fire Tower &
Additional Antennae

Trombatore Trail

Bearwallow
Gap

28    P

# 29 Florence Nature Preserve

This hike loops through a protected nature preserve where you can enjoy a little bit of everything in one circuit. First, ascend along a cascading stream to visit an old cabin site. Stop by a view, then circle around to a better panorama. Cap it off with stops at two waterfalls, all nestled in a natural world of Southern Appalachian splendor.

**Start:** US 74A trailhead
**Distance:** 5.3-mile balloon loop
**Difficulty:** Moderate
**Elevation change:** +-1,260 feet
**Maximum grade:** 15 percent downhill grade for 0.4 mile
**Hiking time:** About 3 hours
**Seasons/schedule:** Daily sunrise to set, fall through spring for best hikes
**Fees and permits:** None

**Dog friendly:** Leashed dogs allowed
**Trail surface:** Natural
**Land status:** Private preserve open to public
**Other trail users:** None
**Maps to consult:** Florence Nature Preserve; USGS Bat Cave
**Amenities available:** None
**Cell service:** Decent
**Trail contacts:** Conserving Carolina, (828) 697-5777, conservingcarolina.org

**Finding the trailhead:** From downtown Asheville, take I-240 east to exit 9, Blue Ridge Parkway/Bat Cave, joining US 74A. Take US 74A east for 13.8 miles to the trailhead on your left, 0.9 mile past the Upper Hickory Nut Gorge Community Center. The parking area is limited so be considerate. Trailhead GPS: 35.473442, -82.332412

## The Hike

Dr. Tom Florence made a career as a physician in Atlanta, Georgia, but he came Carolina way whenever he could, to rest and refresh here in the beautiful Southern Appalachians. Specifically, he came up to a tract near the hamlet of Gerton, just east of the Blue Ridge in Henderson County. He bought his parcel of paradise back in 1966 and continued to add to the acreage. He and his wife, Glenna, built a cabin to spend the summers, then eventually built a permanent home on the property that ultimately expanded to 600 acres along the south slope of Little Pisgah Mountain.

The Florence family grew to love their special tract of land. As Dr. Florence got into his upper years, the thought of keeping the land natural appealed to him. About this time he heard of what was then called the Carolina Mountain Land Conservancy. Ultimately, he donated all but 30 acres of land to the conservancy, retaining a parcel for his family home. Today, the conservancy manages the donated property. They have developed a trail network exploring the scenic swath where forests grow tall, streams run clear and free, and rocky crags offer vista points.

Ironically, although the land was saved from modern development—normally meaning high-dollar mountain home communities—the terrain here in the upper

Hickory Creek valley was once home to over ten individual hardscrabble farms, where Carolina mountaineers hoed corn and tobacco and vegetables, just trying to get along. Additionally, the Old Buncombe Turnpike crossed here. This primitive road once connected mountain communities to the west such as Asheville to the Piedmont and lowlands to the east, before the railroads and later interstates came along.

The land is within the Upper Hickory Nut Gorge. Today, you can access Florence Nature Preserve from the official trailhead on US 74A, and connect to a network of blazed trails coursing through the former Florence property. The hike switchbacks up a north-facing, wildlife-rich slope above Hickory Creek, then comes alongside an

*This slide cataract at Florence Nature Preserve cuts a slender channel.*

unnamed tributary draining the slopes of Little Pisgah Mountain. Make an attractive ascent through this stream valley, passing the stone foundations of a forgotten cabin. After breaking the 3,000-foot barrier, take the spur trail to a rock outcrop with a partial view down the Hickory Nut Gorge and beyond. The hike then visits a former field, now growing up with trees. From there it wanders along a ridge where pink lady slippers rise among the oaks and pines. The second mountain view is superior. Here, several rock outcrops give you mainly westerly views of the Blue Ridge and the Tennessee Valley Divide. Streams on this side of the divide flow directly into the Atlantic Ocean, whereas streams on the other side of the divide ultimately feed the Mississippi River and flow into the Gulf of Mexico.

Speaking of water, the end of the hike takes you past a pair of waterfalls, very different from one another. The first cataract makes a 30-foot drop down a 60-foot-long stone channel, looking like someone carved the channel in clay with his or her finger. The next spiller is a two-step more typical drop of about 15 feet into a clear, gravel-bordered plunge pool, putting an exclamation point on the trek.

While hiking here, look for relics of the past from the former farms, whether they are piles of rocks or flattened out spots for bits of metal. Admire but leave them be. You will also see grown-over roads from days gone by. The trails are not officially named but they are marked with color-coded blazes. A trail map is available online.

## Miles and Directions

**0.0**   From the gravel parking area with the conspicuous stone chimney and trailhead sign, take the yellow-blazed singletrack trail into rocky, north-facing woods, rich with wildflowers in spring. Earth and wood steps ease the numerous switchbacks.

**0.3**   Pass a rocked-in spring just below the trail. Look for a low-slung rockhouse just past the spring.

**0.4**   Span a trickling branch on a short stone slab bridge. Keep angling up the slope of Little Pisgah Mountain.

**0.8**   Reach a flat alongside an unnamed tributary of Hickory Creek. Keep up the right bank of the creek.

**0.9**   Cross the unnamed creek and reach the Blue Trail and the loop portion of the hike. Head right, ascending along the stream in mixed woods with rhododendron. Ahead, pass a little 3-foot waterfall.

**1.2**   Come to the foundation of an old cabin on your right, just after bridging a little feeder stream. Examine the squared-off stone spot, root cellar, and chimney remnants. Imagine cleared land encircling this little home in the hollow. Keep uptrail.

**1.3**   Reach a trail intersection. The Yellow Trail goes left to the White Trail, shortcutting the loop. Stay straight on the Blue Trail.

**1.5**   Keep straight on the Blue Trail after intersecting the White Trail.

**1.7**   Split right on the Orange Trail, tracing an old road to an outcrop.

**1.9**   Reach the outcrop known as Tom & Glenna Rock with limited views to the east, down the Hickory Nut Gorge. Backtrack.

**2.1**   Rejoin the Blue Trail.

**2.2**    Cross the unnamed creek on a wide road bridge, then enter a closing meadow and trail intersection. Turn left on the Red Trail, descending along a wooded ridgeline.

**2.5**    Keep straight after meeting the White Trail. Make a brief uptick, then resume heading downward. Look for pink lady slipper flowers in this vicinity. Rhododendron becomes more prevalent.

**3.1**    Level off, then meet the Orange Trail. Join the Orange Trail, climbing to a little rocky knob. Here, outcrops provide views south and west, south of the other side of Hickory Creek valley and west of the Blue Ridge, at this point the ridge dividing Buncombe County and Henderson County. Backtrack.

**3.3**    Rejoin the Red Trail. Drop more steeply. Come very near private property.

**3.6**    Make a hard left, and level off, joining an old roadbed.

**3.7**    Pass a pair of cabins, private property within the Florence Nature Preserve. The trail widens as you are now following the gravel cabin access road, part of Kelly Hill Road.

**4.0**    Stay left as Kelly Hill Road curves to the right. Rejoin singletrack trail.

**4.1**    Cross a stream, then climb. Turn into another tributary.

**4.2**    Come to the spur trail leading right and down to the first waterfall, the slender chute. After visiting the fall, bridge the stream.

**4.3**    Bridge the stream again below the two-tier waterfall with a gravel-bordered little pool. Ascend along the left bank of the stream.

**4.4**    Complete the loop portion of the hike. Backtrack.

**5.3**    Arrive at the trailhead, completing the balloon loop.

## CHIMNEY ROCK PARK

Many hikers take this same road heading for Chimney Rock Park, a formerly private entity folks have been visiting for a century, now owned by the state of North Carolina, but run much as it was by the Morse family, who sold the park in 2007, after opening it in 1902. The admission fee is much higher than your average state park, but it does have some significant natural features worth visiting via park trails. Hickory Nut Falls, Exclamation Point, and Gneiss Cave are three such highlights worth visiting. Hickory Nut Falls, on Fall Creek, dives over a vertical lip on Chimney Rock Mountain, dropping an impressive 400 feet. Chimney Rock Park is also known for being a "star" of the 1992 movie *The Last of the Mohicans*. The final 17 minutes of the movie were filmed at the park. Interestingly, it is hoped that a network of trails will link many of the Conserving Carolina properties—including Florence Nature Preserve—not only to one another but also to trails in Chimney Rock Park. For more information, please visit www.chimneyrockpark.com.

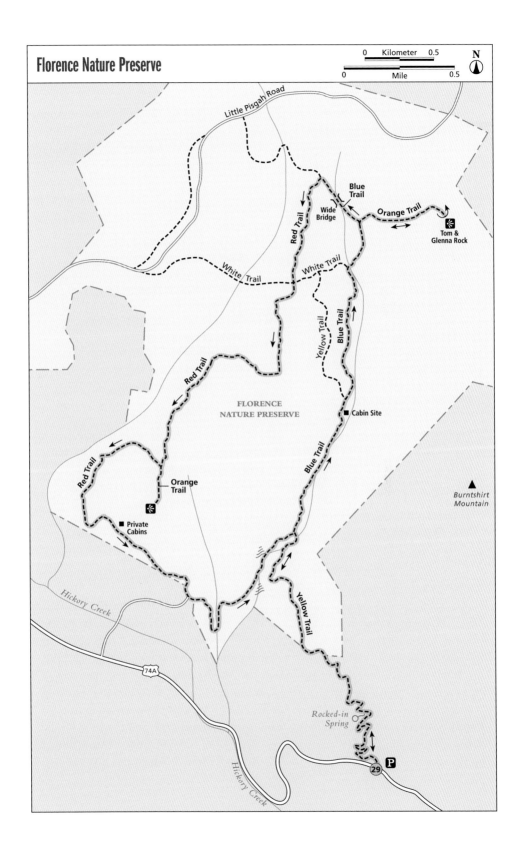

# Florence Nature Preserve

0 Kilometer 0.5

0 Mile 0.5

N

Little Pisgah Road

Red Trail

Blue Trail

Wide Bridge

Orange Trail

Tom & Glenna Rock

White Trail

White Trail

Yellow Trail

Blue Trail

Red Trail

FLORENCE NATURE PRESERVE

Cabin Site

Red Trail

Orange Trail

Blue Trail

Burntshirt Mountain

Private Cabins

Hickory Creek

74A

Yellow Trail

Rocked-in Spring

P

29

Hickory Creek

# 30 Rattlesnake Lodge Hike

This fun little trek takes the Mountains-to-Sea Trail to the relics of a yesteryear mountain retreat by the name of Rattlesnake Lodge, built by one of North Carolina's earliest national park proponents. First, you will leave a mountain gap, then switch-back up Bull Mountain, passing open rock slab slopes presenting views of the Swannanoa River valley and adjacent mountains. Reach the ruins of Rattlesnake Lodge after a gentle uptick where you can explore this highland getaway that once included a pool, water-driven generator, and even a tennis court!

**Start:** Bull Gap
**Distance:** 2.8-mile there-and-back
**Difficulty:** Easy
**Elevation change:** +-560 feet
**Maximum grade:** 8 percent grade for 0.6 mile
**Hiking time:** About 1.5 hours
**Seasons/schedule:** 24/7/365
**Fees and permits:** None
**Dog friendly:** Leashed dogs allowed
**Trail surface:** Natural

**Land status:** Blue Ridge Parkway
**Other trail users:** None
**Maps to consult:** National Geographic #779 Linville Gorge, Mount Mitchell Pisgah National Forest; USGS Craggy Pinnacle
**Amenities available:** None
**Cell service:** Iffy
**Trail contacts:** Blue Ridge Parkway, (828) 348-3400, www.nps.gov/blri

**Finding the trailhead:** From Asheville, take I-26 north to exit 21, New Stock Road. Immediately reach a traffic light, then turn right and reach a second light. Turn left here on Weaverville Road, US 19 Business, passing Ingles grocery store on your right. Follow Weaverville Road for 0.8 mile, then turn right on Reems Creek Road. Follow it for 4.4 miles, then turn right on Ox Creek Road. Follow Ox Creek Road for 3.5 miles to reach a small parking area on the left at Bulls Gap. If this parking area is full, continue for 0.3 mile farther and reach a second parking area. Trailhead GPS: 35.669889, -82.471142

## The Hike

This hike is chock-full of history. It follows an early mountain road leading to the summer home of Dr. Chase P. Ambler, who in addition to being a fine physician was also an outdoors enthusiast and a driving force in establishing the public lands surrounding Asheville that we use today. Dr. Ambler was a founding member of Appalachian National Park Association, a philanthropic outfit dedicated to preserving North Carolina's mountain lands for future generations. Out of this effort were born Pisgah National Forest, Great Smoky Mountains National Park, and the Blue Ridge Parkway. Ironically, Dr. Ambler's property, after going through several hands, ended up being part of the Blue Ridge Parkway, the lands through which this hike follows.

*This wall was part of the barn at Rattlesnake Lodge.*

First, you start at a place called Bull Gap, named for being the area where North Carolina's last wild bull buffalo was shot back in 1799 by a fellow named Joseph Rice. The hike—which gains 600 feet from Bull Gap to the Rattlesnake Lodge—then travels a road built by Dr. Ambler around 1900 to reach the 318-acre mountain retreat he dubbed Rattlesnake Lodge. The lodge included not only a main house but also several outbuildings and ingenious methods of providing the house with water and electricity. You will see the remains of these structures, including a barn, swimming pool, chimneys, a springhouse, and even the waterpower generator building.

Dr. Ambler put a lot of time and effort into this retreat, first building the road, then quarters for a construction crew who set about leveling the mountainous terrain for the buildings, developing springs, and building the actual structures. Interestingly, the building wood used was hand-hewn chestnut cut on the property. Moreover, even the furniture, from bed frames to chairs, was constructed on-site using local wood.

This cove high in the Blue Ridge Mountains in the shadow of Rocky Knob was purportedly a haven for rattlesnakes. Wishing to protect his family, Dr. Ambler put a $5 bounty—a week's wages at the time—on rattlesnakes, and skins aplenty came in from the local area. The skins ended up decorating the living room ceiling of the lodge, giving the getaway a name. And until 1920, Rattlesnake Lodge stayed the summer home of Dr. Ambler and his offspring. They often entertained guests and enjoyed the lodge during the other seasons as well.

Rattlesnake Lodge was a continual work in progress. It was overseen by a caretaker who lived on the property year-round. Dr. Ambler ran cattle here and kept horses as well. He added another 1,000 acres to his 318 acres comprising Rattlesnake Lodge. Trails crisscrossed the property and connected to other places, including Mount Mitchell.

Desiring a true retreat, Dr. Ambler kept the trail from Bull Gap to Rattlesnake Lodge primitive. To that end, a carriage house was constructed at Bull Gap, where the doctor and his guests could leave their horse-drawn carriages after the ride from Asheville, then either walk or ride a horse to Rattlesnake Lodge. On your hike, you will follow much of the road constructed by Dr. Ambler, though steeper sections use switchbacks and foot trail. The route you take is now the Mountains-to-Sea Trail, North Carolina's long-distance master path. After passing the crumbled remains of the carriage house, you head up the slope of Bull Mountain. While working up the side of Bull Mountain, the Mountains-to-Sea Trail leads along a steep slope passing by open rock outcrops, adding view possibilities. It isn't too long before first arriving at the barn site and then coming to the old swimming pool. From there you will pass by the lodge site and outbuilding foundations. Take your time and explore all the building sites. And if the distance isn't far enough for you, consider taking the blue-blazed spur trail from Rattlesnake Lodge a half-mile down to the Blue Ridge Parkway. This spur path travels alongside the upper reaches of Bull Creek, where you will find a scenic sloping cascade just before the spur reaches the Parkway and the Tanbark Ridge Tunnel.

## Miles and Directions

**0.0**   From the small parking area at Bull Gap, walk south through the gap on an old road once linking Ox Creek valley to the Swannanoa valley. Pass the crumbled remains of Dr. Ambler's carriage house, then turn left, joining the Mountains-to-Sea Trail. Begin climbing switchbacks on the south slope of Bull Mountain. The Blue Ridge Parkway lies below.

**0.3**   A steep, partly rock, slope avails a view to the southwest of Rice Knob and to the south, down Bull Creek valley. Continue in oaks with occasional evergreens.

**0.4**   Make a big switchback to the left.

**0.7**   Cross a big rock face with open views of the Swannanoa River valley to the south and Swan Mountain rising to the east.

**1.0**   The Mountains-to-Sea Trail takes you between a pair of boulder gates flanking both sides of the trail. Look for magnificent and sturdy white oaks rising in the forest.

**1.2**   Come to the outlying area of Rattlesnake Lodge, reaching the old barn foundation. Here, horses and cattle were quartered and a pigpen was downhill. The rock wall foundation of the barn is still evident. Continue along the Mountains-to-Sea Trail to reach the Rattlesnake Lodge.

**1.4**   Come to the balance of Rattlesnake Lodge, viewing the concreted swimming pool for the dwelling. Ahead is the site of the lodge and a leveled front yard. Soon pass the blue-blazed spur trail leading right a half-mile to the Blue Ridge Parkway, just west of the Tanbark Ridge Tunnel. Continue looking around, appreciating the springhouse, generator area, tool house, and amazing rock work. Find the tennis court site uphill. The Mountains-to-Sea Trail continues around the cove to rise and meet Swan Mountain. After exploring heartily, turn around and backtrack.

**2.8** Arrive at the trailhead, completing the hike.

# DR. AMBLER'S INNOVATIONS–OLD AND NEW

It was the early 1900s and times were changing. Being a bright innovative man with means, Dr. Ambler used the technology of the time and other conveniences, as well as old-time techniques, to make his lodge a comfortable home for his wife, children, and frequent guests. Rock retaining walls and foundations were "dry constructed," meaning no concrete was used, just careful hand placement of stones, definitely an old way of doing things. However, Rattlesnake Lodge had hot water storage, yet the water was heated by a wood-powered stove. A shallow swimming pool was gravity fed by chilly mountain springs through underground pipes. The covered springhouse had a grooved shallow rock depression you can see today to store milk and other perishables. A bridge stretched from the second floor of the lodge to a hill, where paths meandered through gently sloping gardens on the way to a leveled tennis court. Woe to the person who hit a tennis ball off the court and down the mountain.

However, his most modern innovation may have been the water-driven generator. It provided electricity for the dwelling. Far uphill a spring-fed reservoir stood, covered to keep out leaves, critters, and general debris. A pipe flowed downhill to a tool shed, under which stood a water-driven generator. You can still see the cement platform upon which the generator stood. This generator powered lights at the remote dwelling, standing at 3,700 feet in the Blue Ridge Mountains, well before most of the country had electricity in their primary homes.

# Rattlesnake Lodge Hike

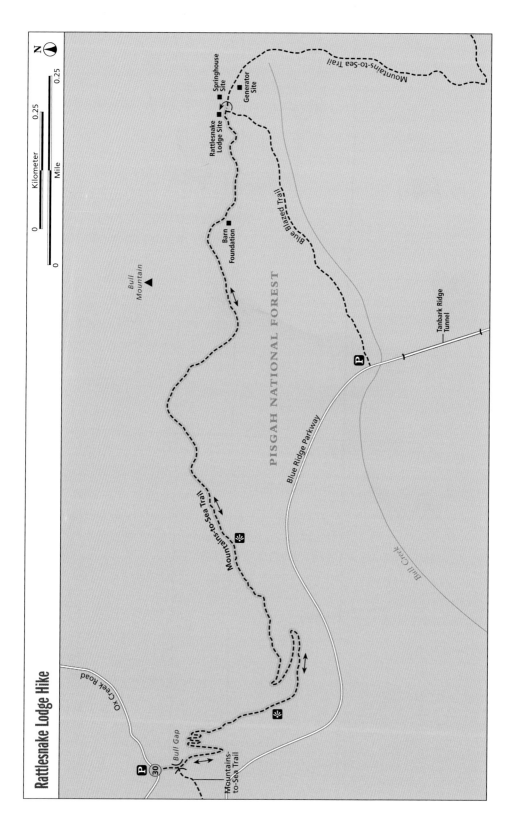

Bull Mountain

PISGAH NATIONAL FOREST

Blue Ridge Parkway

Bull Creek

Tanbark Ridge Tunnel

Mountains-to-Sea Trail

Blue Blazed Trail

Springhouse Site

Generator Site

Rattlesnake Lodge Site

Barn Foundation

Mountains-to-Sea Trail

Ox Creek Road

Bull Gap

30

Mountains-to-Sea Trail

N

Kilometer

0      0.25

Mile

0      0.25

# 31 Little Snowball Mountain

This trek starts off the Blue Ridge Parkway within easy striking distance of Asheville and traverses the lesser-trod Snowball Trail to an outcrop known as Hawkbill Rock. Here, you can peer down the Reems Creek watershed down to Weaverville and beyond. Other points of view include the parkway, Craggy Gardens, and even Mount Mitchell. Continue beyond Hawkbill Rock along a lonely, picturesque ridge to reach the site of the Little Snowball Mountain fire tower before backtracking to the trailhead.

**Start:** Beetree Gap near Craggy Gardens Picnic Area
**Distance:** 7.2-mile there-and-back
**Difficulty:** Easy to moderate
**Elevation change:** +-1,176 feet
**Maximum grade:** 13 percent grade for first 0.7 mile
**Hiking time:** About 3.8 hours
**Seasons/schedule:** 24/7/365 save for winter Blue Ridge Parkway closures
**Fees and permits:** None
**Dog friendly:** Leashed dogs allowed

**Trail surface:** Natural
**Land status:** National park, national forest
**Other trail users:** None
**Maps to consult:** National Geographic #779 Linville Gorge, Mount Mitchell, Pisgah National Forest; USGS Craggy Pinnacle
**Amenities available:** Craggy Gardens visitor center and picnic area nearby
**Cell service:** Fair
**Trail contacts:** Blue Ridge Parkway, (828) 348-3400, www.nps.gov/blri

**Finding the trailhead:** From Asheville, take the Blue Ridge Parkway northbound 15 miles to turn left toward the Craggy Gardens Picnic Area (not the visitor center), on your left at milepost 367.6. Drive up the Craggy Gardens Picnic Area access road for 0.3 mile to reach Beetree Gap, where Stoney Fork Road, FR 63, splits left. Park here, then join the Mountains-to-Sea Trail leading left, south, from the gap. Parking is limited so be considerate. Trailhead GPS: 35.699939, -82.398911

## The Hike

This hike takes place in the greater Craggy Gardens area, off the Blue Ridge Parkway, in an area where a multitude of worthwhile hikes can be undertaken. People often take shorter hikes to the viewpoints around Craggy Gardens or to Cascade Falls and Douglas Falls. Hikers often make their way to Hawkbill Rock via the Snowball Trail, but few go beyond the viewpoint along the ridge of Snowball Mountain to where a fire tower once stood. Even though views are limited at the tower site, the ridge walk is scenic, as you cruise a tapered highland crest under regal woods, through shady gaps, under laurel tunnels, and past an interesting spring to the tower site.

*Peering into Reems Creek valley on a bright autumn afternoon*

Our trek starts on the venerated Mountains-to-Sea Trail, North Carolina's master path extending from Clingmans Dome in the Smoky Mountains, then wandering through the Southern Appalachians east into the Piedmont and all the way to the Outer Banks, astride the Atlantic Ocean. However, this hike soon diverges from the Mountains-to-Sea Trail and joins the Snowball Trail, named for Snowball Mountain, Snowball Gap, and Little Snowball Mountain. Exactly how the name Snowball was associated with the ridgeline is now lost to time.

The ridgeline was most famously known for having the Little Snowball fire tower. Originally erected in 1934 by the Civilian Conservation Corps, the 21-foot metal

structure was in use for a half-century. Unknowingly, fire tower spotters were perched above Big Ivy, where the tower was later moved. Nevertheless, until the 1970s spotters peered forth from on high, in search of mountain conflagrations. After that, the tower was sold, moved off the mountain by hand, and stored in Big Ivy until its 2006 reconstruction at the Big Ivy Community Center. Today, visitors can see the live-in interior of the tower, with its stove and all.

The view from Hawkbill Rock may not be 360 degrees as was the panorama from Little Snowball fire tower, but it'll come in a close second. The outcrop opens to the southeast, where the Reems Creek watershed is encircled by the Blue Ridge

Parkway and the ridge of Snowball Mountain. The maw of the valley opens southwest, where Weaverville and the French Broad valley extend in the distance. Peering south, Snowball Mountain rises tall along with the rest of the Blue Ridge. Looking back northeast, you can see Craggy Pinnacle and all the way back to Mount Mitchell.

Interestingly, much of Snowball Mountain is the Pisgah National Forest boundary. However, a little before you reach Hawkbill Rock, you come to land purchased by the Southern Appalachian Highlands Conservancy. They bought 90 acres in the immediate area to preserve "scenic views for recreational visitors, clean water sources for area residents and habitat for native species." The area is close to not only this hike, but the land purchase also keeps views natural from the nearby Blue Ridge Parkway. The Southern Appalachian Highlands Conservancy was originally founded in 1974 to purchase and protect a route for the AT atop Roan Mountain, the lofty, grassy ridgeline dividing North Carolina and Tennessee near Bakersville, North Carolina. The mission has grown and expanded for the philanthropic outfit. To date, the organization has protected almost 70,000 acres of the Southern Appalachians in the Tar Heel State and its neighboring state of Tennessee. The rest of the hike to the fire tower site straddles this boundary betwixt national forest and conservancy land.

Continuing out the ridge, you will trek northwest on a long gentle descent to Snowball Gap and the hike's low point of 4,365 feet. From here, you follow the old fire tower access jeep road, traveling along the east side of Little Snowball Mountain. You then pass an ingenious spring used by tower watchers. The spring was concreted in, elevating the water level and a pipe added for a permanent 24/7/365 water fountain with an iron door above it, accessing the main spring itself. It isn't far to the tower site from the spring, now a forlorn knob with four concrete supports that once stabilized the tower. In winter you will be able to see the surrounding mountains and valleys, but your best look remains from Hawkbill Rock.

## Miles and Directions

**0.0**    From Beetree Gap, head west on the Mountains-to-Sea Trail, away from the Craggy Gardens Picnic Area. Ascend a narrow wooded ridge, clad in haw, sugar maple, yellow birch, sprinkled with red spruce.

**0.1**    Intersect the Snowball Trail. Keep straight here, as the Mountains-to-Sea Trail veers left toward Potato Field Gap. The Snowball Trail continues to gently climb. Slip over to the north side of Snowball Mountain in a rich wildflower area.

**0.3**    Switchback up to regain the crest of the ridge. After the second switchback, a short spur leads left to a limited southerly view.

**0.5**    Pass a Department of Interior survey marker. Leave the Blue Ridge Parkway and enter the Pisgah National Forest.

**0.7**    The trail reaches a view to the east of the Craggy Mountains just before reaching the high point on Snowball Mountain. Begin working downhill toward a gap separating Snowball Mountain from Hawkbill Rock, leaving the spruce trees behind.

**0.9**    The descent steepens, yet is tempered by loping switchbacks. The ridgeline narrows and is grown up with galax and mountain laurel.

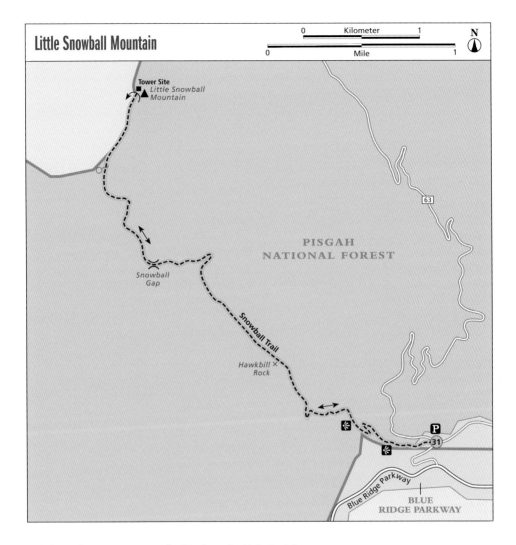

# Little Snowball Mountain

0 — Kilometer — 1

0 — Mile — 1

N

Tower Site
■ Little Snowball
▲ Mountain

63

PISGAH
NATIONAL FOREST

Snowball
Gap

Snowball Trail

Hawkbill ✕
Rock

P
31

Blue Ridge Parkway

BLUE
RIDGE PARKWAY

**1.1**   Come to an outcrop beside the trail with limited views.

**1.2**   Briefly level off in a gap. Then descend right of the gap before climbing.

**1.3**   Reach the knob of Hawkbill Rock after a final steep but short climb over bare rock. Once atop the rock, head left for multiple vistas of the surrounding lands from varied perches, part of the greater Hawkbill Rock. Continue out the Snowball Trail, mostly downhill.

**2.5**   Come to Snowball Gap. Continue the Snowball Trail, joining the old tower access road. Swing around the east side of Little Snowball Mountain.

**3.2**   Pass a concreted spring to the left of the trail. Regain the crest of the ridge.

**3.6**   Come to a knob and site of the Little Snowball fire tower.

**7.2**   Return to Beetree Gap, completing the hike.

# 32 Cascade Falls and Douglas Falls

This hike takes the top-down approach as it visits two exciting yet disparate waterfalls, dropping 1,300 feet on the way. First, leave the Blue Ridge Parkway's scenic Craggy Gardens area, then join the Mountains-to-Sea Trail before breaking off to the lesser-used Douglas Falls Trail. Switchbacks aplenty lead you first to the long-spilling Cascade Falls, a slide cataract the path crosses in mid-descent. Continue down, passing through old-growth woods and gigantic boulders en route to Douglas Falls, a 60-foot show of water that dives from a sheer rock cliff into a stone cathedral.

**Start:** Craggy Gardens Visitor Center
**Distance:** 6.6-mile there-and-back
**Difficulty:** Moderate to difficult
**Elevation change:** +-1,597 feet
**Maximum grade:** 12 percent downhill grade for 0.4 mile
**Hiking time:** About 3.6 hours
**Seasons/schedule:** 24/7/365, save for Blue Ridge Parkway winter closures; late spring for wildflowers and bold waterfalls
**Fees and permits:** None
**Dog friendly:** Leashed dogs allowed

**Trail surface:** Natural
**Land status:** National park, national forest
**Other trail users:** None
**Maps to consult:** National Geographic #779 Linville Gorge, Mount Mitchell, Pisgah National Forest; USGS Craggy Pinnacle, Montreat
**Amenities available:** Visitor center, gift shop, restrooms open during warm season
**Cell service:** Okay
**Trail contacts:** Blue Ridge Parkway, (828) 348-3400, www.nps.gov/blri

**Finding the trailhead:** From Asheville, take the Blue Ridge Parkway northbound 18 miles to the Craggy Gardens Visitor Center, on your left at milepost 364.6. Do not go to the Craggy Gardens Picnic Area, south of the visitor center. Look for the Mountains-to-Sea Trail on the southwest corner of the paved parking area. Trailhead GPS: 35.699445, -82.380057

## The Hike

Most people who visit Douglas Falls take the easy route from the Pisgah National Forest's FR 74, accessible via the community of Dillingham. But not only do they miss overall better scenery, they also miss Cascade Falls, a very long cataract that is hard to measure, since it is a slide that flows over a narrow rock slab through woods. But it is safe to say that Cascade Falls ranges in excess of 100 feet. And if you start at Craggy Gardens, you will have a chance to survey Cascade Falls for yourself—since the trail cuts through the middle of Cascade Falls, giving you a look at the upper half and lower half.

Wise hikers will choose the best time to make this trek. Being lesser used, this upper route to Douglas Falls can be overgrown in late summer. In winter, you may find the parkway closed. However, the parkway's official website offers real-time road

*Douglas Falls rashly plummets from a moisture-sheened cliff.*

closure information, eliminating a needlessly frustrating drive. Late spring through early summer is the best time to undertake this highland waterfall trek that starts over a mile high and never gets below 4,000 feet. In spring, the trails won't be overgrown, flowers will be coloring the trailside floor, and the waterfalls will be brashly flowing. In mid-June the Craggy Gardens area turns purple with Catawba rhododendron blooms covering its altitudes.

The hike leaves the Craggy Gardens Visitor Center to soon join North Carolina's master path—the Mountains-to-Sea Trail—as it cruises the side slopes of 5,892-foot-high Craggy Pinnacle. The route leads over Big Fork Ridge, then picks up the signed but fainter Douglas Falls Trail. It descends in a series of carefully crafted switchbacks into the headwaters of fittingly named Waterfall Creek. Trail construction is expensive and labor intensive. Respect the resource and don't shortcut the switchbacks. Shortcuts cause trail-damaging erosion.

The switchbacks end just before hopping over the uppermost reaches of Waterfall Creek. Behold a slide cascade crashing as you cross, a warmup cataract before coming to Cascade Falls—a surprisingly long waterfall that seemingly has no end—either up or downstream of the trail crossing. Dashing water raves over an irregular rock slab, sometimes widening, sometimes narrowing, flanked by brush and trees. Observe metal poles embedded into the rock as you bisect the falls. A hand cable once ran across the embedded poles to aid the slick traverse of Cascade Falls. Be especially careful in high-water or frozen conditions. Otherwise, you will be measuring the lower part of the falls by counting how many times you bounce on your behind while sliding down the cataract.

Beyond Cascade Falls, tramp along the side slope of 5,860-foot Bullhead Mountain, another high peak of the Craggy Mountains, affectionately known as the Craggies. You are 4,700 feet high. Cross a couple of feeder branches, the second of which is the stream that produces Douglas Falls. This watercourse—pleasantly following gravity's orders—belies its future as a worthy waterfall. Ahead, look for old-growth hardwoods towing in the forest. Big boulders occupy the slopes as well.

The sounds of 60-foot Douglas Falls drift upward while you are in the boulders. Stay with the trail as it switchbacks down to the falls. Very few will disagree that Douglas Falls is worth the hike. Here, the nameless branch spews in a white taper from an overhanging ledge into an open-to-the-sky, forest-surrounded clearing, finally smashing into a rock jumble below. Nimble walkers can squeeze behind the falls by the cliff. Grab views of the spiller from all directions.

# Miles and Directions

**0.0**    Pick up a connector path from the southwest corner of the Craggy Gardens Visitor Center parking area, aiming for the Mountains-to-Sea Trail. The singletrack footpath shifts among outcrops under maple, birch, and buckeye. In summer, ferns, mosses, stinging nettle, and hobblebush rise from the forest floor.

**0.1**    Intersect the Mountains-to-Sea Trail. Turn right, northbound, working your way on a narrow, rocky, and rooty track, dipping below Craggy Gardens Visitor Center. The path leaves Blue Ridge Parkway property and enters the Pisgah National Forest, though you will notice no difference in terrain or management thereof. The trail curves around boulder-strewn Big Fork Ridge where gray- and smooth-trunked beech rise above a grassy forest floor.

**0.7**    Big Fork Ridge narrows and you drop toward Waterfall Creek among wind-sculpted yellow birches.

**1.0**    Intersect the Douglas Falls Trail. Drop left, leaving the Mountains-to-Sea Trail. Begin working downhill using numerous switchbacks.

**1.6**    Step over uppermost Waterfall Creek. Look upstream for an unnamed 25-foot slide cascade, partly hidden in vegetation.

**1.9**    Come to the middle of Cascade Falls after cutting through a rhododendron copse. Be careful crossing the rock slab over which water flows. Be very careful crossing in high-water or icy condition.

**2.2**    Cross an unnamed tributary of Waterfall Creek. Watch for oaks finding their place among the northern hardwoods as you continue descending.

**2.6**    Work over a rib ridge, then reach yet another creek. This is the stream of Douglas Falls.

**2.8**    The trail takes you by a notable old-growth red oak. Look for partial views down the Waterfall Creek valley, then cross a spring seep dribbling through a pebble garden.

**3.0**    The Douglas Falls Trail makes a hard switchback to the left. Note the faint remains of the formerly maintained, now abandoned, Bullhead Ridge Trail that continues straight at the switchback.

**3.3**    Come to Douglas Falls after switchbacking down past some massive boulders and passing through a campsite. Here, you can see the unnamed stream rashly plummet off a sheer, moisture-sheened cliff, splattering into an always-soaked rock pile, then gather and push onward to meet Waterfall Creek. Enjoy straight-on looks as well as sideway shots of Douglas Falls, where you can admire the stream spraying from the rock face. You are still above 4,200 feet here. Relax, then prepare to regain the lost elevation. Backtrack.

**6.6**    Arrive at the Craggy Gardens Visitor Center, completing the hike.

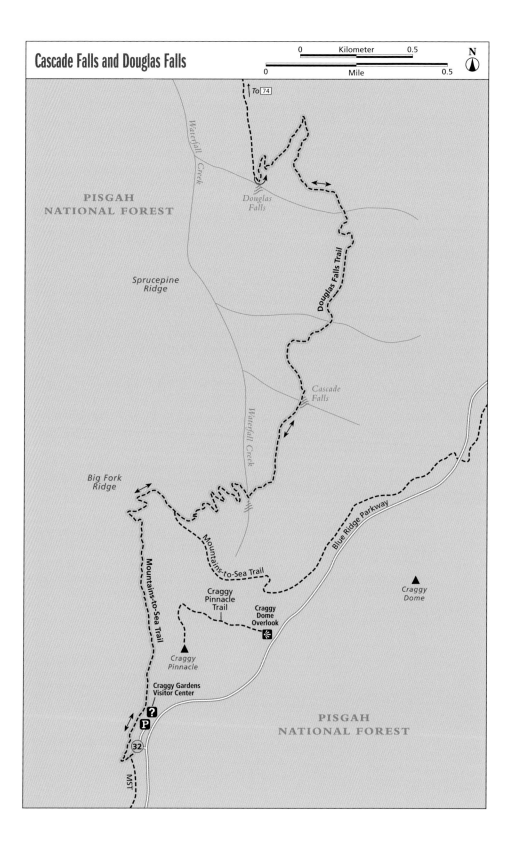

# Cascade Falls and Douglas Falls

0    Kilometer    0.5

0    Mile    0.5

N

*To* 74

*Waterfall Creek*

**PISGAH NATIONAL FOREST**

*Douglas Falls*

*Sprucepine Ridge*

Douglas Falls Trail

*Cascade Falls*

*Waterfall Creek*

*Big Fork Ridge*

Blue Ridge Parkway

Mountains-to-Sea Trail

Mountains-to-Sea Trail

Craggy Pinnacle Trail

Craggy Dome Overlook

*Craggy Dome*

▲ *Craggy Pinnacle*

Craggy Gardens Visitor Center

**PISGAH NATIONAL FOREST**

32

MST

# ADDITIONAL RECREATION AT CRAGGY GARDENS

This hike starts at the Craggy Gardens, a quick getaway from Asheville to a botanically rich mountain atop the Blue Ridge Parkway. The Craggy Gardens are a blend of rock outcrops, grassy balds, and brushy heath balds with wind-stunted woods adding to the vegetative blend. The variety of scenery and vista possibilities, along with the spectacular blooming rhododendron, makes it a Blue Ridge Parkway highlight. Since you are already at Craggy Gardens for this hike, why not explore more while you are here?

The Craggy Gardens Self-Guiding Trail runs in conjunction with the Mountains-to-Sea Trail, going the opposite direction as our hike to Douglas Falls. It makes a 1.4-mile there-and-back hike through a mosaic of environments. The interpretive path also passes a trailside shelter where a spur finds an overlook. Blueberries ripen in July up here. If you keep going on the Mountains-to-Sea Trail, you will end up at the Craggy Gardens Picnic Area, a charming dining locale. The Craggy Pinnacle Trail starts a half-mile north of the visitor center. It leaves the Craggy Dome Overlook, passes a developed spring, and climbs 0.7 mile through stunted hardwoods to reach a brushy heath bald, standing at 5,640 feet, where you can soak in views in all four cardinal directions. Blooms decorate this mountain, too. Therefore, while hiking to Cascade Falls and Douglas Falls, try to save a little energy for additional exploration of the Craggy Gardens.

*A straight-on view of Douglas Falls*

# 33 Point Lookout Trail

This is a great rainy/wet day hike on a paved trail that traces a long closed high-way through the mountains above Old Fort and Black Mountain. The track, popular with hikers and bicyclists, ascends the valley of Swannanoa Creek through attractive woods, winding amid coves before rising to a shoulder of Bernard Mountain where you will find Point Lookout, a fantastic and long appreciated vista. From there, the Point Lookout Trail continues, going over a railroad line to end near Swannanoa Gap. Your return trip is downhill all the way.

**Start:** Parking area near Piney Grove Baptist Church
**Distance:** 7.2-mile there-and-back
**Difficulty:** Moderate
**Elevation change:** +-912 feet
**Maximum grade:** 5% grade for 3.6 miles
**Hiking time:** About 2.9 hours
**Seasons/schedule:** 24/7/365, solitude in winter
**Fees and permits:** None
**Dog friendly:** Yes, on leash only

**Trail surface:** Asphalt
**Land status:** National forest
**Other trail users:** Bicyclists
**Maps to consult:** National Geographic #779 Linville Gorge, Mount Mitchell Pisgah National Forest
**Amenities available:** None at trailhead
**Cell service:** Decent
**Trail contacts:** Pisgah National Forest, (828) 689-9694, www.fs.usda.gov/nfsnc

**Finding the Trailhead:** From Asheville, take I-40 east to Exit 72, Old Fort/Mountain Gateway Museum, then head left on US 70/Main Street for .4 mile, then turn left onto NC 1400/Old US 70 and follow it for 2.8 miles to end at the trailhead parking area on your left, near Piney Grove Baptist Church. Do not park in the gravel lot on Sunday mornings during church services. Trailhead GPS: 35.635083, -82.224350

## The Hike

To reach many hikes around Asheville, we use the interstates that zip us through town and onward to enjoy some precious time in the great outdoors. There was a period when Asheville and the rest of the country had to use winding two lane roads to get from Point A to Point B. In North Carolina, US 70 was (and still is) a primary east-west route, stretching from the Atlantic Ocean to the Tennessee state line. The part of US 70 east of Asheville, near the hamlet of Old Fort, wound its way up the Swannanoa Creek valley en route to the town of Black Mountain. The road passed Point Lookout with its spectacular view to the east, and stopping there became a rite of passage for travelers. Hotels even sprang up around Point Lookout (people weren't in such a hurry back then). Later, the interstates came and a portion of I-40's route used the old US 70 route, closing part of US 70. An adjacent part of US 70 passing

*This stretch of trail has seen all sorts of traffic over the decades.*

through the Pisgah National Forest was closed down, gated on both ends, left to grow over, melding back to the woods on the slopes of Bernard Mountain and the valley of Swannanoa Creek.

Locals began using the old concrete highway for hiking and bicycling, tracing the abandoned highway that had seen parades of automobiles chugging their way into the mountains from the Piedmont, and vice-versa. The highway had lived through untold numbers of cars breaking down on the climb—radiators steaming, gas tanks on empty, smoke bellowing from the tail pipe until the engine ran no more. And then it became a quiet woodland access for those who knew its secrets.

But word about the "secret" trail to Point Lookout got out. Subsequently, a plan developed to open old US 70 as an official trail managed by the US Forest Service, whose property through much of the trail ran. The road was stabilized, landslides cleaned up and culverts scoured. Finally, the old concrete highway was topped with a layer of asphalt, making for a smoother track. And in 2008, the newly christened Point Lookout Trail was opened.

Old US 70 had a second chance. Instead of cars and trucks, hikers and cyclists wound its curves and traveled under its leafy roof. Occasional breakdowns might be a turned ankle or a sprung chain instead of a blown engine or steaming radiator. Why

# Point Lookout Trail

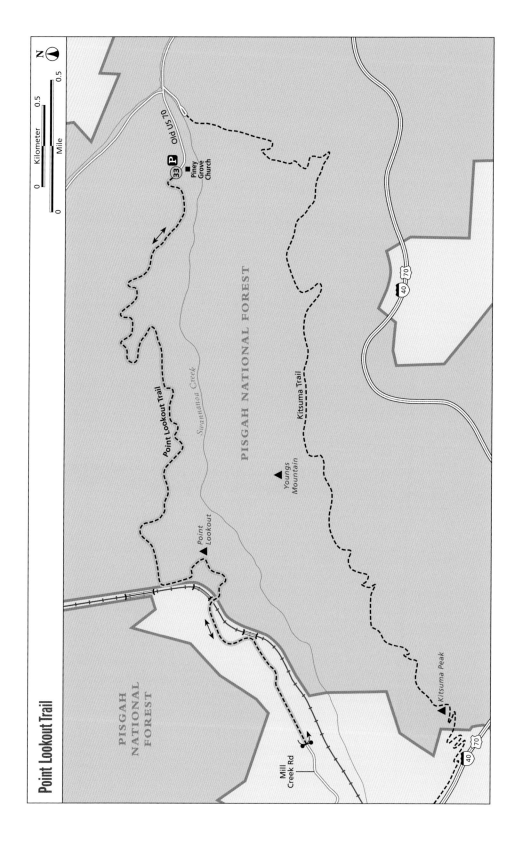

PISGAH NATIONAL FOREST

Mill Creek Rd

Point Lookout Trail

Swannanoa Creek

Point Lookout

PISGAH NATIONAL FOREST

Youngs Mountain

Kitsuma Trail

Kitsuma Peak

33

P

Old US 70

Piney Grove Church

40 70

40 70

N

0        Kilometer        0.5
0          Mile          0.5

don't you give the Point Lookout Trail a chance? I enjoy its sense of history, woodland scenery, and the challenge. It's a great alternative when other trails are muddy or your hiking partner wants something a little more "civilized." It is also a great winter alternative, since its elevations stay below 2,600 feet. Additionally, resting benches are located throughout the trek should you desire a breather, or just want a place to soak in the mountainside splendor.

And about the return trip . . . it is downhill the entire way back. Make sure to stop at Point Lookout on the way up and on the way back down. Make your own adventure on the Point Lookout Trail.

## Miles and Directions

**0.0** From the gravel parking area open to the public but used by Piney Grove Church on Sunday mornings, walk west on Old US 70 just a short distance to a gate (there's a house on the left at the gate). Hike around the gate and begin ascending the Point Lookout Trail, recycled US 70. Immediately enter attractive hardwood forest with Swannanoa Creek down in the hollow to your left and Bernard Mountain rising to your right.

**0.2** Gated Forest Road 4026 goes left. Stay with the asphalt Point Lookout Trail, westbound. The atmosphere is serene here, nestled between Youngs Mountain to your left and Bernard Mountain to your right.

**0.5** Pass a bluff, blasted to allow US 70 to ascend the mountain. Trek into wooded coves where streams flow under the trail via culvert. You might call this a mountain greenway, with elevation change included.

**1.0** Make a sharp left curve, crossing a major unnamed tributary of Swannanoa Creek in thick rhododendron. Begin angling up a shoulder ridge of Bernard Mountain. Enjoy a view east as you pass a fenced area along the trail with a steep slope.

**1.2** Turn back west, gaining the crest of the shoulder ridge. Swannanoa Creek splashes below. More views open ahead. Walnut trees are common. The variety of trees makes this a great autumn color destination. However, kudzu covers still other areas.

**2.2** Come near Norfolk Southern Railway.

**2.5** A gravel track leads acutely right and is used by railroad personnel for track management.

**2.6** Come to Point Lookout. Here a spectacular view stretches into the horizon, over the Swannanoa River valley east through the mountains toward the Piedmont. A signboard details interpretive information and a pair of flagpoles flies North Carolina and American flags. Soak in a view from observation benches. Beyond, turn back into the Swannanoa Creek valley.

**2.9** Hike above the rail line where it emerges from a tunnel.

**3.3** Begin a long straightaway.

**3.6** Reach the west terminus of the Point Lookout Trail at Mill Creek Road. A gate divides the trail from the road. There is shoulder parking along Mill Creek Road, but it is not recommended. Backtrack, soaking in the trailside scenery.

**7.2** Arrive at the trailhead, completing the historic trek.

# 34 Mount Mitchell State Park Loop

This circuit hike takes you to the highest point east of the Mississippi River—Mount Mitchell. Start near the park restaurant traversing rare spruce-fir forest and take the historic Old Mitchell Trail to the summit, where prolific panoramas can be had on clear days. Descend along Lower Creek on the also historic Camp Alice Trail. Finally, join an old logging railroad bed on the Commissary Trail, where still more views open. Along the way you pass the info-rich park office.

**Start:** Mount Mitchell State Park restaurant
**Distance:** 4.1-mile loop
**Difficulty:** Moderate
**Elevation change:** +-1,170
**Maximum grade:** 15 percent for 0.7 mile
**Hiking time:** About 2.5 hours
**Seasons/schedule:** 7 a.m. to 10 a.m. daily, whenever the skies are clear and Blue Ridge Parkway is open
**Fees and permits:** None
**Dog friendly:** Leashed dogs allowed

**Trail surface:** Natural
**Land status:** State park
**Other trail users:** None
**Maps to consult:** Mount Mitchell State Park; USGS Mount Mitchell
**Amenities available:** Restrooms at trailhead
**Cell service:** Weak
**Trail contacts:** Mount Mitchell State Park, (828) 675-4611, www.ncparks.gov/mount-mitchell-state-park

**Finding the trailhead:** From Asheville, take the Blue Ridge Parkway north 34 miles to milepost 355. Turn left on NC 128 into Mount Mitchell State Park. Follow the scenic highway 3.0 miles, to the park restaurant parking area on your right. Trailhead GPS: 35.752805, -82.273604

## The Hike

Mount Mitchell has been determined to be the highest point east of the Mississippi River without doubt. The mountaintop stands at 6,683 feet along the crest of the Black Mountains. However, there was once a great controversy as to the true high point in the East. Some thought it was Grandfather Mountain, an impressive crag to the northeast of Mount Mitchell. Others thought it was Clingmans Dome in the Smokies, yet still others thought it was a peak such as Mount Washington in New England. Here in Carolina, the debate was primarily between Grandfather Mountain and what became Mount Mitchell. Back in 1835, Dr. Elijah Mitchell, of the esteemed University of North Carolina, made his way to the top of Black Mountains and determined that they were indeed higher than Grandfather Mountain. However, Thomas Clingman, a North Carolina senator, onetime student of Dr. Mitchell and later to be Confederate general, challenged his former mentor as to the high point. To end the controversy once and for all, in 1857, Elisha Mitchell headed up to the Black Mountains to once again measure the high point. Elisha may have used what is now known as the Old Mitchell Trail—the very path upon which this hike begins—to scale the summit. His climb went well but on the way back the professor tumbled from a cliff, landing at the base of a 40-foot waterfall, where he drowned.

Dr. Mitchell was vindicated posthumously, while Thomas Clingman got nearby Clingmans Peak named for him as well as the Smokies high point of Clingmans Dome. To honor Professor Mitchell's efforts, the high point in the Black Mountains was named after him. Mitchell was later buried at the peak. Being the high point only added to the attraction for people visiting the Black Mountains. The range is a place where flora and fauna replicate Canada. Long ago, when the climate was colder, plants such as red spruce and Fraser fir, birds such as juncos, and critters such as red squirrels found a home in the Southern Appalachians. After the climate warmed again, the flora and fauna survived on "sky islands" such as the Black Mountains.

Hikers have been coming to scale the Black Mountains since the 1830s, when what became the Old Mitchell Trail was a primary route along the crest. The trail actually started down along the Swannanoa River and worked its way up to the ridgeline, ending at Mount Mitchell. Therefore, when you hike this path you are walking in the footsteps of early Southern Appalachian explorers. What is left of the Old Mitchell Trail starts at the park office. Mount Mitchell State Park was established in 1915 when area citizens cried foul upon seeing the Black Mountains being denuded of vegetation after loggers arrived in the early 1900s equipped with band saws and efficient methods of timber removal via logging railroad lines.

Prior to this, North Carolina did not even have a state park system, therefore the state park system and Mount Mitchell State Park were established simultaneously. Consequently, the preservation of Mount Mitchell not only led to saving North Carolina's highest peak but also to the protection of all the other parcels in the state park system, from the Atlantic Ocean to the Piedmont to the Appalachian range.

Of course, early users of the Old Mitchell Trail did not start near a park restaurant, as you do on this hike (check ahead for restaurant hours, as they are seasonal). Nor did early hikers walk by a developed tent campground. But eventually they made their way to the top of Mount Mitchell, despite the irregular, rooty, and rocky terrain that remains rugged to this day, despite the plethora of stone steps, wooden walkways, and other conveniences used by modern trail builders.

Mount Mitchell is graced with a low-slung stone observation tower with a 360-degree panorama of the surrounding mountains. To help you get your bearings, signs are posted pointing out notable places on the horizon. On the very clear days—when you should be doing this hike—the views extend to impressive lengths, from the Black Mountains in the near as well as the immediate state park facilities, to far-flung peaks on the horizon, and easily identifiable landmarks such as Table Rock as well as distant points well into Tennessee.

Most visitors to the observation tower will be coming via the short and busy Summit Trail, accessed from a parking area just below the peak of Mount Mitchell. However, once you backtrack on the Old Mitchell Trail, the crowds once again

*Spruce-fir forest gives way to colorful deciduous trees on Mount Mitchell.*

*A visual guide atop Mount Mitchell helps you identify distant peaks.*

thin out. Then join the Camp Alice Trail, a rough path once used by early tourists in the 1930s and '40s to access the top of Mount Mitchell from Camp Alice, a converted tourist camp that was formerly a logging camp located near Lower Creek. This stream, emerging from springs on the highest mantles of Mount Mitchell, tumbles down in cascades that sing into your ears.

After tackling the Camp Alice Trail, join the Commissary Trail, a wide double-track path that most hikers will welcome after the irregular pathways thus far. The gravel track follows an early 1900s logging line that was later converted to haul tourists to Mount Mitchell instead of logs from Mount Mitchell. Since the 1930s, tourists have been using the Blue Ridge Parkway to reach the state park, the same as most of us do today.

The hiking is easy on the Commissary Trail, despite the gradual uphill. Nearly continual views open to the east along the path. The first part of the Commissary Trail is the only part of the hike where you are less than 6,000 feet in elevation. You then rejoin the Old Mitchell Trail near the park office, and trace the crest of Black Mountain back to the park restaurant parking area.

# Miles and Directions

**0.0**    From the state park restaurant parking area, join the Old Mitchell Trail northbound, heading away from the park restaurant building. Walk among darkly shaded red spruce and Fraser fir trees, broken with brushy clearings presenting views.

**0.4**    Pull away from the park road, which you have been paralleling. Keep northbound on the singletrack path. Parts of the trail are rough and irregular and even use land bridges to pass ultrarugged segments. Note the many skeletal tree trunks and dead evergreens from the balsam wooly adelgid, an exotic insect.

**0.8**    Meet the Camp Alice Trail, your return route. For now stay left on the Old Mitchell Trail, still climbing in perpetually shady lush woods.

**1.0**    The Campground Spur Trail comes in after a couple of switchbacks. Stay right with the Old Mitchell Trail.

**1.2**    Join the Summit Trail, heading right. This wide concrete path is quite a change from the Old Mitchell Trail. Throngs of walkers may also be ascending the Summit Trail. Pass the park environmental education building and also the spur leading left to the Balsam Nature Trail, a signed interpretive walk informing hikers about the boreal forest atop Mount Mitchell.

**1.4**    Reach the low-slung observation platform atop Mount Mitchell. The four cardinal directions and signage help you identify sights on the horizon, including the Commissary Trail, upon which you are fixing to walk, as well as other destinations included in this guide. Backtrack down Mount Mitchell 0.6 mile to the Camp Alice Trail intersection.

**2.0**    Descend on the Camp Alice Trail, the path mountain enthusiasts took in the 1930s and '40s to top out on Mount Mitchell from Camp Alice, the logging-camp-turned tourist-camp. Come alongside Lower Creek, falling in noisy cascades.

**2.3**    Reach a trail intersection at Lower Creek. To your left, across Lower Creek, the Camp Alice Trail continues east. Turn right, not crossing the creek, and join the Commissary Trail, a wide gravel path. Head south, making a gentle uptick. The footing is good, allowing you to look around. Views extend to your left, easterly, across the South Toe River valley to points beyond.

**3.5**    Arrive at a pole gate and the rear of the state park office. A short walk around the office leads to the parking area and the signed Old Mitchell Trail. Join the Old Mitchell Trail, northbound.

**4.1**    Return to the park restaurant parking area after passing the restaurant, with its tempting food smells. Complete the hike, perhaps indulging in a post-hike dining experience.

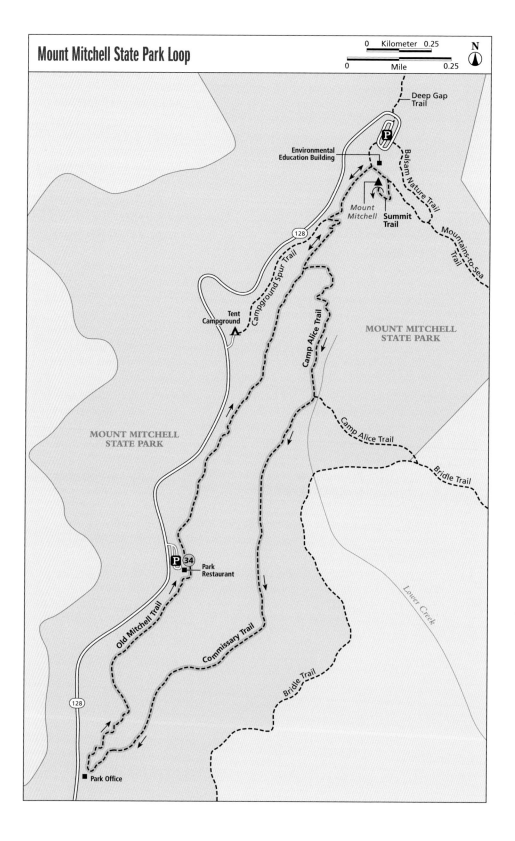

# Mount Mitchell State Park Loop

0   Kilometer   0.25
0          Mile          0.25

N

Deep Gap Trail

P

Environmental
Education Building

Balsam Nature Trail

Mount
Mitchell

Summit
Trail

Mountains-to-Sea Trail

128

Campground Spur Trail

Tent
Campground

Camp Alice Trail

MOUNT MITCHELL
STATE PARK

Camp Alice Trail

Bridle Trail

MOUNT MITCHELL
STATE PARK

Lower Creek

P 34

Park
Restaurant

Old Mitchell Trail

Commissary Trail

Bridle Trail

128

Park Office

# 35 Black Mountain High Country Hike

This hike starts at Mount Mitchell State Park, where you begin on the shoulder of the East's highest peak, then travel along the crest of the Black Mountains, scaling several mountains above 6,500 feet. The ridge running track traverses spectacular view-delivering outcrops on an uneven, rugged, and slow trail. The undulations are more down than up, therefore after arriving at your turnaround point at grassy Deep Gap, you will be challenged on the hike back. Allow ample time for your return or consider backpack camping at Deep Gap.

**Start:** Mount Mitchell State Park Picnic Area
**Distance:** 7.6-mile there-and-back
**Difficulty:** Difficult due to rugged trailbed and elevation change
**Elevation change:** +-1,760 feet
**Maximum grade:** 17 percent grade for 0.8 mile
**Hiking time:** About 5 hours
**Seasons/schedule:** 24/7/365, whenever the skies are clear and Blue Ridge Parkway is open
**Fees and permits:** None
**Dog friendly:** Leashed dogs allowed

**Trail surface:** Natural
**Land status:** State park, national forest
**Other trail users:** None
**Maps to consult:** National Geographic #779 Linville Gorge, Mount Mitchell, Pisgah National Forest; USGS Mount Mitchell
**Amenities available:** Restrooms, water, picnic tables, and shelters
**Cell service:** Decent
**Trail contacts:** Pisgah National Forest, Appalachian Ranger District, (828) 689-9694, www.fs.usda.gov

**Finding the trailhead:** From Asheville, take the Blue Ridge Parkway north 34 miles to milepost 355. Turn left on NC 128 into Mount Mitchell State Park. Follow the scenic highway nearly to the Mount Mitchell parking area. Very near the top, turn right and see the state park picnic area on your left. Follow the paved path into the picnic area and beyond as it turns gravel. Trailhead GPS: 35.767366, -82.264668

## The Hike

Check the weather forecast before you take this hike at Mount Mitchell—the peak is cloaked in fog, rain, or snow 8 out of every 10 days. Snow has been recorded every month of the year; 104 inches of the white stuff fall annually. But that's life at the top of the highest point in the East, right here in Asheville's backyard.

If you get lucky and come here on a clear day, you will be well rewarded. Not only can you bag the highest point in the East, but also this hike takes you over four more officially named peaks, the lowest of which is 6,548 feet! Yet another peak has fantastic views. The Black Mountains are not only high but also biologically significant. When the last Ice Age retreated north, cold-weather plants and animals retreated with them—except for those that survived on the highest mantles of the

*A view opens along the crest of the Black Mountains.*

South—Mount Mitchell, Clingmans Dome, and Roan Mountain, to name a few. These lofty ridges became cool-climate islands where the rare red spruce–Fraser fir ecosystem still thrived in Dixie.

Unfortunately, this spruce-fir complex has been under attack by the balsam wooly adelgid, a pest killing many trees. Despite the damage, the landscape is still scenic

and you can hike through a mix of environments—spruce-fir forests, moss and fern patches, grassy spots, naked rock outcrops, and wind-sculpted Catawba rhododendron. Mountain ash and yellow birch find their places. Moss grows in the shadows.

The first 0.4 mile is a nature trail, then after that the hike gets tougher as you trace a primitive track over irregular rock slabs occasionally requiring all fours. You will first top out on Mount Craig at 6,647 feet, the second highest peak in the East, 37 feet less than Mount Mitchell and 4 feet higher than the Smokies' high point of Clingmans Dome. The views are expectedly spectacular. Look back on Mount Mitchell and the Blue Ridge Parkway from this peak named for the North Carolina governor who established this state park. The next peak is wooded Big Tom, named for renowned guide and bear hunter Tom Wilson.

Prepare for a slick and steep drop off Big Tom. The crest is truly rugged. After passing the Buncombe Horse Trail Connector, climb Balsam Cone where the 6,611-foot mount sports views of Potato Hill and Maple Camp Bald. Look for houses and farms in the lowlands. The Black Mountain Crest Trail fully leaves the state park, then tops out on Cattail Peak. Spruce and fir grow in dense ranks. After topping out on Potato Hill, with first-rate panoramas—including from where you came—the hike makes a prolonged downgrade.

It is 750 feet down to Deep Gap. The grassy clearing of Deep Gap has views of its own and is a potential camping area. Stony Deer Mountain rises in the distance. Water can be had down the Colbert Ridge Trail, 0.1 mile north of Deep Gap. Camping areas are scattered about. Old Deep Gap Road, a now-unmaintained path, leaves acutely left from Deep Gap and also avails water. From here, the Black Mountain Crest Trail continues along the ridge crest to end at Bowlens Creek, 8 miles north of Deep Gap. Allow plenty of time for rest and climbing your way back to Mount Mitchell State Park.

## Miles and Directions

**0.0**   From the state park picnic area trailhead join the Black Mountain Crest Trail, a gravel track heading north into a dense fir forest. Stone steps make the footbed easy for hikers.

**0.4**   Dip to a gap and the end of the nice footbed, though stone steps have been placed on the trail. The path quickly becomes more difficult and you begin crossing the first of many irregular rock slabs atop the Black Mountain crest.

**0.9**   Top out on Mount Craig. Stay on the path, preserving the fragile plants along the rock outcroppings. Additional northward vistas open ahead.

**1.1**   Surmount Big Tom. A very sharp descent follows, parts of which necessitate ropes.

**1.6**   Come to a trail intersection. Keep straight on the Black Mountain Crest Trail as the Buncombe Horse Connector Trail leaves right.

**1.9**   Reach Balsam Cone. Descend and leave the state park, entering Pisgah National Forest.

**2.4**   Pass a tall overhang, then come to the top of Cattail Peak, covered in woods.

**3.0**   Reach the top of Potato Hill. Take the side paths heading west and east to extensive views.

**3.8**   Reach Deep Gap, a grassy flat with camping potential. Water can be had from spur trails here. Backtrack.

**7.6**   Arrive at the trailhead, completing the hike.

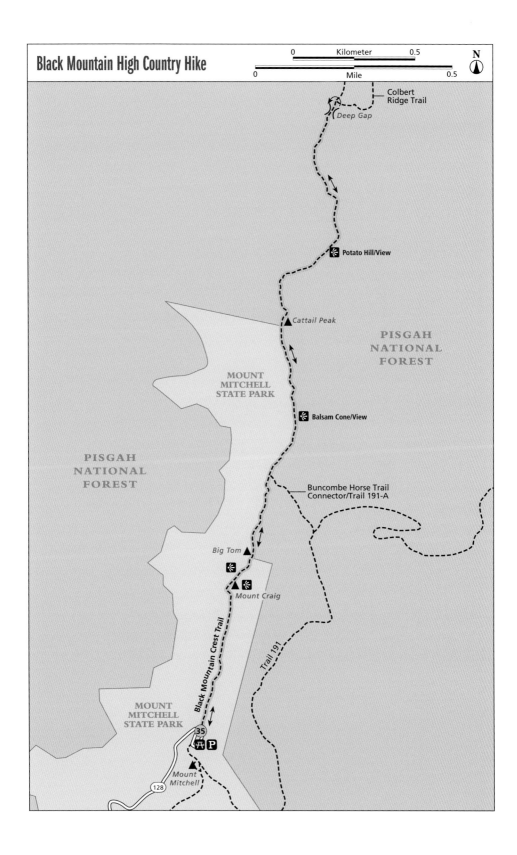

# Black Mountain High Country Hike

0     Kilometer     0.5
0     Mile     0.5

**N**

Colbert
Ridge Trail

*Deep Gap*

Potato Hill/View

▲ *Cattail Peak*

PISGAH
NATIONAL
FOREST

MOUNT
MITCHELL
STATE PARK

Balsam Cone/View

PISGAH
NATIONAL
FOREST

Buncombe Horse Trail
Connector/Trail 191-A

*Big Tom* ▲

▲ *Mount Craig*

Trail 191

Black Mountain Crest Trail

MOUNT
MITCHELL
STATE PARK

35

P

▲

*Mount
Mitchell*

128

# ABOUT MOUNT MITCHELL STATE PARK

Did you know Mount Mitchell State Park has the highest campground in the East? The climate, flora, and fauna are more like Maine than down in Dixie. Recognizing the unique characteristics and status as highest point in the East, then North Carolina governor Locke Craig made Mount Mitchell North Carolina's first state park. Add in a tent-only campground, park restaurant with million-dollar views, gift shop, picnic area, and more trails, then sprinkle in superlative highland scenery, and Mount Mitchell State Park is a Southern Appalachian highlight.

Mount Mitchell's tent-only campground is situated at 6,300 feet among stunted and weather-beaten mountain ash along with Fraser fir and spruce. The nine campsites splinter off the gravel path. Although small and relatively close together, the sites are private because of thick understory growth. There is little canopy overhead, as the trees become gnarled the higher they grow. Two water spigots and a restroom with flush toilets are situated along the walk-in trail.

I recommend camping here to engage in other activities in addition to your hike. If you have not done it yet, make the quick walk to the Mount Mitchell observation tower, elevation 6,684 feet. Here lie the remains of Elisha Mitchell, who fell to his death from a waterfall after measuring the height of the mountain on June 27, 1857. From the tower, views extend in all directions, including along the crest of the Black Mountains where this hike travels. Back near the parking area, check out the museum that details the natural history of Mount Mitchell.

Other hiking trails wander through the state park. Leave the campground on the Campground Spur Trail, then make a 4.1-mile loop with the Old Mount Mitchell Trail and Commissary Trail. The Balsam Nature Trail and Mount Mitchell Trail create a circuit under 2 miles.

Mount Mitchell State Park is surrounded by the Pisgah National Forest and is also adjacent to the Blue Ridge Parkway. This setup makes for large parcels of public lands well beyond the 1,860-acre state park. Still other national forest trails link to the state park trails, allowing additional hiking opportunities.

# 36  River Loop with Setrock Creek Falls

This fun hike circles the upper South Toe River as it flows beneath the shadow of Mount Mitchell. The walking is not too steep or long, and includes a side trip to 60-foot Setrock Creek Falls. You will first climb away from the river, then walk along wooded slopes and brushy bluffs before descending to span the South Toe River on a bridge. After that, circle back down the valley, coming directly alongside the waterway in places. Finally, pass through Briar Bottom Group Camp and Black Mountain Campground, in addition to visiting the aforementioned Setrock Creek Falls.

**Start:** Trailhead across from Black Mountain Campground entrance

**Distance:** 4.1-mile loop

**Difficulty:** Easy-moderate

**Elevation change:** +-779 feet

**Maximum grade:** 13 percent grade for 0.4 mile

**Hiking time:** About 2.5 hours

**Seasons/schedule:** 24/7/365, spring for bold falls and river

**Fees and permits:** None

**Dog friendly:** Leashed dogs allowed

**Trail surface:** Natural, some pea gravel

**Land status:** National forest

**Other trail users:** Campers at Black Mountain and Briar Bottom

**Maps to consult:** National Geographic #779 Linville Gorge, Mount Mitchell, Pisgah National Forest; USGS Old Fort, Celo

**Amenities available:** Campground, restrooms near trailhead

**Cell service:** None

**Trail contacts:** Pisgah National Forest, Appalachian Ranger District, (828) 689-9694, www.fs.usda.gov

**Finding the trailhead:** From Asheville, take the Blue Ridge Parkway north to milepost 351.9. Here, turn left on FR 472, South Toe River Road, and follow it 4.4 miles to Black Mountain Campground, on your left. The trailhead is on the right just beyond the left turn into the campground. Trailhead GPS: 35.750817, -82.220138'

## The Hike

This hike starts at Black Mountain Recreation Area, a concentration of outdoor opportunities in the Pisgah National Forest along the South Toe River, at the base of Mount Mitchell. This area includes a large-group campground as well as an additional campground for individual campers. A fine network of trails laces South Toe River valley, including North Carolina's master path—the Mountains-to-Sea Trail—and a track leading to the top of Mount Mitchell, as well as trails for casual bicyclists. The South Toe River flows form the aquatic centerpiece of the Black Mountain Recreation Area. On this river, visitors can fish for trout, tube the shoals, and swim the pools during the warm season. Additional watery features include Setrock Creek Falls, Camp Creek, and other unnamed streams and cascades. Furthermore, the Blue

Ridge Parkway and its attractions are just a few miles distant, and perhaps may be your scenic driving route from Asheville.

You will see much of the recreation area during this hike. Even though you are on a sizable river, the elevation is still up there. Your starting point is over 3,000 feet. The trek starts just across from Black Mountain Campground and rises away from sonorant South Toe River. After a pair of intersections, your climbing is mostly done. You will then head upriver while crossing intermittent streambeds flowing down from Cove Ridge. The trail is mostly in the forest, but it does pass above a field offering a view and also bounces along an evergreen-clad bluff overlooking the South Toe River. Eventually, the trail drops down to the FR 472 bridge, your conduit to cross the river. The loop then turns downriver, crossing boulder-strewn Camp Creek. It then passes an unnamed branch flowing between Whiteside Ridge and Flynn Ridge. This stream has a very high, multitiered but hard-to-access waterfall for those who want to scramble to it.

Beyond this stream, the River Loop meanders to the banks of the South Toe where you can enjoy this surprisingly large waterway. Next, the River Loop enters Briar Bottom Group Camp, a large camping area with multiple shelters reservable by groups. Then you reach the spur to Setrock Creek Falls. It is but a short distance from the River Loop to this hike highlight—a four-tiered cataract that spills a total of 60 feet, ending in a plunge pool before skittering downstream to feed the South Toe River. Don't try to climb along this waterfall. It is a dangerous proposition and people get hurt here every year. After Setrock Creek Falls, you walk parallel to the river beside some gravel bars to Black Mountain Campground. Its auto bridge takes you back over the South Toe River to complete the hike.

With so much to do in the vicinity in addition to this hike, consider incorporating other recreational activities into the River Loop. You could spend an entire summer day exploring here. Moreover, a night in Black Mountain Campground would cap it off. The area as a whole will be busy during the warm season, but think of it as like-minded recreationalists all enjoying this beautiful swath of the Pisgah National Forest north of Asheville.

## Miles and Directions

**0.0** From the trailhead across the road and just downriver from the entrance to Black Mountain Campground, join the River Loop as it leaves south and uphill, entering woods and running in conjunction with the Mountains-to-Sea Trail and the Green Knob Trail.

**0.3** Come to a trail intersection after the biggest climb of the hike. Here, the Mountains-to-Sea Trail heads left while we curve right with the River Loop. Continue ascending on a sharp slope. The singletrack path becomes rocky.

**0.4** Reach yet another intersection. Here, the Green Knob Trail heads left for the Blue Ridge Parkway while the River Loop climbs a bit more then levels off, and then turns southwest, roughly paralleling the South Toe River. Bisect occasional drainages running off Cove Ridge.

**1.3** Step over a tributary of the South Toe River, then quickly pass above a grassy wildlife clearing with a view across the valley. Ahead, the trail curves onto a steep bluff tightly grown with mountain laurel and rhododendron. More views open above the evergreens.

**1.8** The River Loop drops to reach bottomland and makes a hard right.

**1.9** Reach gravel FR 472. Turn left here and immediately cross the South Toe River on the road bridge. Just past the bridge, the signed River Loop splits right away from the forest road,

*Setrock Creek Falls takes many forms on its 60-foot descent.*

# River Loop with Setrock Creek Falls

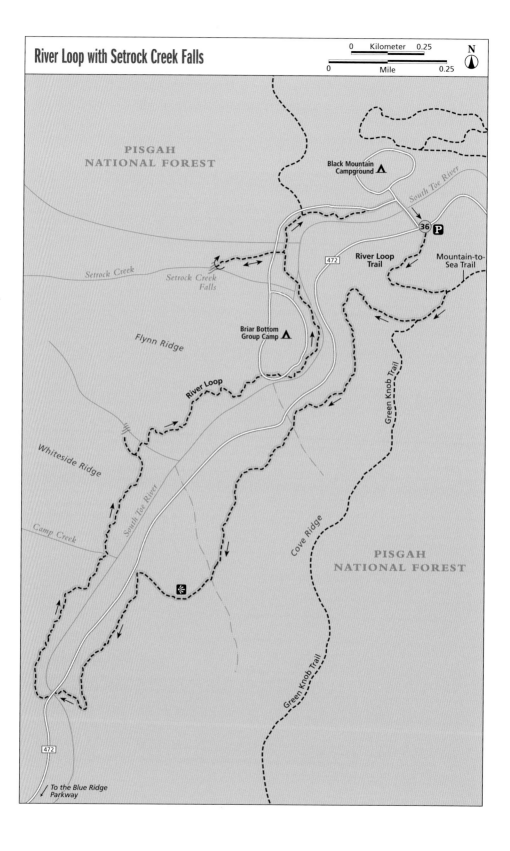

0   Kilometer   0.25

0   Mile   0.25

N

PISGAH
NATIONAL FOREST

Black Mountain
Campground ▲

South Toe River

36 P

Setrock Creek

Setrock Creek
Falls

472

River Loop
Trail

Mountain-to-
Sea Trail

Flynn Ridge

Briar Bottom
Group Camp ▲

River Loop

Green Knob Trail

Whiteside Ridge

South Toe River

Camp Creek

Cove Ridge

PISGAH
NATIONAL FOREST

Green Knob Trail

472

To the Blue Ridge
Parkway

near a dispersed campsite. Curve back northeast, now heading downriver in tall woods with a thick understory of rhododendron.

**2.4**    Come to Camp Creek. The clear stream draining the east slope of Mount Mitchell spills across the trail, then drops through an attractive boulder garden. Rock-hop Camp Creek.

**2.6**    Come to an unnamed creek. If the water is flowing boldly, you will hear a pair of tall and narrow falls crashing from above. A rough manway leads up the left bank to a 40-foot fall with a curtain drop followed by an irregularly angled cascade. Above that is an even higher, taller cataract. If the leaves are off the trees, you will be able to easily see these unnamed cataracts. Cross this stream, then mostly descend.

**3.0**    Come directly alongside the South Toe River amid doghobble thickets. Quickly reach the Briar Bottom Group Camp, with facilities from water spigots to bathrooms to picnic shelters. Keep straight and cross the group camp loop road, then veer right to cross the road a second time, joining the pea gravel Briar Bottom Bike Loop. Cruise riverside bottoms availing river access.

**3.4**    Bridge Setrock Creek.

**3.5**    Head left on the Setrock Creek Falls Trail, just before crossing an iron hiker bridge. Head left and shortly cross the group camp road again. The path changes to singletrack beyond the group camp road crossing.

**3.6**    Come to the base of 60-foot Setrock Creek Falls. Watch the water as it slaloms over the multiple stages of the cataract. Backtrack and rejoin the River Loop, crossing the iron hiker bridge over rhododendron. Pass under a powerline and walk along a fenced bluff.

**3.9**    The Mount Mitchell Trail leads left to the top of the highest point in the East. Keep straight on the River Loop, making a level trek along bottomlands.

**4.0**    Emerge on the access road to Briar Bottom Group Camp. Stay straight, reaching the Black Mountain Campground. Head right and cross the bridge over the South Toe River.

**4.1**    Arrive at the trailhead, completing the hike.

# OTHER HIKES AT BLACK MOUNTAIN RECREATION AREA

Black Mountain Recreation Area, where this hike starts, is an excellent trail hub for hikers who want a variety of trails and destinations. The Green Knob Trail leaves the same trailhead and takes walkers 2.8 miles up to the Blue Ridge Parkway and a fire tower. Though the tower-viewing box is now closed, hikers can still gain worthy 360-degree views of the Black Mountains, Mount Mitchell, and other adjacent ranges. The Mount Mitchell Trail breaks off from the River Loop and fights 5.6 miles up a series of connecting ridges to the top of 6,684-foot Mount Mitchell, gaining 3,600 feet in the process! And if that is a little too strenuous, try the 0.7-mile Devils Den Nature Trail. It starts at the rear of Black Mountain Campground and makes a much shorter loop through woods and a boulder garden. And there are still more hike possibilities here at Black Mountain. Start with the River Loop and I bet you'll be back here for more trekking.

# 37 Crabtree Falls

This loop hike leads from a popular campground on the Blue Ridge Parkway down to an impressive high cataract—Crabtree Falls—that plunges 70 feet over a rock face, misting visitors when its flow is up. Spring is a good time to visit the falls, for not only bold flows but also to see the forty-plus species of wildflowers, from lady slippers to jack-in-the-pulpits to a few relic crabapple trees that gave the area its name. It's a little over 500-foot elevation change down to the falls. Your return trip explores the upper Crabtree Creek valley.

**Start:** Crabtree Falls visitor center trailhead
**Distance:** 2.7-mile loop
**Difficulty:** Easy-moderate
**Elevation change:** +-643 feet
**Maximum grade:** 12 percent for 0.8 mile
**Hiking time:** About 1.5 hours
**Seasons/schedule:** 24/7/365, winter through early summer
**Fees and permits:** None
**Dog friendly:** Leashed dogs allowed
**Trail surface:** Natural

**Land status:** Blue Ridge Parkway
**Other trail users:** Campers at Crabtree Falls Campground
**Maps to consult:** National Geographic #779 Linville Gorge, Mount Mitchell, Pisgah National Forest; USGS Celo
**Amenities available:** Picnic area nearby, restroom, water in campground
**Cell service:** Iffy up high, none near falls
**Trail contacts:** Blue Ridge Parkway, (828) 348-3400, www.nps.gov/blri

**Finding the trailhead:** From Asheville, take the Blue Ridge Parkway north to milepost 338.9. Here, turn left into the Crabtree Falls Area. Immediately turn left and reach the upper trailhead parking. Trailhead GPS: 35.812731, -82.143569

## The Hike

Back in the 1930s, when developing the Blue Ridge Parkway, Crabtree Falls was one of North Carolina's natural assets the Park Service knew they wanted to include. Except back then it was called Murphy Falls. Just to make things more complicated, official USGS Quad maps called Crabtree Falls "Upper Falls." The Park Service renamed the falls after Crabtree Creek, on which it is located. Others contend the falls were named for an early colonial settler named John Crabtree. Name aside, this gorgeous 70-foot cataract that spills over a widening ledge is one of my favorite sights on the parkway.

Crabtree Falls makes a worthy hike destination. A loop trail leads to the falls, allowing you to cover new ground the entire route while seeing the cascade. Crabtree Falls is the centerpiece of a recreation area that includes a campground located just off the parkway. The campground, situated at 3,600 feet, makes a fine hot weather getaway. It is open during the warm season. The campsites have a picnic table, fire ring,

*Crabtree Falls displays its aquatic splendor in late fall.*

lantern post, and level tent pad. Water spigots and restrooms are spread out among the seventy-one tent and twenty-two RV sites. A designated picnic area is located less than a mile south on the parkway for those who want to dine outside.

The crabtrees that once covered the partly wooded meadows of the recreation area continue to fall to the winds of time and relentless reforestation. However, some of the crabtrees still show off their blossoms here atop the Blue Ridge. After leaving the upper trailhead adjacent to the parkway, you will pass through some relic

*Crabtree Falls on a summer day*

meadows being kept open by the Park Service with periodic mowing. Beyond the meadows, the hike skirts by the campground entrance station. Here, your descent begins in earnest. The trail falls away through rhododendron, then passes an abandoned trail, formerly creating an additional loop. A series of switchbacks on a steep wooded slope moderates the decline. Parts of the trail use well-placed, sturdy but narrow stone steps to lose altitude. Depending on water volume, the roar of Crabtree Falls may be filling your ears.

Then Crabtree Falls comes into view, a froth of white spreading over rock strata. The 70-foot parade of lather crashes into a pool, then splits around a small, rock island atop which stands one of the most photographed trees—a yellow birch—along the Blue Ridge Parkway. A wooden walkway bridge crosses Crabtree Creek, doubling as a first-rate observation/photography platform. And from this bridge waterfall enthusiasts will be snapping pictures and video using whatever devices they have on hand, from smartphones to big ol' cameras sitting atop tripods, trying to get the perfect shot. And Crabtree Falls is exceptionally photogenic—the stream fearlessly diving over a bare cliff, spilling in sheets, dashing from rock to rock, then regrouping to slalom in shoals and flow under the observation bridge.

Some waterfall visitors go back the way they came, the backtrack being shorter. However, you will be going against the flow of hikers, which could be important on those busy, fair weather Saturdays. Moreover, additional viewing opportunities of Crabtree Falls are ahead as you climb stairs away from the creek. More switchbacks lead up past an overhanging rockhouse. Come to a linear outcrop where you can walk out and look down on the falls as it makes a big drop. This precarious view is better when the leaves are off the trees. You then head up the perched upper valley of Crabtree Creek. The stream drains this elevated valley between Sevenmile Ridge and the Blue Ridge, making a surprisingly large waterway for a 3,500-foot elevation. And upper Crabtree Creek speeds along in shoals and pools. The loop crosses Crabtree Creek on a hiker bridge before finally turning away from Crabtree Creek to cut through the campground. Beware of old, closed connector trails. Soon you will hear the cars on the Blue Ridge Parkway, marking your return to the trailhead.

Spring and late fall are the best times to visit Crabtree Falls. In spring, you will be rewarded with wildflowers rising from the refreshed soil and a normally fast-flowing Crabtree Creek that will put extra pepper into Crabtree Falls. In late fall, the leaves are off the trees, the crowds have thinned, allowing you to view the Crabtree Falls through the woods from afar and up close without having to jostle for elbow room on those ideal warm-weather days. Also, you can better see the geology of the land, the rock strata that make waterfalls happen. Early morning is a good time during the warm season as you will also beat the crowds. Additionally, since Crabtree Falls is on the west side of the Blue Ridge, it takes a while for the sun to hit the falls, making for better photography conditions in the morning. No matter the weather, season, or time of day, do carve out a few hours to visit this jewel of the Blue Ridge Parkway.

*This view reveals the Blue Ridge Parkway above. Crabtree Falls tumbles beneath the tree cover below.*

# Miles and Directions

**0.0**  From the upper trailhead near the closed Crabtree Falls visitor center, take the asphalt Crabtree Falls Trail downhill. Lights to access the area amphitheater line the path.

**0.1**  Pass the amphitheater on your left and the asphalt ends. Keep straight and enter a field/woods mix. A trail comes in on your left and is your return route. For now, continue through the woods and fields. Look for relic crabtrees.

**0.2**  A spur trail leads left toward the B Loop of Crabtree Falls Campground. Stay right toward Crabtree Falls. Pass some campsites on your left.

**0.3**  Cross the campground entrance road and come near the campground entrance station. Rejoin the hiking trail leaving from the back left corner of the parking area near the entrance station. You are now descending to the falls under a cloak of rhododendron and black birch.

**0.5**  Stay right as a closed alternate loop trail leaves left. The closed loop should grow fainter with time. Continue descending off the west side of the Blue Ridge.

**0.7**  Stone steps aid your descent on this steep, rocky, and rooty mountainside.

**0.8**  A hiker bridge takes you over a steep streamlet. More stone steps lead down on a switch-back to the right. The stream you just bridged flows over the trail. Depending on water levels, you may need some fancy footwork to keep your feet above water.

**0.9**  Make a big switchback to the left. Continue descending.

**1.1**  Come to Crabtree Falls. The setting is gorgeous as the 70-foot cataract plunges over the side of a precipice and widens on its splashy fall. If the water and wind are up, you will soon be tickled with mist. Continue across the combination bridge/waterfall observation platform, admiring the plunger from multiple angles. Climb away from the falls on stone steps and short switchbacks. Alternate views of the falls open when the leaves are off the trees.

**1.3**  Come along an overhanging rockhouse. Just ahead, reach a rock outcrop that extends left to a potentially dicey precipice with a top-down leaf-off view of Crabtree Falls, as well as the Blue Ridge Parkway above. Ahead, come alongside Crabtree Creek, viewing lesser cascades.

**1.6**  A boardwalk leads over a tributary of Crabtree Creek. Next, cross Crabtree Creek on an iron hiker bridge. Keep upstream on the left bank. Walk past more alluring waters.

**2.0**  Top a hill then curve left, ascending along a tributary of Crabtree Creek.

**2.4**  Pass the other end of the closed loop trail, then shortly enter B Loop of the campground. Keep straight here, bisecting the campground and look for the trail between sites #82 and #84 on the far side of the campground. Open onto mixed fields and woods. Ahead, the trail splits; head left toward the amphitheater. A right will lead you back toward the visitor center. Pass the amphitheater, then backtrack.

**2.7**  Arrive at the trailhead, completing the hike.

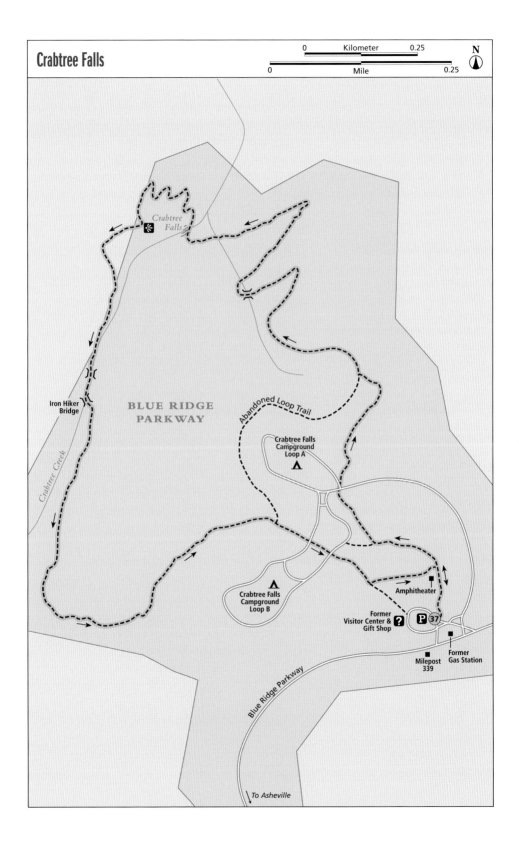

# Crabtree Falls

0   Kilometer   0.25

0   Mile   0.25

N

Crabtree
Falls

BLUE RIDGE
PARKWAY

Iron Hiker
Bridge

Crabtree Creek

Abandoned Loop Trail

Crabtree Falls
Campground
Loop A

Crabtree Falls
Campground
Loop B

Amphitheater

Former
Visitor Center &
Gift Shop

P   37

Milepost
339

Former
Gas Station

Blue Ridge Parkway

To Asheville

# 38 Trails of Linville Falls

Explore a total of over 4 miles of trails centered on renowned 150-foot Linville Falls, off the Blue Ridge Parkway. From the visitor center you first view Upper Falls, then soak in elevated looks at the main portion of Linville Falls backed by a panorama of Carolina mountains. Return to the trailhead, then take the more challenging track to Linville Falls and its big, stone-rimmed plunge basin, then grab an additional elevated perspective. Finally, pay a little visit to 12-foot Duggers Creek Falls to complete the aquatic tour.

**Start:** Linville Visitor Center

**Distance:** 4.1 miles there-and-back with a loop and spurs

**Difficulty:** Moderate

**Elevation change:** +-968 feet

**Maximum grade:** 19 percent grade for 0.2 mile

**Hiking time:** 2.5 hours

**Seasons/schedule:** 24/7/365, save for Blue Ridge Parkway winter closures

**Fees and permits:** None

**Dog friendly:** Leashed dogs allowed

**Trail surface:** Natural, some gravel

**Land status:** National park

**Other trail users:** None

**Maps to consult:** National Geographic #779 Linville Gorge, Mount Mitchell, Pisgah National Forest; USGS Linville Falls

**Amenities available:** Picnic area nearby, restroom, water, book store/visitor center in season

**Cell service:** More on than off

**Trail contacts:** Blue Ridge Parkway, (828) 348-3400, www.nps.gov/blri

**Finding the trailhead:** From Asheville, take I-40 east to exit 72, Old Fort. Join US 70 east for 11 miles to turn left on US 221 north near Marion and follow it 22 miles to meet the Blue Ridge Parkway. Turn northbound on the BRP and follow it for 1.1 miles to turn right onto the access road for Linville Falls visitor center and follow it for 1.5 miles to dead end at the trailhead. Trailhead GPS: 35.954856, -81.928047

## The Hike

Linville Falls is arguably the signature cataract for the Blue Ridge Parkway in North Carolina. After all, it has its own visitor center and campground centered around it, and a fine set of nature trails of varying difficulties that add up to over 4 miles of hiking if you do them all. Moreover, these paths are not just aimless walks in the woods. The trails lead to multiple vantages of 150-foot Linville Falls from near and far, up and down, below and beside. Photographers have a heyday trying to get the best shot of the white froth that first spills as Upper Falls, then flattens out in a pool before entering a slender swirling drain-like defile, then opening as an explosive force of white, making a final 45-foot dive off stripped rock into an enormous plunge pool.

*Linville Falls as seen from the Plunge Basin*

Superlative scenery comes along with each waterfall view, a melding of rock, water, and forest looks deep into the Linville Gorge and of the mountains framing the Linville River. Add in old-growth hemlock and white pine trees to the mix. Given to the National Park Service by benefactor John D. Rockefeller Jr., the cataract and over 1,000 adjacent acres became part of the Blue Ridge Parkway. The access, trail system, and campground were subsequently developed. This access is often closed during winter, but you can access the trail system via a Pisgah National Forest trailhead off Wisemans View Road, which is off NC 183 near the falls.

The trail system comprises two primary paths, each on respective sides of the Linville River. Each route offers views, but one is decidedly more difficult than the other. The Erwins View Trail is easier, is more popular, and is designed to handle large numbers of less able hikers. However, do not blow it off just because it is easy and popular. Absorbing the views along the Erwins View Trail helps you create a mosaic of perspectives of Linville Falls. Leave directly from the visitor center on a wide easy path, shortly bridging the surprisingly large and wide Linville River. The waterway's size is remarkable considering that the watershed is above 3,000 feet upstream of Linville Falls.

A spur takes you to Upper Falls and is a point doable by almost everybody. Here, a large rock slab and promontory allow hikers to view Upper Falls and its wide pool. Visitors can also peer down into the main body of Linville Falls as the waters funnel together into a swirling, tunnel-like rock chute where whitewater boils down and out of sight. And to think that Linville Falls handles the most volume of any waterfall spilling off the Blue Ridge!

The next three vistas on the Erwins View Trail are elevated panoramas. On the way, you pass through a grove of preserved old-growth hemlocks. The Chimney View allows a look at the primary drop of Linville Falls and the rock basin plunge pool, where continual washing from the falls limits vegetation growth. Next comes the Gorge View. This outcrop gives you a non-waterfall downstream perspective of the upper Linville Gorge, the river below, and the wooded gorge walls falling off the Blue Ridge.

Erwins View are actually two separate but adjacent viewpoints and are true magnificent mountain prospects. Here, Linville Falls forms a centerpiece of water and rock, framed by thick forests, contained in an outer frame of distant mountain ridges extending to the horizon. Wow!

You have to return to the visitor center to begin the lesser-used, more challenging Plunge Basin Trail. It explores the other side of the Linville River, making an initial steady climb and leaving most waterfall visitors behind. First, visit the plunge basin and the base of Linville Falls. The trail here is primitive as it squeezes past narrows, then descends a cliffline using stairs. From there, an irregular, extremely rocky trail takes you to the river's edge, where some final rock scrambling brings hikers face-to-face with the falls, a true reflection of nature's power and majesty, spilling from an opening in a rock cleft, widening and diving in white chaos as the spilling cataract echoes off the stone walls and makes continual waves in the plunge pool.

The final look at Linville Falls is from a rock outcrop just above the plunge basin. Work your way from the river to this stone outlook. Here, you are close to the falls but above the final plunge, lending a final perspective to your tour of Linville Falls.

But wait—there is more. Though puny by comparison, Duggers Creek Falls and the trail to it put an exclamation point on your Linville Falls adventure. The short path passes near the parking area, then turns up Duggers Creek, where a faucet-like Duggers Creek Falls makes its tapered dive into a slot canyon through which you view the spiller. From there, the hike leads amid outcrops before returning to the trailhead.

*Looking downstream from Gorge View*

Hikers relax along the Linville River below Linville Falls.

# Miles and Directions

**0.0** From the visitor center, walk under the breezeway on the wide Erwins View Trail. Ahead, cross the Linville River on a pedestrian bridge.

**0.3** Bridge a small tributary of the Linville River.

**0.4** Keep straight as a spur trail goes right to Wisemans View Road. Just ahead, turn left toward Upper Falls. The trail narrows.

**0.5** Open onto a large, wide outcrop with a view of Upper Falls to your left and the top of the main falls to your right. Backtrack, then continue on toward Chimney View. Pass under some preserved old-growth hemlocks.

**0.8** Split left to Chimney View. Descend to two overlooks on an outcrop with a raised view of Linville Falls as well as good looks upriver and downriver. Backtrack.

**1.0** Rejoin the main trail near a rain shelter and continue toward Erwins View and Gorge View.

**1.1** Come to the Gorge View. This non-waterfall look avails a downstream view of upper Linville Gorge. Resume toward Erwins View, ascending steps.

**1.2** Reach Erwins View and one of the finest vistas on the Blue Ridge. Backtrack all the way to the visitor center.

**2.1** Join the Plunge Basin Trail after leaving the trailhead. Walk a narrower, steeper path, immediately passing the Duggers Creek Falls Trail.

**2.2** Keep straight at a connector heading left to intersect Duggers Creek Falls Trail.

**2.4** Head left at the next intersection toward the plunge basin. This path traverses a wooded hillside, then narrows at some outcrops through which you squeeze. Descend steps. The trail becomes rocky and rough.

**2.8** Reach the base of the falls after scrambling along the Linville River. At high water levels, rock scrambling may prove difficult. Boulders aplenty provide ample seating. Note the shaded defile to your right, an almost cave. Backtrack.

**3.2** Head left toward the Plunge Basin Overlook. Walk under arbors of mountain laurel.

**3.4** Reach the Plunge Basin Overlook, with an elevated, close view of the falls. Backtrack toward the visitor center.

**3.9** Veer right onto the Duggers Creek Falls Trail just before reaching the visitor center. Cruise alongside the parking lot.

**4.0** Leave left on the Duggers Creek Falls Trail, after meeting the Connector Trail. Ascend.

**4.1** Bridge Duggers Creek. Look upstream from the bridge at faucet-like Duggers Creek Falls. Climb from the bridge, circling around an outcrop. Descend to the park access road. Cross Duggers Creek on the road, then head left, rejoining foot trail. Arrive at the parking lot on the opposite end of the lot from the visitor center, ending the hike.

# Trails of Linville Falls

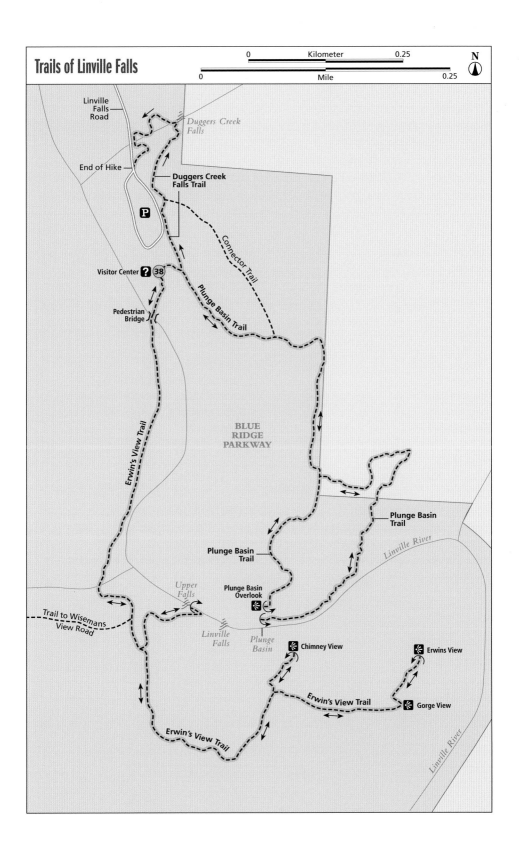

0     Kilometer     0.25

0     Mile     0.25

N

Linville
Falls
Road

*Duggers Creek
Falls*

End of Hike

**Duggers Creek
Falls Trail**

P

Connector Trail

Visitor Center ? 38

**Plunge Basin Trail**

Pedestrian
Bridge

Erwin's View Trail

BLUE
RIDGE
PARKWAY

**Plunge Basin
Trail**

*Linville River*

**Plunge Basin
Trail**

*Upper
Falls*

**Plunge Basin
Overlook**

Trail to Wisemans
View Road

*Linville
Falls*

*Plunge
Basin*

Chimney View

Erwins View

Erwin's View Trail

Gorge View

Erwin's View Trail

*Linville River*

# 39 Linville Gorge Wilderness Hike

Take a hike in legendary Linville Gorge to the Tower of Babel, where fantastic views await from a stony perch deep in the Linville Gorge Wilderness. Travel along the gorge slope on a rugged path that makes for slow going. Pass a river access and panoramas of the gorge, as well as a waterfall and big pool. Your ultimate destination is worth the challenging trail. The Tower of Babel is a notable stone knob nearly encircled by the Linville River. Soak in views of the wild canyon and mountains in the distance.

**Start:** Pine Gap Trailhead
**Distance:** 5.8-mile there-and-back
**Difficulty:** Difficult due to rugged trail
**Elevation change:** +-928 feet
**Maximum grade:** 18 percent grade for 0.2 mile
**Hiking time:** About 4.5 hours
**Seasons/schedule:** 24/7/365, whenever the skies are clear
**Fees and permits:** None, except for backpackers in season
**Dog friendly:** Leashed dogs allowed

**Trail surface:** Natural
**Land status:** National forest
**Other trail users:** A few kayakers, anglers, and rock climbers
**Maps to consult:** National Geographic #779 Linville Gorge, Mount Mitchell, Pisgah National Forest; USGS Linville Falls
**Amenities available:** None
**Cell service:** A little near the trailhead
**Trail contacts:** Pisgah National Forest, Grandfather Ranger District, (828) 652-2144, www.fs.usda.gov/nfsnc

**Finding the trailhead:** From Asheville, take I-40 east to exit 85 near Marion. Join US 221 north for approximately 24 miles to the town of Linville Falls and NC 183. Turn right on NC 183 east and follow it for 0.7 mile to gravel Kistler Memorial Highway. You will see a sign indicating Linville Falls and Linville Gorge Wilderness. Veer right here and follow the gravel road for 0.9 mile to the Pine Gap trailhead on your left. **Note:** Along Kistler Memorial Highway, a gravel road, you will pass the Pisgah National Forest access for the trails of Linville Falls, and the Linville Gorge Wilderness information cabin before reaching the Pine Gap Trail trailhead. Trailhead GPS: 35.940319, -81.930402

## The Hike

Linville Gorge is a "must"-hiking destination for residents of greater Asheville. The deeply carved valley is a federally designated wilderness and certainly exudes qualities expected in such an untamed place. The terrain is rugged and rocky, and wildfires regularly sweep through the gorge. The Linville River slices its way through a brawling chaos of rocks, boulders, and cliffs, occasionally slowing in inviting pools, then hurtling through unruly rapids. The trail system reflects the wild and rugged nature of the gorge. Being a designated wilderness, the Pisgah National Forest maintains the trail system at a more primitive standard. When you combine the primitive pathways along with the rocky terrain and inevitable fallen trees, it results in slow travel for the wilderness hiker. Therefore, allow ample time to make this hike and include time to relax and enjoy your hard-earned scenery.

Linville Gorge Wilderness is popular not only with day hikers but also with backpackers. However, permits are required to backpack the wilderness during summer and holiday weekends. Backpacking permits can be obtained by calling the Grandfather Ranger District office at (828) 652-2144. Interestingly, your starting point—the Pine Gap Trail—is also utilized by kayakers. These intrepid paddlers actually carry their boats down to the Linville River via this trail. To facilitate this, improvements were made to the Pine Gap Trail, making it easier for kayakers to tote their boats the half-mile to the river. Brush was cleared in a wider swath from the path and footing was improved—rocks were removed and the trailbed smoothed out. This has made the first part of the hike a little more user-friendly than days gone by. The upstream access off the Blue Ridge Parkway requires boaters to either paddle through or around Linville Falls, both dangerous propositions that all but a very few maniacs avoid. Furthermore, the National Park Service, which manages the Linville Falls area, officially prohibits boating on its part of the Linville River, making the Pine Gap Trail the uppermost legal entry point.

The trails at Linville Gorge are also used by anglers who are looking to fish for trout, smallmouth bass, and bream in challenging waters, as well as rock climbers who dare the stony cliff faces so abundant in this jewel of the Blue Ridge.

Being hikers, we will enter the gorge on foot. The improved Pine Gap Trail leads past an overlook, revealing the depth and magnitude of the gorge and keeps angling downhill using switchbacks to make the Linville River after a half-mile. This is where the paddlers jump in the water and descend nearly 2,000 feet before exiting near Lake James at the NC 126 Bridge. You can check out the river, too, here.

The Pine Gap Trail continues following the Linville River, then turns away to cut across a bend and comes to a signed trail intersection in aptly named Pine Gap, where aromatic evergreens rise in tall ranks. Here, hikers join the rugged Linville Gorge Trail, tracing the winding course of the Linville River among pine, mountain laurel, and oaks. The trail then comes to the edge of a cliff, where excellent upstream panoramas open.

Ahead, a few switchbacks lead to the river itself. Enjoy trailside looks into the mix of stone and water. Next on the highlight list is an unnamed 15-foot waterfall just around the bend. A spur leads to an elevated rock ledge where you can peer down to the combination tier and slide cascade with a huge recovery pool ideal for dipping.

The hiking is still slow and challenging while working alongside rock walls, over outcrops, and fallen trees. The river is making tortuous bends. Then you reach the signed trail intersection next to the Tower of Babel. Here, a rockhouse is downhill to your left. Visit the rockhouse. The network of user-created trails can prove confusing. However, a little persistence will take you to the top of the outcrop, where the maw

Author overlooks Tablerock and Linville Gorge as seen from the Tower of Babel.

of Linville Gorge opens wide, with Hawkbill Mountain and Tablerock rising in the yon. Below, the Linville River is nearly encircling the tower. Allow plenty of time for the slow backtrack to the trailhead.

## Miles and Directions

**0.0**   Join the Pine Gap Trail, a singletrack path leaving the southeast corner of the parking area. The narrow way descends over an improved surface but still with plenty of roots, rocks, and imperfect footing.

**0.1**   A rock outcrop to the left of the trail provides your initial vista into the Linville Gorge. Hike along the base of sheer stone bluffs.

**0.5**   Reach a spur trail going left to the Linville River after a few switchbacks. Visit the river if you please. Boulders overlook slow pools and beckon hikers to the moving aqua amid still stone.

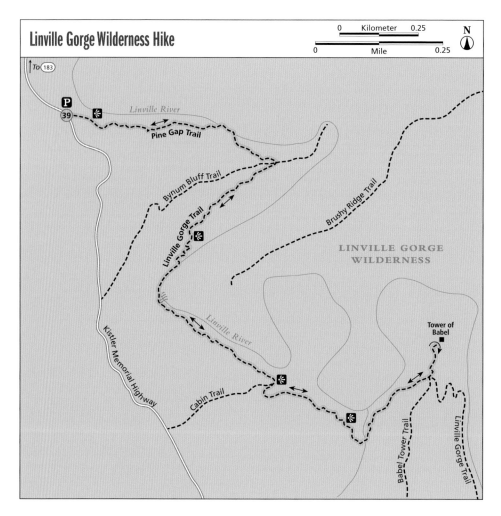

**0.8** Come to a four-way trail junction in Pine Gap. Here, a spur trail leads left 0.2 mile down to the inside of a bend in the Linville River, where a rocky bar faces a vertical bluff. The Bynum Bluff Trail leads acutely right up the nose of a rocky ridge to Kistler Memorial Highway. Join the Linville Gorge Trail. It curves slightly right here, turning southwest with the bend of the river.

**1.1** The trail takes you next to a rockhouse.

**1.2** Reach a rocky precipice. Hikers can peer upstream into the river gorge with Brushy Ridge and Long Arm Mountain rising in the background. Note the rapids and pools below.

**1.3** Come to the Linville River at a big rock slab after passing by a dripping cliffline. Gain a close-up look at the wild waterway.

**1.4** Pass an unnamed 15-foot waterfall as the trail and river curve left. A spur leads to the cataract with a big plunge pool. Continue cruising beneath bluffs.

**1.7** A spur descends left to the river. Stay with the Linville Gorge Trail.

**1.9** Pass a spur trail leading left to a view along a narrow outcrop just before coming to the Cabin Trail. It makes a nearly 1,000-foot climb in a mile before reaching Kistler Memorial Highway. Stay with the Linville Gorge Trail as it curves around a hollow.

**2.2** Come alongside a rock promontory with a down gorge view of the Tower of Babel rising from the heart of the gorge.

**2.3** Step over a clear, perennial stream and turn downstream along it. Ahead, look for a user-created spur leading left to the river. Stay right with the Linville Gorge Trail.

**2.8** Come to a four-way intersection just after passing a rockhouse to your left. The Babel Tower Trail leaves right while the Linville Gorge Trail keeps straight. A wide rock flat stands to your left, above the rockhouse. Take yet another trail leading left and downhill, then climb into the rock flats. Circle around the left side of the pinnacle, cloaked in scraggly pines, and find a steep primitive path leading to the Tower of Babel.

**2.9** Arrive at the top of the Tower of Babel. Widespread panoramas open down Linville Gorge, with Tablerock and Hawkbill Mountain rising dramatically into the sky. Additional vistas can be had looking upstream. Backtrack.

**5.8** Arrive back at the trailhead.

# 40 Lake James State Park Hike

This state park trek gives western Carolina hikers a chance to explore a different environment—the Piedmont-like lands bordering Lake James. This particular hike takes trail walkers along rolling shores, where views open across the clear water with piney peninsulas in the near and the rising Blue Ridge in the distance. Elevation changes are minimal, and the state park offers additional trails and activities, sure to make your trip here a worthwhile endeavor.

**Start:** Near the East Shelter of Paddys Creek area
**Distance:** 3.4-mile loop
**Difficulty:** Easy to moderate
**Elevation change:** +-261 feet
**Maximum grade:** 4 percent grade for 0.4 mile
**Hiking time:** About 2 hours
**Seasons/schedule:** Dec to Feb: 7 a.m. to 6 p.m.; Mar, Apr, and Oct: 7 a.m. to 8 p.m.; May to Sept.: 7 a.m. to 9 p.m.; Nov: 7 a.m. to 7 p.m.; fall through spring to avoid crowds
**Fees and permits:** None for entrance or hiking; fee for swim beach when lifeguards on duty

**Dog friendly:** Leashed dogs allowed
**Trail surface:** Mostly natural
**Land status:** State park
**Other trail users:** None
**Maps to consult:** Lake James State Park Trails; USGS Oak Hill, Ashford
**Amenities available:** Restroom, picnic tables, swim beach, and concessions in season
**Cell service:** Good
**Trail contacts:** Lake James State Park, (828) 584-7728, www.ncparks.gov/lake-james-state-park

**Finding the trailhead:** From Asheville, take I-40 east to exit 90, Nebo/Lake James. Turn right and join Harmony Grove Road, then pass over the interstate. After 0.6 mile, reach an intersection and stay right on Harmony Grove Road, following it for 2.2 more miles to reach the intersection with US 70 in Nebo. Turn left and follow US 70 west just a short distance, then turn right on NC 126. Follow NC 126 for 5.0 miles, passing the Catawba River section of Lake James State Park to turn right into the Paddys Creek area. Follow the main park road for 2.2 miles to dead end at the large swimming beach area with a large parking lot. Drive along the lowermost parking area past the concession/ranger station/swim beach entrance to the signed East Shelter. Park here near the shelter. Trailhead GPS: 35.750977, -81.874862

## The Hike

If you look at a map of Lake James, there is something strange looking about it. Rather than your typical reservoir where a river is dammed and flooded, Lake James was created by damming the Catawba River and the Linville River, then linking them by canal, giving it that unusual look. The canal linking the two dammed waters created a 6,812-acre impoundment. This dam building occurred in the 1920s by Duke Power for the generation of electricity, which the dam continues to provide to this day. Its location at the base of the Blue Ridge Mountains makes Lake James one of the most scenic impoundments in North Carolina. From many locales one can see Lake James in the foreground with the Southern Appalachians rising in the distance. The best views are arguably from the lake into the heart of Linville Gorge, simply a superlative vista that should grace North Carolina newcomer and tourist brochures from Kitty Hawk to Murphy.

However, back in the 1920s people weren't thinking of vacationing here and purchasing lakefront and mountain land on which to build houses with scenery in mind. Nevertheless, as all western North Carolinians know, that situation has changed. Land prices have gone through the roof. A century later, locals and transplants alike are seeking to build their homes with panoramas of undulating mountains and placid waters on now-expensive properties.

That is precisely what makes Lake James State Park so valuable. Set along the shores of Lake James in two parcels, the preserve offers visitors the type of scenery desired by homebuilders. Today, you can come and engage in outdoor recreation, soaking in this marvelous landscape and not even have to pay an entrance fee!

Luckily, local legislators saw the value of creating a shoreline state park. In 1987, Lake James State Park came to be. After the land was acquired, the park was developed with aquatic and land recreation in mind. Trails were laid out for hikers like us, and a separate set of pathways were constructed for mountain bikers. This creates a good situation for both parties. A total of over 10 miles of hiking trails was constructed and about 15 miles of mountain biking trails built. These pathways traverse hills bordering peninsulas extending into the lake. The rolling lands are low by western Carolina standards and exhibit characteristics as well as flora and fauna of both the Piedmont and Appalachians. For example, you will see the red clay associated with the Piedmont as well as trees that find a home in the Piedmont like shortleaf pine, sweetgum, and winged elm, offering a different experience than hiking in the mountains to the west.

Hiking here is an excellent winter proposition and enjoyable spring and fall as well. However, hiking at Lake James State Park in the summer can be very hot, and boat traffic on weekends can make the lake noisy. Nevertheless, I do suggest coming here for an extended visit, as the park has an excellent walk-in tent camping area in the Catawba River Area of the park as well as drive-up tent camping in the Paddys Creek Area. The camps have hot showers and flush toilets. Trails emanate directly from the campground area, adding to the hiking possibilities.

Multiple picnic areas make dining here a breeze. There is even a picnic shelter at the trailhead, as well as multiple shaded lakeshore picnic tables. Anglers will enjoy vying for largemouth and smallmouth bass as well as walleye. Kids will have a ball fishing for bluegill and sunfish from a fishing pier located near the trailhead. Although you may not have a motorboat, the park does rent canoes and kayaks, allowing boat-less visitors to paddle and fish the alluring shoreline. You can rent your boat near the trailhead as well. Finally, a large swim beach is located here as well.

There is a fee in effect when lifeguards are on duty. However, if they are not working, there is no fee.

This hike uses the Mill Creek Trail, the park's longest hiker-only path. The adventure will take you directly through the swim beach when making your loop. However, the trek starts by heading away from the swim beach and facilities, making a counterclockwise loop. It then skirts the first of many quiet coves as the Mill Creek Trail roughly parallels the shoreline. You have opportunities for multiple views of the lake, especially when curving along the Mill Creek arm of the impoundment,

*A trailside beach overlooks Lake James.*

including vistas of the Blue Ridge rising in the distance. The Mill Creek Trail then turns away from the water and works over a low peninsula and returns to the water at the Paddys Creek arm of the lake, where more panoramas await. The final part of the trek leads through the main facilities of this area, including the aforementioned swim beach, concession area, boat rental, ranger office, picnic areas, and shelters. This area will get crowded on warm summer weekends. Plan accordingly, but do come here; it adds a new perspective to hiking in the greater Asheville area.

# Miles and Directions

**0.0**   As you face the signed East Shelter at the greater swim beach/ranger office and conces- sion area, head left on the gravel Mill Creek Trail, immediately crossing the asphalt track leading down to a fishing pier. The path quickly becomes natural surface, bordered by tightly grown young pines. Shortly come along an embayment of Lake James.

**0.1**   Leave the embayment and head up a wooded intermittent drainage. Notice the red clay, shortleaf pines, and sweetgum trees characteristic of the Carolina Piedmont. Curve around the embayment.

**0.5**   Briefly return to the shoreline, then split left, bisecting a peninsula stretching into the lake. Mountain laurel, American holly, and clubmoss are common along the path.

**0.8**   Reach a bench and lake overlook. View a cove in the near and mountains in the distance. Continue to curve with the lake's curves along the sloping shoreline.

**1.5**   Turn around the head of a rhododendron-choked spring. Head back toward the lake, then curve away yet again.

**1.7**   Come very near the Paddys Creek area campground.

**1.8**   Lake James is back in view. Walk among young spindly trees, regenerating in former farmland.

**2.0**   Cross the paved main park road of the Paddys Creek area. Quickly reenter woods. Start a gentle downhill.

**2.7**   Reach a trail intersection. Here, Paddys Creek Trail leads right, up the Paddys Creek arm of Lake James. Our hike, however, turns left, toward the developed facilities of the swim beach area.

**2.9**   Curve around a small cove, then cross a little creek on a pedestrian bridge.

**3.0**   Come to the end of the natural surface trail and find another fishing pier. A spur trail goes left up to the parking area. Keep straight on an asphalt track, then reach the swim beach. Hike along the swim beach, enjoying distant views. Come near the large concession build- ing/ranger office.

**3.2**   Leave the beach area. Keep easterly, walking amid picnic tables with the lake to your right and the parking area uphill to your left.

**3.4**   Arrive at the East Shelter and the parking area, completing the hike.

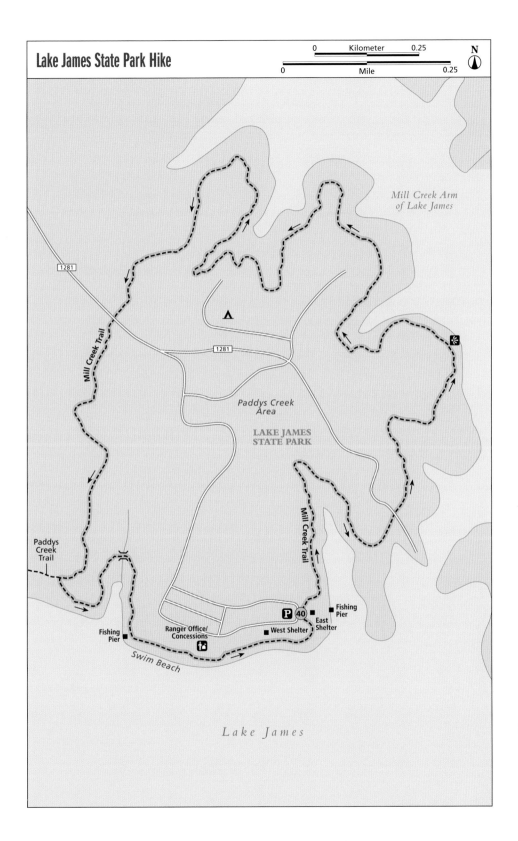

# Lake James State Park Hike

0    Kilometer    0.25
0    Mile    0.25

*Mill Creek Arm of Lake James*

1281

Mill Creek Trail

1281

*Paddys Creek Area*

**LAKE JAMES STATE PARK**

Paddys Creek Trail

Mill Creek Trail

Fishing Pier

Ranger Office/ Concessions

P 40

West Shelter

East Shelter

Fishing Pier

*Swim Beach*

*Lake James*

# Hike Index

# About the Author

**Johnny Molloy** is a writer and adventurer based in Johnson City, Tennessee. His outdoor passion started on a backpacking trip in Great Smoky Mountains National Park while attending the University of Tennessee. That first foray unleashed a love of the outdoors that has led Molloy to spending most of his time hiking, backpacking, canoe camping, and tent camping for the past three decades. Friends enjoyed his outdoor adventure stories and one even suggested he write a book. He pursued his friend's idea and soon parlayed his love of the outdoors into an occupation. The results of his efforts are over eighty-five books. His writings include hiking guidebooks, camping guidebooks, paddling guidebooks, comprehensive guidebooks about a specific area, and true outdoor adventure books throughout the eastern United States, including hiking guides to North Carolina's national forests, Great Smoky Mountains National Park, the Triad, and the Triangle.

Molloy also writes for varied magazines and websites. He continues writing and traveling extensively throughout the United States, endeavoring in a variety of outdoor pursuits. His non-outdoor interests include American history and University of Tennessee sports. For the latest on Molloy, please visit www.johnnymolloy.com.

# THE TEN ESSENTIALS OF HIKING

American Hiking Society

American Hiking Society recommends you pack the "Ten Essentials" every time you head out for a hike. Whether you plan to be gone for a couple of hours or several months, make sure to pack these items. Become familiar with these items and know how to use them. Learn more at **AmericanHiking.org/hiking-resources.**

 1. **Appropriate Footwear**

 6. **Safety Items** (light, fire, and a whistle)

 2. **Navigation**

 7. **First Aid Kit**

 3. **Water** (and a way to purify it)

 8. **Knife or Multi-Tool**

 4. **Food**

 9. **Sun Protection**

 5. **Rain Gear & Dry-Fast Layers**

 10. **Shelter**

## PROTECT THE PLACES YOU LOVE TO HIKE

Become a member today and take $5 off
an annual membership using the code **Falcon5.**

AmericanHiking.org/join

American Hiking Society is the only national nonprofit
organization dedicated to empowering all to enjoy,
share, and preserve the hiking experience.